LAST OF THE DINOSAURS

Maurice Bamford

LAST OF THE DINOSAURS

The Kevin Ashcroft Story

Scratching Shed Publishing Ltd

First published by Scratching Shed Publishing Ltd in 2008
Registered in England & Wales No. 6588772.
Registered office:
47 Street Lane, Leeds, West Yorkshire. LS8 1AP

www.scratchingshedpublishing.co.uk

ISBN 9780956007520

Unless stated otherwise, all photographs are from the personal
collections of Kevin Ashcroft and Mike Latham

Cover: Kevin Ashcroft and Peter Smethurst carry four year old mascot
Gary Ashcroft aloft, after Leigh beat Leeds to win the Rugby League
Challenge Cup Final at Wembley, London, on 15th May 1971.
(Photo © Getty Images)

A catalogue record for this book is available from the British Library.

Typeset in Warnock Pro Semi Bold and Palatino

Printed and bound in the United Kingdom by
L.P.P.S.Ltd, Wellingborough, Northants, NN8 3PJ

Acknowledgements

The idea that I should write this biography of Kevin Ashcroft was arrived at after a conversation with the highly-respected sports journalist, broadcaster and historian Mike Latham. Mike is a sports fanatic who specialises in rugby league, soccer and cricket. A dedicated long-time supporter of Leigh RLFC, Mike supplied me with every detail of Kevin's distinguished playing and coaching career and was a constant help during its production.

Another fantastic help, of course, was Kevin Ashcroft himself. Communicating by telephone, we would regularly speak for long periods of time, only short bursts of which were spent actually recapping Kevin's career. The remainder was taken up by laughter, as we swapped tales of the characters who once bestrode our game like giants. Kevin generates a natural warmth and humour. Add to that his many years in professional rugby league, both as a player at the highest level and a coach of some of the biggest clubs in the game, and the reader will have an idea of what a pleasure it has been to take this long and unforgettable journey through the greatest game among the greatest men. A special mention too to Kevin's wife, Janet, who so often waited for Kevin and I to finish our conversations as they were about to go out into town.

There has been many a telephone call to the former Leigh chairman, Mr. Brian Bowman, who was always on hand to help with any query. Thanks are also due to my wife Rita, who acted as a dictionary so many times in spelling the big words I so rarely use.

A final note of gratitude must go to Mr. John Wilkinson, chairman for so many seasons at Salford City Reds; that fine all-round international John Woods; and arguably the best player of all-time, Alex Murphy, for their testimonials to our central character - the one and only Kevin Ashcroft.

Contents

Foreword - by John Wilkinson OBE ix
Introduction - by Maurice Bamford xiii

The Last of the Dinosaurs

Chapter One...19
Chapter Two 35
Chapter Three...49
Chapter Four...75
Chapter Five...117
Chapter Six...161
Chapter Seven 177
Chapter Eight..225
Chapter Nine 233

Kevin's Dream Teams..237
Epilogue..239
Afterword - by Kevin Ashcroft.......................................243

Testimonials

An appreciation - by John Woods 247
The Last Word - by Alex Murphy OBE 249

FOREWORD

BY JOHN WILKINSON OBE

It is indeed an honour to be asked to contribute the foreword to this biography of a rugby league legend, who exceeded himself as a player, coach and a great ambassador of our beloved game.

My first contact with Kevin was in the late 1970s, when he was managing at Locker Industries, a company owned by Brian Pitchford, the Warrington chairman.

At that time, I was a service engineer, repairing and supplying welding equipment, and an avid Salford supporter. Kevin and I had many conversations on the subject of rugby league during my visits to the firm. So when Alex Murphy OBE - then the coach at Salford - signed Kevin to play in the number nine position, a firm friendship grew.

When Alex resigned as head coach and Kevin took over in the role, he was instrumental in my taking over the chairmanship of this great club on 18th January 1982.

Unfortunately, two months into my tenure, Kevin was

approached by Warrington, one of his former clubs, to take over the coaching responsibilities there. It was a hard decision for him to make, as Brian was Kevin's boss and desperately needed his services. When Kevin left the Willows, it was a bitter blow to myself and the club, but the circumstances dictated.

In July 1984, Salford again had a vacancy for a head coach and Kevin had become available. It was a good move for Salford and Kevin, who worked well in tandem with Tommy Grainey as his assistant and Bob Welding as 'A' team coach. I can honestly say that the following six years were possibly my most enjoyable in the game. Those three gentlemen were great to be around and I will always appreciate the loyalty and commitment they gave to me and our club. We saw promotion to the first division in the first season, two Lancashire Cup finals and a Challenge Cup semi-final appearance against Wigan (when they were in their pomp), played at the old Burnden Park ground in Bolton.

Over the years, I have found as a club chairman that the hardest decision to make is when you part company with your head coach. If you have both shown true loyalty and results have not been good, it is a very difficult and sad time. The supporters vent their frustration and the outcome is that the coach loses his position.

Kevin gave the Salford club six years of wonderful service under my chairmanship and, I can honestly say, our friendship is as strong today as it was when we first met in the late 'seventies.

I was so proud to be asked to be the guest speaker at a tribute dinner for Kevin, recently held at the Lowton Civic Hall, Leigh. It was a great occasion, strongly attended by the many people who Kevin has come into contact with during a wonderful career. It was particularly nice to be in the company of Leigh's 1971 Challenge Cup winning team, who travelled far and wide to be part of this nostalgic evening.

So, Kevin, thank you for your tremendous contribution to our great game. Thank you too for the times we shared at Salford and your esteemed friendship, which will be treasured for a lifetime.

John A. Wilkinson OBE
Chairman
Salford City Reds

INTRODUCTION

As our game moved inexorably towards the Super League era, with its wholesale changes in laws, skills and even the time of year in which it was played, one never envisaged that over one hundred years worth of wonderful earthy characters were, like the dinosaur and dodo before them, about to die out forever.

One train of thought is that full-time employment and the tremendously high contracts paid to modern players is one reason for the demise of these ultra-tough, hard and yet extremely humorous men. Another is simply that the age in which such fine sportsmen were produced gradually made way, in a natural progression, for the game we see today. Either way, that the loss of employment away from rugby league has had some input on the personality of its players is a possibility that can't be ignored. From the launch of Super League in 1996, the game's whole persona changed. Weekly television coverage and increased media interest totally remoulded the sport and its century of traditions.

Among the casualties were the individual characters our game produced - men with jobs and a strong social life away from rugby league football. The ordinary supporter would meet his or her heroes in most aspects of normal life, walking through town or out for the odd drink and, in most cases, would find the player very approachable. It was quite normal to meet a player, enquire about his health and reiterate ones support for him and his team-mates. The supporter would most often receive a friendly word in return and this bred a feeling that the supporter was part of their favourite team. The fact that the players had 'ordinary' jobs, away from football, helped to maintain a two-feet-on-the-ground attitude and kept the players in touch with the real world and its individual problems.

Despite today's players being bigger, fitter and stronger than their predecessors, between its conception in the late 1800s and the arrival of summer Super League in 1996, the sport produced players with a different level of skill. Rugby league was a far more brutal game than it is now, and while one may consider that a step forward it did somehow cater for the entertainment of the spectator of those days. The game was a little slower too, mainly because of the tactical innovations introduced by the styles of coaching employed. Tackling - or 'dee-fence' as it is now called - was far tougher, with a vastly greater number of high tackles overlooked, hence the cauliflower ears, broken noses and facial scar tissue worn as medals of honour by the old-timers. Overall, the skill factor - and this is a very debatable point - is considered by most former players to have been higher in the pre-Super League era than it is today.

What follows is the biography of one player from that era. His name is Kevin Ashcroft. He was a hooker for his county and country, with a CV that reads, whether as player or coach, as a great success story.

In Kevin's day, every position on the field required its own set of skills. A hooker's brief was, first and foremost, to gain at least his share of the ball from what were then highly-competitive set scrums. His instructions in the 'loose' were to attend to the vital role of dummy-half at as many play-the-balls as possible, and hit the correct side of the field without being told. He was also expected to run the football out and away from the dummy-half position to gain forward ground, support any break by a team-mate and, on defence, produce rock solid tackling in and around the immediate vicinity of the play-the-ball.

As for winning the ball, the scrums in those days were competitive to a very high degree. The hooker was expected to be alert, have the speed of foot to strike for the ball like a cobra and, above all, be blessed with razor sharp instincts of self-preservation. The simultaneous full-blooded head-butts of an opposing front row; the sly and hurtful punch from the opponents' second row; the stray elbow flashing across ones face just before the scrum was formed or after it had begun to break away; plus the ever dangerous collapsing scrum were just some of the dangers that faced the hooker at every set-piece.

No doubt such a tough battleground helped to shape the characters whose part in each game, and at every scrum, was to assume the position of a crucified man, with arms draped around his two props' necks, as both packs reared up and charged like stags in the rutting season, to meet, head on, without flinching, in a sickening collision that was intended to maim one of the competing sets of forwards, with the hooker the number one target. Those who do not remember competitive scrums may think this description overblown, but I can assure you that it did happen, exactly as described. The chances of an all-out brawl between the two forward packs was always bubbling away under the surface and, rest assured, both hookers would be prominent in any such fracas. For that was the nature of their position.

The book before you tells the story of just such a man; one of the most colourful and in-your-face hookers that rugby league has ever produced.

While serving the game in almost every crucial position, whether as player or coach on the international, county and club scene, media manager, commercial manger or radio personality, Kevin Ashcroft's strong suit has always been his sense of humour. His tough exterior sometimes hides the funny side of a man who is always a pleasure to meet, or call on the phone.

As when he played, Kevin is on the ball in his evaluation of the modern game and its players, having seen service with some of the top clubs of his era. As a player he was an enigma and one of the first hookers to invent a style of play that suited him and his character. He broke the game down to fit his playing strengths and therefore became a 'modern day hooker' in the old-fashioned game, yet he could also be classed as one of the last of the old-time rakes. His astute dummy-half play, no-nonsense powerful tackling, in-built reading of a game and tactical awareness would surely have earmarked him as Super League class today. In comparing Kevin to present-day hookers, perhaps the one to whom he is most similar is Matt Diskin, of Leeds Rhinos. Kevin may well have the drop on Matt with his overall strength and physique, but both are comparable in dummy-half play, strong tackling, picking the best way to point the attack and superb opportunists.

In his pomp, Kevin played with and against some of the finest and toughest front-rowers ever seen. The list includes top hookers like Tony Fisher, Peter 'Flash' Flanagan, Keith Bridges, Bob Dagnall, Tony Karalius, Johnny Ward, Clive Dickinson and Colin Clarke to name but a few. Among the best props, meanwhile, were Cliff Watson, Stan Owen, Jim Mills, Dennis Hartley, Terry Clawson, Arthur Beetson, Bill Martin, Brian Edgar, Frank Foster, plus many more.

So, here is the tale of Kevin Ashcroft, a man guaranteed to bring a ray of sunshine into any meeting. The sort of happy hooker that, once upon a time, rugby league was all about. I hope you enjoy his story.

Maurice Bamford
March 2008

CHAPTER ONE

Kevin Ashcroft is never without a quick word or quip. When, at the end of a long, distinguished and successful career some idiot called him a dinosaur, Kevin answered without hesitation: 'Thanks very much, did you know that dinosaurs ruled the world for millions of years'.

Kevin first saw light of day on 5th June 1944. Another major event occurred around that time too, but D-Day pales into insignificance when compared with this man's arrival. The Ashcroft family home was in Earle Street, in the small industrial area of Earlestown, one-and-a-half miles north of Newton-le-Willows.

Originally, Earlestown was built to house the navvies who worked on the Manchester to Liverpool railway. With the railroad finished, the place developed into the home of the giant Vulcan ironworks, a huge complex of furnaces and steam trip hammers that fed the hungry bellies of Britain with iron, thereby helping to build an Empire on which the sun never set. Running parallel to the ironworks was the

Viaduct wagon works, another big, noisy factory and work base.

The Ashcroft family consisted of mum Bessie, dad Billy and Kevin. The young Ashcroft attended Earlestown District School and then moved up to the Council School, which was the normal progression of education in those days. It was at the Council School that Kevin came under the tutelage of Mr. Ben Higham, a good man and a sports-minded teacher who loved his pupils to follow the Corinthian code and excel at sports, occasionally to the detriment of lessons. As Kevin remembers: 'I received the best of both worlds, as I left that school with the ability to play sport and knew my one times table.'

Billy Ashcroft, Kevin's dad, had served in His Majesty's Royal Navy during the Second World War and saw life in that most dangerous of services, the submarines. Kevin's mum, Bessie, had been an international swimmer and represented Lancashire and England in several events. Bessie's dad and Kevin's grandad Billy Harrison, meanwhile, was a Leigh lad who, in his youth, had been a tough old street fighter for money. Life was hard in Billy Harrison's day. There was no money and no work, so the fit, tough kids took to making a few bob as best they could. Billy would take on all-comers for 'brass'. He would also make a few shillings in that most brutal of all street corner sports, 'clog shin kicking'. Billy, like most of his age group, always wore clogs.

A typical shin kicking contest involved two clog-wearing contestants. Each sat on a chair facing the other and took it in turns to kick the shins of his opponent, until the contestant who was prepared to continue the longest was declared the winner. The gladiators who took part in this brutal competition took their battle scars to the grave, as their shins were gnarled and dented forever. On Sundays,

Billy always had a special pair of clogs to wear. These 'Dandy Clogs' were made of shiny black leather and decorated around each sole by a row of brightly polished brass studs.

A tough old boy was Billy Harrison. When Billy's wife Mary, Kevin's grandma, died, the old man was left to live alone in Leigh as best he could. Bessie travelled through to care for her dad every day from Earlestown.

Kevin takes up the story: 'He was a rum old lad was my grandad. He had followed Leigh rugby league all his life and had tales galore about the characters in and around the club. At the back end, he loved watching big Stan Owen play. He used to say, "Yon fella's a hard lad", meaning Stan. As his health failed, he would ask me to bring him cigarettes from the corner shop. Then my mam would play hell with me for bringing them for him, but my grandad wanted a smoke so I did as I was asked.'

Kevin's dad, Billy Ashcroft, had a mate in Earlestown, a Scots lad called Jock McPhillips, who was a keen boxer and had been a professional fighter in Scotland. Jock ran a boxing club in the Sea Scouts main hall and Billy thought that teaching his son the noble art of self defence would hold the lad in good stead as he grew up in a rough time. So Billy took his son down to watch the training and young master Ashcroft quickly became hooked.

Under the shrewd coaching of Jock McPhillips, Kevin developed into an aggressive young scrapper who was soon a star of his weight division. The Earlestown Sea Cadets boxing team, at ten various weights, became well known and won many competitions. Kevin boxed at the lightest weight, seven stone, and within a short time the Sea Cadets had won their way to the 1954 ABA finals. Boxing firstly at regional level, then over in Preston for the quarter and semi-finals in which Kevin beat a lad called Dougherty to go through to the finals at the Albert Hall in London, Kevin became ABA champion of his weight when he beat his opponent in the final.

It was around this time that young Kevin ventured into the world of big business. His forte was catering but, to set the scene, one needs to know about his business partners.

Earle Street was a row of houses with all sizes of families living there. A few doors down from the Ashcrofts lived a large family with the surname of Garry. The Garry family consisted of five sisters and seven brothers. A couple of doors further down were the Duttons. They were a fair-sized family too, but not as big as the Garrys. Kevin was mates with both families but his best mate was 'Lion' Garry, so named for his ability to climb anything in the known world.

At the end of Earle Street was an old-fashioned corner shop which made and sold delicious meat pies on the premises. The family who owned and ran the shop was called Roștron. Now, this was one of those shops that, as a kid, one would stand around outside just to soak up the aroma when they were baking. Over the road from Rostrons was the Viaduct wagon works. Between them and the Vulcan ironworks, the little corner shop made a fortune selling their delicious pies.

Setting up the Earle Street mafia was easy. Kevin and 'Lion' were the Godfathers and everyone else the soldiers. The catering idea was a joint venture between Kevin and 'Lion'. They realised that Rostrons made their pies twice a day. The morning bake was for the men buying one for their breakfast. The second bake was for dinner time, when the workmen rushed over to the shop for their midday pie. Rostron's back yard was spotlessly clean. It backed onto the Ashcoft's backyard and was separated only by a wooden fence which had a gap under the bottom rail to stop it rotting. Those gorgeous pies were taken out into the yard to cool. They were in flat trays and easily slid on the spotless yard floor.

Ever the opportunists, Ashcroft and Garry Ltd devised a method of sliding the trays up to the dividing fence, thence under it and off to the works big gates to sell their plunder. Business was brisk each morning, as the two young entrepreneurs sold the pies at twopence each. The shop could not explain the loss of the morning trade and the two bushrangers continued to coin in the pennies until they were spotted by a bobby on the beat, who checked with Rostrons and the game was up. Kevin knew the business had gone belly up when he was confronted by a huge policeman and his straight-as-a-die dad. The end product was a warning from the bobby and a good hiding from Billy. It was a good scam while it lasted and it was nice to have a few bob in ones pocket, but Kevin had learned that crime did not pay.

* * *

Back at the Council school, the word had gone around that there was an ABA champion on the premises and every afternoon, on the way home, there would be another contender after his title. Kevin says: 'Some afternoons they were queuing up to fight me. I think I had more fights than Archie Moore. Most kids are the same weight at that age, give or take a few pounds, but one or two were bigger lads. Anyway, I was still ABA champion at the end.'

When Kevin was thirteen years old his mum and dad decided to move over to Leigh to be nearer his grandad, Billy. The move meant that Kevin again had to change schools. He was registered at Manchester Road School and there came under the attention of the respected headmaster, Mr. Bert Causey. Mr. Causey would have a profound influence on Kevin's whole lifestyle. He was a strict disciplinarian who, above all, cared sincerely for the welfare and future of all his pupils. The headmaster's passions were learning and sport, so Kevin thought he would be alright with his boxing ability and knowing his one times' table.

As a young man, Mr. Causey had been sought after to turn professional as a wing threequarter, but decided on an academic career despite having a deep love for the game of rugby league. In making that choice, Mr. Causey was launched on a lifetime's quest of helping youngsters to take the straight path. The headmaster won tremendous respect from every youngster he came into contact with, including Kevin. 'The great man guided many kids into professional rugby league and even when these players were battle-hardened, tough professionals, everyone addressed him as either "Sir" or "Mr. Causey",' remembers Kevin. 'It was never, ever, Bert. To the day Mr. Causey died, we all used the prefix "Sir" when addressing him.'

Kevin also tells of the control Mr. Causey held over Manchester Road School. 'If we were in class and Mr. Causey walked across the playground, he could see into the classroom through the floor-to-ceiling windows. As he strode across the play area the word would go out in a whisper, "Sir is here". The class would stand to attention by their desks. Should any boy not stand when he entered, it was spotted and that boy would be summoned to appear before him and a light clip on the ear administered. The boy remembered next time.'

Mr. Causey spoke to Kevin about having another string to his bow and advised him to take up rugby league as his secondary sport. Kevin fancied the idea as all he was doing then was practising boxing (a good job, too - given how the fact that he had won the ABA championship was not missed at his new school and the unofficial 'championship bouts' for Kevin's 'belt' continued). A fair description of Kevin's ability as a boxer back then would be a tough battling kid who could bang a bit.

When fourteen years old and in his final year under the great headmaster, Kevin finally took Mr. Causey's advice about playing the rugby game. The former Wigan centre, Albert Wood, started a junior team at the Roman Catholic club of St. Mary's in Leigh and he asked Kevin to come along. Mr. Causey had coached Kevin in the art of scrum-half play so, when he joined St. Mary's, it was as a half-back. Kevin enjoyed himself tremendously and the rough and ready camaraderie suited him well.

Meanwhile, he continued to box and, at the age of fifteen, the highly-respected promoter Harry Levine contacted Billy Ashcroft to ask if his son would join his stable of boxers - some of them the brightest prospects around. Billy was a streetwise father and thought hard about this offer for his son's future. In the end, though, he thanked Harry Levine for his interest and told him that the only stable Kevin would be joining was the Burtonwood Engineering Company, where Billy had been able to gain Kevin an apprenticeship. Even so, the young Ashcroft was clearly no mug at the fighting game and in time was selected to spar against the world champion, Hogan 'Kid' Bassey.

Given that Kevin was so good a scrapper it came as a surprise when, the morning after a night out with his mates to celebrate his eighteenth birthday, he awoke with the biggest black eye ever. The birthday party had been a pub crawl around Leigh and all had taken onboard a substantial amount of alcohol. It had been a very foggy night and, eventually, the group headed back to Mr. and Mrs. Ashcroft's home for a meal and bed. In fact, it was so foggy that Leigh Council had hung paraffin lamps out to assist travellers. Having had their fill of Kevin's mum's food, the lads made their way to sleep it off in Kevin's bedroom.

Kevin later recalled that he'd had a restless night's sleep and remembered, in a half-awake stupor, seeing black cobwebs hanging from the ceiling of his room. Knowing how houseproud his mum was, he thought it was the beer making him see things. Come the morning, however, Kevin came back to the land of the living and found himself unable to open his sore eye. Then he realised that one of his mates had foolishly brought one of the lamps from the street into his bedroom and that the fumes had caused the black cobwebs to hang from the ceiling, ruining the spotless painted plaster.

When his dad came in to see how the mates were coping with their hangovers, he said to Kevin: 'That's a great shiner you've got Kevin, were you fighting last night?' Kevin couldn't remember, but said he thought that they had not been carrying on. 'No lad,' his dad confirmed. 'It wasn't a fight. Your mam came in to see how you were and saw the lamp doing the damage. She took the lamp outside, came back in and smacked you with a punch that would have sickened Joe Louis. If I were you, I'd get your mates to give you a hand redecorating.' This they did and the mystery of the black eye was solved.

* * *

Kevin maintained his connection with St. Mary's rugby league team and was becoming talked about as a prospect when he played in a knockout competition in Leigh, known as the Shaw Cup, which St. Mary's won. Amongst the spectators was Gwyne Davies, the cracking stand-off half and local Leigh lad who had then signed for Dewsbury. Gwyne was the brother of Alan Davies, the great centre who played at Oldham and Wigan, as well as Great Britain and Lancashire. Gwyne was a wonderful player too. It must have come from their father, the former Leigh half-back Harry 'Cocky' Davies, who had signed for the club in 1930. Harry worked for one of the Leigh board of directors as a joiner and it was said that his favourite run from a scrum was around the blind side when, on almost every occasion, he was smashed into advertising boards that were demolished on impact. It was Harry's job the following Monday morning to repair the broken boards, thereby making a few quid for his boss and keeping himself in work.

Gwyne Davies had a car, so travelling to Dewsbury for training was not that difficult for Kevin. And, after a couple of trial games, he was signed as a professional player for the Dewsbury club as a very promising scrum-half for the princely sum of £100. Of that fee, £50 was paid on signing and another £50 after three first-team games. Kevin's problem at Dewsbury, though, was that the club had just signed a scrum-half from Hunslet, Ally Newall, and he was the club captain. Even so, by now Kevin was just nineteen years old, so he had plenty of time in which to make his mark as a number seven. He didn't know it then, but he was about to embark on a wonderful career that would take him around the world twice on all-expense paid trips, and see him become a highly respected sportsman at both county and international level.

The Dewsbury side he joined was full of excellent young players, mostly signed from local junior rugby. All were destined to make a name for themselves in the tough, brutal game that was, in those days, rugby league football. Of the youngsters learning their trade, Bob Hirst, Kevin Osborne, Brian Firth, John Harvey, Colin Byrom, Bob Walker, George Newsome, Gwyne Davies and Ally Newall were the regular backs, while Trevor 'Tank' Walker, Brian Taylor, Jim Naylor, Brian Smith, Barry Rushworth, Les Jones, 'Dick' Lowe, Peter Mullins and Doug Manners were in the pack. Kevin could even see a difference in the standard of rugby between St. Mary's and Dewsbury's 'A' team. Players were bigger, faster and vastly more experienced. He met players who had come to the end of their careers because of age, players who had served an apprenticeship in this level and were ready for the big time, and players who could not raise their game to move their careers onward and upward.

Coaching the Dewsbury side was former international forward and Wigan star, Charlie Seeling Jr, who had been impressed by Kevin's work as a half-back. One day, coach Seeling pulled Kevin out of training and told him that the regular hooker for Dewsbury, Brian Smith, was injured and that the club was stuck for a replacement in the number nine jersey. Now Kevin knew how important the hooking role was and told the coach that he had never played there before. Charlie Seeling, though, put Kevin at ease and told him that he thought playing hooker would push the young man on in the world of rugby league.

Encouraged, Kevin said he would do it, so coach Seeling put his young charge in the practice scrum, giving him tips and showing him all the trade secrets. His first game for Dewsbury in that position was to be against Bramley at Crown Flatt on 12th October 1963, a baptism of fire if ever there was one. A key figure for the Bramley 'Villagers' then was the big, tough prop Dave Horne. This fearsome man was a renowned scrummager, standing well over 6ft tall and weighing in at around eighteen stones. He was as strong as a bull and, being well-seasoned, would do whatever was necessary to gain winning money. Dave Horne's hooking partner was iron man Dennis Morgan, a Featherstone lad originally who had moved around the league to several clubs, each paying Dennis his worth as a ball winner. Morgan knew every trick in the book and alongside Dave Horne was almost invincible. One can only sympathise with

Kevin. A hooking novice, he was up against arguably one of the better props in Yorkshire and a real battle-hardened old pro.

Kevin tells the story: 'Those two butted, kicked and punched me throughout the game and, no matter what my prop did to protect me, they really gave it to me. I was black and blue, but I learned a lot from Dennis Morgan about getting into the correct position early in the scrum. I also learned about hooking the ball from behind the opposing hooker's legs. Several times, Dennis appeared to let me win the ball, then he would sweep those big legs behind me and take both the ball and me almost out of the pack.' It was indeed a great experience for the young Ashcroft. Although beaten for the ball by two to one, Kevin played his part in a 14 points to 8 victory. He was a quick learner in that kill or be killed position and, in this tough game, did enough in attack and defence to warrant keeping his place until the more experienced Brian Smith returned.

As it happened, Kevin played in the following two games, a 6-4 win against Salford at the Willows and a 13-5 home defeat to a very strong Castleford outfit. But those three games in the first team earned Kevin his second payment of £50. He couldn't wait to get to Tuesday evening training to get his hands on the fifty quid. He went straight to the secretary's office and faced the rather miserable Tom Clerk with the brash confidence of someone so sure of himself. Tom, a straight-faced character, said: 'The chairman, Brearley Bailey, has your money and he won't be in until next week. You will get it then.' What a disappointment! Gwyne Davies advised Kevin to ask again on Thursday when they went to training and Kevin did just that. Tom Clerk was as evasive as ever with his excuses: 'Mr. Bailey has been in and gone home - he said he would see you next Thursday.' Suddenly, Kevin could smell a rat. 'Will the chairman be in on Saturday for the match?' he asked. 'If he is, he can bring it then can't he?' 'I've told you next Thursday,' snapped the secretary and Kevin had to leave it there. Back in the 'A' team, Kevin dashed the following Thursday to see Tom Clerk. 'Is it here?' he asked. The secretary looked at Kevin over his glasses, as he usually did, and said in a sarcastic way: 'We aren't running off with your £50. Mr. Bailey has been called away suddenly and will see you next week.'

That was it. Kevin demanded to get in touch with the chairman immediately and, whilst he was speaking to Tom Clerk, in walked the vice-chairman Mr. Roy Harter. Now, Roy was a former player at the club and knew the way of things. 'How much do we owe you Kevin?' he asked. '£50 Mr. Harter, it's my contract money,' Kevin replied. Roy Harter turned to Tom Clerk and asked: 'Has Kevin fulfilled his contract requirements?' The sullen secretary nodded. 'Right then, Tom, give me the petty cash box,' and he withdrew £50 and gave it to Kevin with a handshake and hearty congratulations. Kevin had learned another lesson. Club secretary's were well known for being tight with club funds. Tom Clerk had given Kevin the run-around for two weeks and, if Roy Harter hadn't shown up when he did, it would have taken him a lot longer than that to get his deserved money.

Kevin's travelling partner and good mate was the aforementioned Gwyne Davies. Gwyne was an excellent footballer, not as powerful as his brother Alan, but everything else was in place. A prodigious side-stepper with wonderful skills, a good turn of pace and first class hands, he was the perfect stand-off half. He was also a character in his own right and as explosive as gelignite. Kevin tells of Gwyne being engaged to one of the prettiest young ladies in Leigh for twenty-three years. Then, during an extended holiday abroad, he met another very wealthy lady much older than he, wed her, returned home to Leigh and calmly told his previous fiancée: 'I have some news for you love. I'm married.' It was as simple as that. Gwyne's wife was a good ten years older than he and, after a few years together, she died, leaving the top-class stand-off a very wealthy man. Unfortunately, only three months after the death of his wife, Gwyne too passed away.

'Gwyne was a shrewd one for getting individual bonuses for games,' Kevin recalls. 'We were playing Wakefield Trinity at Crown Flatt and we were behind at half-time by 10 points to 2. I heard Gwyne talking to the chairman about a special deal for him if we won the game. "It will be worth £20 to you Gwyne if we win," said Brearley Bailey. In the second half Gwyne scored two unbelievable tries, both from a long way out. Dick Lowe kicked the goals and we won 12 -10.' Gwyne picked up his £20 bonus after the game.

In the defeat by Castleford, Kevin damaged an ankle. It turned out to be ligament trouble and he missed three matches. Then, being a youngster, he rushed back too soon and the ankle went again in a game up in Cumbria against Whitehaven. Despite winning the match 15-5, it cost him another fifteen games off injured. That was no use to Kevin. He had tasted first team rugby and the added incentive of a few winning pay packets, and he wanted more. Another lesson learned, then, was to make sure you are completely over your injury before you come back.

Eventually, he recovered and was declared fit. After a couple of good 'A' team games he was back in the first team for the final five fixtures of the season. The enforced lay-off had sharpened his enthusiasm and, as he picked up more and more experience in the hooking role, so his own game developed. Those five final matches were against Wakefield Trinity, a 23-8 away loss, two home wins, 10-0 against

Whitehaven and 5-0 against Huddersfield, and a couple of games against Liverpool City and Barrow. The Liverpool clash was a 15-3 away victory, in which Kevin scored the first of the sixty-one tries he would register in his career. The last match brought a strong Barrow side down to Dewsbury, where the Red, Amber and Black's won 13-0, to end the season on a high note.

* * *

Kevin trained hard in the close-season, determined to make up for those missed matches in the last campaign. His form in pre-season training was good, so he was promoted to number one hooker to start the 1964-65 season. A defeat at home to Oldham by 17 points to 4 in the first game was a disappointment. But two days later, Dewsbury recorded a sensational 12-10 win at Belle Vue over Wakefield Trinity. The euphoria soon evaporated when York inflicted a 23-15 defeat at the old Clarence Street ground, and then another disappointment came with a reverse at the hands of Bramley by 19 points to 4. In this game, Kevin set his stall out to erase the misery of his debut last season. And, although his team were beaten, Kevin had possibly his best game ever for Dewsbury.

The opening four games, then, had produced one win and three losses. The next, though, was not only the first round of the Yorkshire Cup, it turned out to be Kevin's last match for Dewsbury. It was also virtually the end of that super footballer, Gwyne Davies's career. The County Cup match in question was against Wakefield Trinity, whom Dewsbury had beaten recently at Belle Vue. The referee was the very experienced Mr. R.L. 'Dicky' Thomas of Oldham and the match was a real thriller. Both sides moved up and down the field in a tremendous exhibition of fast, open football. Then, with the score 11-10 to Trinity and the game going into its final ten minutes, Gwyne Davies beat his opponent directly from a scrum and set off on a brilliant run. As he approached the Wakefield full-back, Gwyne chipped the ball over his opponent's head, raced around him, took it first bounce into his hands and sped over by the Trinity posts for what seemed surely to be the winning score.

The Dewsbury celebrations were short-lived, however, as Mr. Thomas had already disallowed the try. He said that Gwyne Davies had knocked on whilst collecting his own kick through. There was pandemonium on the Crown Flatt playing area, as the Dewsbury players pleaded with the referee to check with his touch judges. But Mr. Thomas was adamant: 'No try'. This was too much for Gwyne, who had argued that it was a fair score. He suggested that if the referee had been unsighted when the incident occurred, he should take advice from a touch judge. Again 'Dicky' Thomas refused and Gwyne seemed to throw a punch at the referee, before turning smartly away and walking off to the dressing rooms. Although suspended sine die, Gwyne was granted a pardon a few years later and returned to rugby league. But the spark had gone and he retired from the game after only a few weeks.

CHAPTER TWO

Unbeknown to Kevin Ashcroft, things had been going on behind the scenes for a month or two. Rochdale Hornets, it seemed, were in need of a good young hooker.

Kevin's grandad's hero, Stan Owen, had by this time left Leigh and joined St. Helens, before moving on to Rochdale soon after. Stan had signed for Leigh from Pontypridd rugby union way back in 1951, but he was still a fearsome prop. As Kevin himself says: 'Once Stan was set in the scrum, nothing would move him.' At Rochdale, Mr. Arthur Walker, the Hornets chairman, had asked big Stan to see if Kevin would come to the club. So, when the prop next saw young Ashcroft, he asked him: 'Why did you go into Yorkshire to play, Ashy? You want to get back into Lancashire and cut out all that travelling'. And that had been that, nothing more.

Until, out of the blue, the Dewsbury chairman Brearley Bailey one day stopped Kevin as he was walking into the dressing room. 'I've agreed terms with Rochdale for you Kevin,' he said. 'So on Thursday you will be training with the Hornets.' At the time, Kevin thought it was a cheek that he had only received £100 and Dewsbury had collected £3,800 in the transfer deal. A profit of £3,700 in ten months, not bad at all. Now, though, he is philosophical.

For one thing, Kevin was only nineteen years of age when he made his first-team debut and played only fourteen games for Dewsbury in all. Obviously, when signing for your first club, everything seems clear in a young player's mind, but a sudden move can catch you unaware. The presence of Stan Owen was another big factor in Kevin's acceptance of the deal. Grandad Billy had related wonderful stories about Stan, and an opportunity to play at the side of his hero would do for Kevin. Even so, all he had to go on was Brearley Bailey's word that a deal had been done, nothing had come from Rochdale. Kevin would look a right mug if he turned up at the Athletic Ground to find the move had fallen through.

'I wondered what it was all about,' says Kevin. 'Then a sudden phone call put it all in perspective. It was Arthur Walker. "We have agreed terms with Dewsbury and Stan Owen will pick you up at your home to go to training next Tuesday evening," he said. "You can sign and train with us at the Athletic Grounds, I look forward to meeting you." Not a word about a back-hander or anything, but it was another adventure. As it worked out I received not a penny piece, but when Janet and I married in the Autumn of 1965, Arthur gave us a set of copper-bottomed pans to move into our new bungalow with.'

Janet Southern, it was, who married Kevin to become Mrs. Janet Ashcroft. In time, the couple would be blessed with a daughter, Donna, and two sons, Gary and Craig. Gary will figure later in one of the most moving and hilarious stories ever told about the game. Janet, though, would watch Kevin's career zoom from its humble beginnings at Dewsbury to the giddy heights of Wembley victories and international stardom - an exhilarating ride.

Her husband is the first to admit that his knowledge of the art and skill of competitive scrummaging was very limited when he arrived at Rochdale. The later image of the streetwise and ultra-professional hooker Kevin Ashcroft was still some way off when the enthusiastic youngster first swung around the necks of his two experienced props, Stan Owen and Peter Birchall. After being transferred from St. Helens to Rochdale after only thirteen games, Stan Owen had made his debut for the Hornets immediately after playing for Saints in the second round of the Lancashire Cup at Barrow in September 1964. Peter Birchall, meanwhile, was also a very solid, tough prop and still a comparatively young man. Between these front-row partners, Kevin honed his hooking skills to a fine edge. The two excellent and respected prop forwards taught Kevin the sneaky tricks that all hookers had in their repertoire and there was so much to learn.

The Rochdale coach at the time was the very good centre turned loose forward, Johnny Noon. As a former member of Oldham's wonderful side of the 1950s and '60s, Noon knew the game thoroughly. Kevin's learning curve, however, was not without hiccups. In one particular game at Fartown, against a robust Huddersfield team, Rochdale, despite having a solid front row, were being licked for possession. The Fartown hooker that day was the terrific ball winner Don Close who, along with his two huge props, was giving young Ashcroft a very rough ride. During one lull in play, Kevin pulled his scrum-half, Johnny Fishwick, to his side and said: 'Is there anybody at all putting the *&^%$ ball in this pack? I haven't seen one *&^%$ feed yet!' That is how good Close was. It was a very tight, dour game and as they were going to a scrum, big Stan growled: 'We need some ball, Ashy, badly.' But hard as Kevin tried he could not get the better of Don Close.

When half-time arrived, Stan and Peter Birchall got their heads together. Stan then put his huge arm around Kevin and said: 'When I give the word, let Closey pinch the loose head.' Now, this was a ploy often used by the experienced hooker of the day. Having the loose head meant that your head was nearest the ball coming into the pack, giving that hooker a distinct advantage. Most hookers tried to steal that position as the scrums formed via sheer strength or devious means. 'Don't forget Ashy, let him pinch the head when I tell you,' Stan reminded Kevin, and out they went for the second half.

With around twenty minutes to play, the two packs began forming for a crucial scrum. 'Now, Ashy. Give him the head and just relax,' growled Stan. So Kevin allowed Don Close to steal the head, relaxed and woke up fifteen minutes later on his way to Rochdale Infirmary, where the half-back Johnny Fishwick later called in to see how his team-mate was. 'Bloody hell Ashy,' he said. 'I saw Don Close pinch the head, then Stan throw a right-hander into Closey, but he hit you on the way through and you shot out of the scrum like a rocket. He saw Closey off too. The punch bounced off you into Don's face.' The plan had worked. Don Close was removed from the Huddersfield front row, the Hornets won some ball in the latter stages of the game and came out winners by a single point, 6-5. Kevin recalls: 'What could I do or say to big Stan? I thought of asking him to be more careful next time, but quickly decided to say nowt and put it down to experience.'

Overall, the impression made upon Kevin by playing alongside the big man was immeasurable. Stan taught Kevin how to scrummage. He taught him how to gain the advantage in any circumstances when confronted by the opposing front row. He showed Kevin the tricks of the trade of the front row union. Followers of the modern game who may not be au fait with the age of competitive scrummaging might well wince if all those 'tricks of the trade' were listed here. But they were many and varied and downright vicious in their application. Punching, raking, kicking, head-butting, biting, kneeing, everything went to ensure the ever-required necessity of winning the ball at every scrum. That was every hooker's desire. At the time Kevin joined the professional ranks, the amount of possession gained from a set-piece was crucial to the end-of-match result. To break even in the scrum count was not really good enough, as it meant a hard slog through the mud, on both attack and defence, in those wintry conditions encountered from November through to March. The aim was to win more than your share.

The hooker's main assets in that aim were his two prop forwards. The pivot of the professional scrum was the field-side or open-side prop. He was the fulcrum by which the scrum-half levered the ball clear from the pack for the use of the backs. The open-side prop's place in the pack was nearest to the scrum-half, who also had the job of feeding the ball in. Strength and nimbleness of foot were paramount in this prop's armoury of skills, as many times he had to contend with the weight of the opposing pack whilst stood on one leg, his other pin heeling the ball back for his hooker. The blind-side prop's job, meanwhile, was to scrummage slightly behind the hooker, thus allowing him to virtually sit on the prop's inside leg as if in an armchair, as they used to say. All very technical, but all very important to the workings of a successful front row.

Stan Owen was a master in the scrum and he put Kevin right as to the intricacies of scrummaging to win. Kevin tells of a trick taught by Stan of the advantages of gaining the 'loose arm'. This was engineered to allow the hooker to be able to swing his feet nearer to the ball as it entered the tunnel of the scrum. With the two packs coming together to form a scrum, Kevin would stand up as the heads of the front rowers met. Then, complaining that he couldn't get into the pack, Kevin would slip his arm from around Stan's neck and push the opposing hooker upwards so he could enter the scrum, never returning his arm back over Stan's neck. This left Kevin with an advantage over his opponent, as he could swing across to the tunnel's mouth with ease. Stan taught Kevin to cheat a wee bit too, as that was the nature of the hooker's game back then.

Almost every hooker had his own party piece that he brought to the scrum. The total disregard to personal safety shown by the hooker in his determination to win the ball resulted in some distasteful and downright foul tactics from his beaten opponents. The most widely used tactic was to trample and stamp on the prostrate rake after he had won the ball. But the experienced hooker knew the dangers and was prepared for the punch, head-butt, rake of the studs, kick or drop of the knees. All these things Stan taught Kevin and, in doing so, helped to produce one of our game's outstanding players.

Kevin tells of his stay at Rochdale: 'My debut for the Hornets was, would you believe, against Dewsbury, my old club, on 28th November 1964 - a 7-7 draw. My final game was in the first round of the Challenge Cup on 4th February 1966, when we lost 18-2 to Hull Kingston Rovers. I managed to score two tries in the eighty-two games I played. We had a number of good Fijians playing at Rochdale then and Voate Drui, Appi [Apisia] Toga or Liatia Ravouvou would step up to the front row if Peter or Stan were indisposed. Another grand prop came to us from Warrington, the tough, no-nonsense Bill Payne.'

* * *

Kevin's emergence under the tuition of big Stan didn't go unnoticed. In April 1965, Kevin and Peter Birchall were selected for Great Britain under-24s to play France in Toulouse.

This was a tremendous achievement as Kevin had played just twenty-nine first-team games before international selection. Great Britain's first-choice hooker at that time was the great Bobby Dagnall of St. Helens, and Kevin was suddenly thrust into the limelight as a genuine contender. The competition for the Great Britain number nine jersey was immensely tough, with Kevin in the mixing pot alongside Bobby Dagnall, Johnny Ward (Castleford), Colin Clarke (Wigan), Peter 'Flash' Flanagan (Hull Kingston Rovers) and Don Close (Huddersfield).

The letter informing Kevin of his selection arrived on 18th March and explained everything: team, remuneration, passports, currency, dress, equipment, personal fitness and the itinerary. Remuneration stated that £15 would be paid for a win, £12 for a draw and £10 for a loss. £1 per day would be paid as subsistence allowance and second-class train fare would be paid on a return ticket from home to Manchester. Passports: 'all players to notify RLHQ if they are in possession of a valid passport. If not then one must be obtained immediately from the local Ministry of Labour Offices, with the cost to be refunded.' Currency: 'a maximum of £50 in notes only may be taken out of the country. Foreign currency notes up to £250 may be taken abroad. The exchange rate is 13.65 NF to the pound [1NF = 100 old Francs = one shilling, five-and-a-half pence]. Please note, continental hotels do not supply soap to the bedrooms. Please take your own.' Dress: 'club or international blazers and flannels would be very suitable for the playing members of the party. Kindly keep the weight of your luggage down to a minimum.' Equipment: 'jerseys, shorts and stockings will be supplied for the match but players must supply all other gear they require. Each player is held personally responsible for returning his own playing gear, jersey, shorts and stockings at the conclusion of the game.' Personal Fitness: 'you will be assumed fit if you do not notify us. If injured between now and the day of departure you must let me know without delay.' Itinerary: 'Please see attached note. If you intend to proceed directly to the airport, please let me know.' The letter was signed: 'Yours faithfully, Bill Fallowfield, sec.'

The itinerary began on Friday 2nd April. It read: '10.00hrs - Assemble Manchester Exchange Station and proceed by coach to Ringway Airport. 11.45hrs - Depart Ringway Airport, lunch on plane. 12.55hrs - arrive Paris. Tour of Paris by mini bus in afternoon. Dinner at Orly Airport. 21.10hrs - Depart Paris. 22.20hrs - arrive Toulouse. Motor coach to hotel. Saturday 3rd April. Motor coach from hotel to stadium [for game]. Sunday, 4th April. 08-00hrs - Leave hotel by motor coach for airport. 09-00hrs - Depart Toulouse Airport, continental breakfast on plane. 10-40hrs - Arrive Paris. 13-10hrs - Depart Paris. 14-10hrs - arrive London Airport, lunch at London Airport. Leeds Party, 19-00hrs - Depart London. 20-00hrs - Arrive Leeds. Manchester Party, 19-30hrs - Depart London. 20-15hrs - arrive Manchester. Liverpool Party, 17-25hrs - Depart London.'

So, so different than today. The teams for Kevin's first international match read thus - Great Britain: Trevor Bedford (Castleford); Rod Tickle (Leigh), Les Thomas (Keighley), Mick Collins (Leigh), Ken Senior (Huddersfield); Phil Kitchen (Whitehaven), Tommy Boylen (Blackpool Borough); Peter Birchall (Rochdale Hornets), Kevin Ashcroft (Rochdale

Hornets), Les Tonks (Featherstone Rovers), Terry Ramshaw (Featherstone Rovers), Mervyn Hicks (St. Helens), Doug Laughton (St. Helens). Subs: Jack Melling (Warrington), Brian Gains (Keighley). The French side was just as tough. It read: Yves Chabert; Gilbert Sagnard, Roger Garrigue, Jean Cabrol, Alain Doulieu; Jacky Casty, Marius Frattini; Jean Sala, Jean Galtier, Dennis Kerbrat, Michel Bardes, Hervé Mazard, Jean-Pierre Clar. The home nation's strength was based around its pack, with a big, strong front row in Sala, Galtier and Kerbrat that was guaranteed to make it hard for the virtually untried Brits. At loose forward, the excellent Clar would be France's leading forward for many years.

Kevin remembers his first international opponents well. 'The French hooker, Galtier, was a tough nut and crazy with it,' he says. 'The problem with the French was that an assault could take place at any time, you were never safe. Our pack was a tough one, though, and would stand against anyone. There were quite a few battles going on but the referee, Mr. G. Jameau, just turned away and let play continue. After a while they quietened down and we began to pressure them with some good football. Ken Senior, Tommy Boylen and Jack Melling scored tries and Big Mervyn Hicks kicked four goals. For them, the wingman Doulieu scored a try and their centre, Garrigues kicked three goals. Their loose forward, Clar, played well I remember, but we were never in danger. It was the first time for a lot of us that we had ever been to France or stayed in an hotel.

Bill Fallowfield was very formal, as one would expect from the top man at Rugby League HQ. On the morning of the match he even made us wear our ties when down for breakfast, and we ate at one long table around which sat all the players and RL staff. No one could start eating until Bill came to the table and he arrived promptly at the time stated: 08-00. He delivered a talk saying he was pleased with us looking so smart and being so punctual. Most of the lads didn't understand what he meant by punctual. Bill went on so long that one of our forwards whispered to me "I bet he will say bloody Grace next," and he did!' On the field, the 17-9 win in Toulouse was a good one, as the French had fancied their chances highly.

Three days after the French game, Hornets played Wigan at the Athletic Grounds, where Peter Birchall and Kevin returned to the pack. The result was a crushing 30-6 win for Wigan. In all, after Kevin's debut game against Dewsbury, Rochdale played a further twenty-one first-team matches and Kevin played in twenty of them, almost always with Stan Owen and Peter Birchall as his props. Kenny Parr and Appi Toga usually formed the Hornets second row, with the loose forward shop looked after by either Johnny Noon, Arthur Gregory or Micky Baxter. The half-backs were chosen from Sid Miller or Johnny Fishwick, and the stand-off job was between Miller, David Evans, Williams or Garforth.

The club's final league placing meant they just managed to land a play-off place against the old antagonists Huddersfield at Fartown, where the Claret and Golds won 36-10. A disappointing year's league and cup records can be summed up: played 37, won 7, drawn 1, lost 29.

* * *

The 1965/66 campaign began with a very good win away to York at Clarence Street, an immediate improvement as Hornets had been beaten there in the previous season. The club's next game, a 17-9 defeat to St. Helens at home, was a more historic affair, in which Kevin had his first real set-to with the great Alex Murphy. Words were exchanged and the two swapped punches.

After beating Keighley 17-3, Rochdale then lost 6-2 at home to Swinton, a game in which Kevin was sent off for persistent 'feet across' in the scrum, earning him a one-match ban. A trip to Oldham's Watersheddings also ended in defeat, 12-7, and then came the first round of the Lancashire Cup. The draw took Rochdale to Blackpool to take on the 'Seasiders' at Borough Park. Blackpool were a tough side to beat on their tight little ground and known as good Cup fighters. Hornets were fully extended in overcoming Borough by 14 points to 9.

Four days later and Swinton were visitors to the Athletic Grounds in round two of the County Cup. In a blood and guts encounter, defences were on top on a heavily-sanded pitch. It was left to Graham Starkey to kick two goals, as Hornets eked out a win by 4-0 in a mud bath. There was one further league game before the Hornets played Leigh in the semi-final of the Lancashire Cup, and that was against Blackpool Borough at Rochdale, where Kevin had a top game in a 9-3 win. The following Thursday evening Rochdale faced Leigh at the Athletic Grounds as planned, and their team was: Joe Chamberlain, Tony Pratt, Johnny Noon, Graham Starkey, Gerry Unsworth, Tony Garforth, Johnny Fishwick, Peter Birchall, Kevin Ashcroft, Voate Drui, Kenny Parr, Appi Toga and Micky Baxter. In a superb display, the Hornets totally outplayed Leigh to win 19-0. Baxter, Pratt and Toga each scored tries, while Starkey (4) and Noon kicked the goals. The scene was now set for a Rochdale Hornets v Warrington Lancashire Cup final.

The semi-final showdown had been a big match for Kevin and gave him the chance to collect his first medal in the professional game. To make it even more special, the game had been against Leigh, the town of his grandad and his own adopted home. Happily, Kevin had been able to deliver a similar performance to the one he had managed on his international debut in France. He recalls: 'I knew we had to win at least fifty per cent at the scrum, which we did, slightly more to be truthful. I felt good at dummy-half and managed to take the ball the right way more often than not. I really enjoyed the tackling and I remember the Leigh players all ran at me, then veered away using their pace. But that is just as I liked it and it helped me throughout the game. The most pleasing thing was that whenever I supported our ball carriers, they slipped me the pass. That makes up for all the graft you put in to get into position. Overall, I was pleased with my contribution.'

Kevin was right in the big time now, with a good debut against France in international football in Toulouse, a place in the County Cup final and a big game at the Athletic Grounds against the New Zealand Kiwi tourists to come on 16th October. The fixture with the touring Kiwis was the first in an arduous three-match programme for Rochdale. The Kiwi game was to be followed by a trip to Whitehaven and then, six days later, the Lancashire Cup final clash with Warrington. But the match against New Zealand was a rough, tough eighty minutes and it gave Kevin his first taste of competition from down under.

Hornets played a full-strength side, despite being only thirteen days from the final. Only one regular player was missing, Tony Pratt being injured. The excellent Fijian wingman, Mike Ratu was his replacement. Kevin recalls: 'The Kiwis put out a huge pack against us. They played three props, all Maori, in Robert Orchard, Sam Edwards and Maunga Emery. They battered us, picked us up and threw us like darts at a dartboard. Their scrum was the strongest six I had ever played against. Only Stan Owen stood his ground. We held them for long periods, but the fact of them being on tour and living together, day in, day out, had built that touring mentality of invincibility. In the end the Kiwis won 10-4 and we were satisfied that we had given it our best shot.' Maunga Emery, incidentally, was the future grandfather of the celebrated modern-day half-back, Stacey Jones, who played with great distinction for New Zealand, Auckland Warriors and Catalans Dragons before his retirement in 2007. Maunga was a big, rough man renowned in Auckland for his strength and fierceness, both on and off the field.

So, the scene was set for Rochdale Hornets to recapture their golden days by taking on 'The Wire' in the big game. As there were only seven teams in the draw from seven first-round games, Warrington had enjoyed a second-round bye on their way to the final, as well as beating Widnes 12-9 away and Oldham 21-10 at home. Rochdale, meanwhile, had beaten Blackpool away, Swinton at home and Leigh at home. The gate was a good one, 21,360, and the referee was a good one too, Mr. Eric Clay of Rothwell. Warrington were as strong as they could be, with a team that read: Geoff Bootle; Ray Fisher, Joe Pickervance, Jackie Melling, Brian Glover; Willie Aspinall, John Smith; Billy Payne, Geoff Oakes, Charlie Winslade, Geoff Robinson, Malc Thomas and Bill Hayes. Hornets too were at strength. Tony Pratt was fit again on the wing and the Rochdale line-up went as follows: Roy Pritchard; Tony Pratt, Graham Starkey, Joe Chamberlain, Gerry Unsworth; Mick Garforth, Johnny Fishwick; Peter Birchall, Kevin Ashcroft, Stan Owen, Kenny Parr, Appi Toga and Micky Baxter, with Voate Drui at substitute (later to come on for Parr).

With the action underway, however, Warrington simply outplayed the brave Hornets to win 16-5. Each Warrington try was scored by a threequarter. The wingmen, Fisher and Glover scored one apiece, while Jackie Melling, who had played for Great Britain under-24s with Kevin, crossed the line twice. Full-back Bootle added a couple of goals. The only Hornets reply was a try and goal by Graham Starkey, ensuring that Kevin's first gold medal in rugby league was a runners-up one. There could be no complaints. The Wire had the edge in the backs and the Hornets had no answer to Warrington's pace and power.

Despite that brave display and the heroic performance against the touring Kiwis before it, by the end of the season Rochdale could boast just thirteen wins in forty games. Kevin played in thirty-four of those and scored one try in a 14-7 win against Liverpool City early in the campaign. More positively, Kevin used his strength and durability to maintain his fitness and continued to develop his game by listening to the advice still given freely by big Stan Owen and putting it into practice. He learned too from the tough, experienced opponents he faced at every scrum whilst labouring at the 'coal face'.

Although Rochdale Hornets were by no means an ultra-successful club, his time there nevertheless gave Kevin the opportunity to soak up no end of important data, all of it adding to his experience in that most important of positions during that era: the hooker. Such info was vital if he was to stay ahead of the many other talented hookers around. Along with all the advice and experience Kevin was busily accumulating, his bubbling in-built enthusiasm, personal toughness and physical strength were gradually seeing him develop not only into a leading club player, but also a true international-quality competitor.

CHAPTER THREE

One never knows what fate has in store. Kevin began the 1966/67 season at Rochdale determined to do well for his club and, also, to add to his one international appearance.

His initial aims were achieved. He played the opening twenty-eight games consecutively, building on his growing reputation as one of the best young hookers around. The second objective though seemed to be a long way off. The same players were being chosen to play for England and Great Britain.

Kevin's advisors told him to get international selection out of his head. Instead, they explained, he should buckle down and put in consistently good performances for his club. 'That's how you break into the big time and win a Great Britain cap,' said Stan Owen. 'Don't worry about it and suddenly it will come. Do well for your club. That is crucial.' However, wheels elsewhere were in motion.

The seeds were first sown on 21st September when Rochdale travelled to Leigh. Although his side were beaten

13-7, Kevin played one of his best games yet for the Hornets. This was duly noted and Leigh began to ask questions about this talented number nine who would surely only get better. In those days, the coach at Hilton Park was the great international and county half-back, the former Warrington star, Gerry Helme, a one-time work colleague of Kevin's father. Soon, however, the great Alex Murphy took over from Helme as Leigh's player-coach, after having fallen out with his until then one and only club St. Helens and moved away from Knowsley Road in acrimonious and complicated financial circumstances.

Kevin read about this in the local newspaper and cringed. 'That's me out at Leigh,' he thought, with very good reason. For earlier in the season, Hornets had lost to St. Helens, 18-16, in a bruising Lancashire Cup clash at Rochdale. And it had been 'Murph' who won it on his own for Saints, thanks to a blinder of a performance. At one stage, trotting back to the halfway line, 'Murph' had questioned Kevin's pace and called him a carthorse, at which insult the pair immediately began a lengthy wrestling match. Now, make no mistake, despite his size, Alex Murphy could scrap - he was a very able fighter. But then again so was Kevin and, when the pair were finally pulled apart, 'Murph' was black and blue and feeling very sore. If that hadn't been bad enough, when Saints then visited Rochdale in the league, the two were soon at each other's throat again.

For home games on a Saturday, the usual routine was that Kevin would work in the morning until 12-30pm, at which time - knowing that his mate would actually clock-off for him at 4-30pm - he would climb the wall between his workplace, Sutcliffe and Speakman, and the working men's club next door, cut across the bowling green and be picked up in Stan Owen's car at the corner shop, and off to Rochdale they would go. On this particular occasion, Kevin had a busy game and, with it being a televised match - Rochdale's first ever - he spent much of his time in the line of the BBC cameras. Back at work on Monday morning, word came through that the boss, Eric Speakman, wanted to see Kevin in his office. Now, Mr. Speakman was a stern sort and Kevin knew instantly when he looked at his face that something was wrong. 'Now then, Kevin,' said the boss. 'You are the kind of man I have wanted to meet for years; a superman! After doing the wages for last week, I see that you left these premises at thirty-one minutes past four on Saturday. Yet at five minutes to four on the same afternoon, I saw you run thirty yards to make a try at Rochdale. That's magic! I just thought I would congratulate you on having a fine game, but please don't do it again.' Breathing a sigh of relief, Kevin went back to work.

Despite Rochdale having trailed 17-0 at one stage, the game had ended in a 17-17 draw. Again, Ashcroft and Murphy were in a running battle throughout, until, that is, the little maestro was forced to leave the field with a broken nose. As Kevin remembers: 'Alex Murphy was not my type of mate at the time. I found him the best footballer I ever played against and the worst person. I thought he was arrogant, self-centred, bloody sneaky and a hard bastard. We'd had a couple of niggles against one another this day, but it was all fifty-fifty. Then he caught me with a punch as I passed the ball. It was a bloody hard one that rattled my teeth. Today they would call it a cheap shot. Anyway, I waited a while until he started on one of those great runs of his. I remembered that he had called me slow and quickly figured that he would try to make me a bigger mug by leaving me stone cold dead with a sidestep. Lo and behold, I chose the right way and landed the perfect stiff-arm tackle, right on his nose. He went down, as we used to say, like a bag of shite and was led off with his usual, "You bastard

Ashcroft, I'll get you". So that's why I thought I would be out in the cold if Alex had anything to do with it.'

But Kevin was totally wrong. Alex Murphy rated Kevin very highly indeed. He had now seen him have at least two cracking games against Saints and spoken to the best hookers around, all of whom gave Kevin a good rap. Upon taking over at Hilton Park shortly after that St. Helens-Rochdale game, he decided to make Kevin Ashcroft one of his first signings.

Kevin's subsequent move to Leigh in February 1967 was as bizarre as the move from Dewsbury to the Hornets. He turned up for training at the Athletic Grounds as usual and the Hornets chairman, Mr. Arthur Walker, looked a little surprised. 'What are you doing here, Kevin?' he asked. 'You were supposed to be at Hilton Park, signing for Leigh this evening.' Kevin was dumfounded and also heartbroken to think that the Hornets would want rid of him, as he was enjoying playing there and had plenty of good mates at the Athletic Grounds.

Rochdale's coach, Johnny Noon, was devastated and played Holy War with the board for letting Kevin go. So much so that, at the end of the season, he left the job. Obviously, for Kevin, it was the money on offer that decided the matter. Away from the game, the Rochdale chairman, Arthur Walker, was in business with Leigh chairman Jack Harding - the pair ran a Manchester nightclub together and were shrewd businessmen both. So, when Mr. Walker told Kevin that he should have gone to Leigh that evening, Kevin weighed it up quickly. 'No one has contacted me,' he said. 'But I had better go across and have a word with them.' When he arrived at Hilton Park, Alex Murphy came over to him. 'Listen Ashy, what's gone is gone,' he said. 'No hard feelings.' And they shook hands. It turned out that the club had negotiated a transfer from the Hornets for £6,800.

Alex made a statement to the Leigh local newspaper about the signing. In answer to the journalist's question, 'Why sign Ashcroft?', he replied: 'Apart from him being the best young hooker around, I signed him because I don't want to have to play against the barmy bastard again. I want him on my side!'

When it was published that Leigh had paid out over six-and-a-half grand for Kevin, there was much micky-taking from his mates, all of whom still lived in the town. Whenever he called in at a local pub for a quiet drink, all the lads would call out: 'Are you getting 'em in Ashy?' The club itself, meanwhile, had embarked upon an almost total rebuilding job. For one thing, in making way for Alex Murphy, coach Gerry Helme had told the board that he wanted to stand down, but not before he had given Kevin's son Gary his gold winners medal from the 1954 Odsal Challenge Cup final replay against Halifax, when at least 102,000 people had watched him win the Lance Todd Trophy. Gerry's only daughter, a very intelligent lady, had no interest in rugby league, so he asked Gary to 'look after it for Uncle Gerry'.

* * *

Once Alex was installed as coach - a position he held until 1971 - he set about putting in place the team that he wanted.

Over the months and years ahead, along with Kevin himself, Leigh welcomed the Hull-born Sid Miller from Rochdale, experienced Charlie Winslade from Warrington, Roy Lester from the Crosfields amateur club, Jimmy Fiddler from Orrell rugby union, Dave Chisnall from Parr Labour Club, Tommy Warburton from Oldham, Dave Eckersley from Leigh colts and two excellent forwards from Wigan in Laurie Gilfedder and Harry Major. Nor was that it. Two more Union players, Derek Watts from Tenbury Wells and big Paul Grimes from Gateshead Fell joined too, as did that fine back-row forward Geoff Lyon from Wigan. The terrific club man Stan Dorrington from the prolific Manchester amateur club, Langworthy Juniors, was another important signing, as were Les Chisnall - a great utility man and brother of David - brought from Huyton , the wonderful goal-kicker Stuart Ferguson from Swansea rugby union, the much travelled forward Geoff Clarkson from Bradford Northern, the excellent Tony Barrow from Saints and, as the cornerstone of the pack, the ultra-enthusiastic Peter Smethurst from Salford. Yet if Smethurst was the cornerstone of the team that Alex built, Kevin Ashcroft was undoubtedly its linchpin.

So much so that when Alex was looking for a vice-captain, he turned to Kevin, who quickly became Prime Minister to Murphy's king. Before, Kevin had always tried to administer unfair tackles upon Alex whenever he could, to 'get' him and blunt his brilliance, hence the broken nose in the Saints - Rochdale game. Suddenly, he was the key man in Alex's masterplan, the great man's confidant, his right-hand man. The combination of these two wonderful characters, Kevin at hooker and Alex feeding the scrum, made an almost unbeatable twosome. 'Murph' had a huge influence on Kevin in no end of ways. When asked many times when both men had retired, 'what did Alex teach you that did the most good for your career?', Kevin would answer immediately: 'he taught me how to cheat'.

Alex would never have swapped jerseys with Kevin and ventured into the 'boiler room' to eek out the ball with foot, calf, thigh, hand or whatever, but the cagey Murphy could assist Kevin with an experienced feed of the scrum, a spin of the ball when feeding, or a bounce off the opposing hooker to land the ball behind Kevin's strike. Where Stan Owen had taught Kevin the art of scrummaging and general front-row play, Alex Murphy too imposed a huge influence over Kevin's future in the game. As an opponent, it was hard enough to deal with 'Murph' feeding the scrum, but to have the determined Ashcroft hooking against you as well made it nigh impossible to win anything in the tight. Theirs was a terrific partnership.

Kevin's debut for Leigh came on 4th March 1967, in a hard-fought 15-12 win at Lawkholme Lane, Keighley. His props that days were big Charlie Winslade at open side and the equally large Mick Murphy at number ten. When one looks at the excellent props Kevin had in club football and at county and international level, then one realises just how true was the old adage that games were won and lost in the front row. Looking back to his first club, Dewsbury, his props there were very good scrummagers: Trevor 'Tank' Walker and Brian Taylor. Then onto Rochdale, with the redoubtable Peter Birchall, Stan Owen and Bill Payne. Now, at Leigh, he had Charlie and Mick, two of the very best pack men around.

At that stage, the Murphy-coached Leigh side took its promptings from the bench, as the great man was as yet unable to take the field for his new club as a result of still being on the playing register at St. Helens. Only a transfer fee paid by Leigh, or any club, could change that. Every single Leigh player wished that were otherwise as his guidance would have taken them to great heights. Even so, Murphy's hand-picked squad of 1966/67 boasted some excellent players. Kevin recalls: 'The team had some very good players in it, a mixture of youth and experience. We had players like Colin Tyrer, Wilf Briggs, Mick Collins, Tommy Grainey, Joe Walsh, Rod Tickle, Gordon Lewis, Terry Entwistle, John Lowe, Mick Martyn, Mick Murphy, Bob Welding, Bill Robinson, Charlie Winslade and Cumbrian

John McVay. We were winning games the club had lost the season before and the rumour was that 'Murph' would be signed as a player in the close-season.'

From finishing twentieth in 1965/66, the club made thirteenth in 1966/67, earning Leigh a play-off place. Unfortunately, when they travelled to St. Helens, they were beaten 37-12. Kevin played in a total of six games in his debut season, missing the win over Barrow at Hilton Park because of a one-match suspension.

Rugby league-wise, then, Kevin had arrived back 'home', and he quickly began to enjoy his game time in the famous cherry and white hoops. Furthermore, this time he'd had the foresight to enquire what was in it for him before signing. Janet and Kevin had very recently moved into a new bungalow and it turned out that a member of the board had several household furnishing shops, via which he agreed to carpet the bungalow throughout as his back-hander. The carpet arrived and was fitted but the couple were in for a shock. 'It was dreadful,' Kevin recalls, 'not at all the carpet we had chosen. In fact when I saw it I thought it was the underlay.' The director apologised for the 'mistake at his end' and assured him that some new carpet would be delivered and fitted. In the meantime, Kevin took up the original carpet very carefully and, as the bungalows were all the same build, sold it next-door-but-one for forty-five quid. So, with the new carpet satisfactory and forty-five pounds in his 'sky rocket' Kevin was delighted.

Kevin's ongoing enthusiasm reached even greater heights the following season when, thanks to a transfer fee in the region of £5,000 paid by Leigh to St. Helens, Alex Murphy was finally allowed to pull on his match boots again. The official date of Murphy's signing as a player was 19th August 1967, the same date, incidentally, that another player who was earmarked for international recognition later in his career arrived at the club, David Chisnall. The pair were joined on September 15th by Laurie Gilfedder and Harry Major from Wigan, followed by Alan Whitworth from Blackpool Borough and Tommy Warburton from Oldham.

Leigh's first game of the 1967/68 season was in the Lancashire Cup, away to Oldham. It resulted in a loss by 17 points to 11. Out of the following ten games, though, Leigh managed eight wins and two losses. One of those wins, a fine 12-9 victory over Wigan at Leigh, was, Kevin recalls: 'Played on a bone-hard pitch and a classic game of rugby league. Murph scored a beauty from half-way and Rod Tickle got our second try, with Tommy Grainey kicking three goals. But it was the calibre of great play that the crowd enjoyed most. There was over 10,000 spectators in Hilton Park.'

The last of those eight wins, meanwhile, was a victory over Salford at The Willows by 5 points to 3 in the first round of the Floodlit Trophy. 'That game was played in the first week in October,' Kevin remembers. 'The pitch was very heavy after days of rainfall. Both sets of backs saw little of the ball, as the game was slugged out between the forwards. Peter Ashcroft got over for us on the wing pretty early on and Laurie Gilfedder kicked a penalty goal. The rest was biff, bang, wallop with penalties given away down to a minimum. There were only two tries in the whole game as defences were bang on top. It was a bloody hard cup tie.'

The official name of this very popular competition was the BBC Floodlit Trophy and it was in its third season, with Castleford the only winners so far, having won it twice. Fixtures were played on Tuesday evenings and shown on BBC2. For Leigh, successfully through to round two, of their following four league games two were won - against Swinton and Barrow - and two were lost, against Rochdale and Hull FC. Murphy's side would face Swinton again in the Floodlit second round at home, where they again won by an identical score to the earlier game of 10-2. Kevin recollects that: 'Murph did his usual big-game thing. He scored a great try and Joe Walsh added another. Laurie Gilfedder kicked two goals and this put us into the semi-final.' It did indeed, setting up a thrilling showdown for Leigh with their deadliest local rivals Wigan at Knowsley Road, St. Helens.

Despite the game being televised, a crowd of over 11,000 trooped into the old ground to witness another brutal battle. 'There was never any love lost between Leigh and Wigan, even more so in a cup tie semi-final,' says Kevin. 'We had talked about our defence before the game and we knew that we would have to tackle like hell to get any sort of a result against the men from Central Park. We did tackle like hell, but so did they. The result was a try-less game but an exciting one. Our pack played wonderfully well and it read, Mick Murphy, myself, Harry Major, Bob Welding, John McVay and Laurie Gilfedder. Laurie kicked four goals and Murph dropped a beautiful goal to give us a 10 points to 2 win and put us through.' Leigh's opponents in the final would be the trophy-holders Castleford, who had beaten Warrington in the other semi-final. As Kevin points out, such big crowds weren't unusual in selected matches. For instance, on Boxing Day, Warrington versus Leigh at Wilderspool drew over 10,000 and, four days later, for the league match, there were over 15,000 in for Wigan versus Leigh at Central Park. In the first round of the Challenge Cup against Warrington at Leigh, 12,000 watched the game, while in round two, again at Leigh, 23,000 packed into Hilton Park. One of the hardest games of the season, though, was that league game at Wigan, three weeks after Leigh's great win in the Floodlit Trophy.

Kevin remembers it well. 'There were several vendettas left over from the Floodlit Trophy win,' he recalls. 'And in all fairness it was not all from the Wigan side. From the start, pockets of fighting players were left behind as play moved on. On occasion, mate would run back to help mate, thus creating a bigger fracas. Play would then settle with tackling even tougher than the Trophy game. Suddenly a player would respond immediately after a tackle, this would lead to a bout of fighting, then another short spell of play, and so on. With the final only sixteen days away it would have been disastrous had anyone received their marching orders.' The officials seemed to recognise this and allowed play to carry on as Wigan regained some self-respect with a hard-earned 8-4 victory.

As the date of the Floodlit final drew nearer, Bradford Northern were the last team to visit Hilton Park, coming away with an unexpected 13-6 win. 'We were at full-strength except for Harry Major, who was out with a pulled calf muscle,' Kevin remembers. 'But Bradford just came at us hard, knowing that we may have had one eye on the Floodlit Trophy. But we had a ten-day breather until the final and the thought of that, and that Bradford were better than us on the day, helped us come to terms with the home defeat.'

The final of the Floodlit Trophy was played on the Tuesday evening of 16th January 1968, at the Headingley home of Leeds RLFC. The referee was Mr. G.F. Lindop of Wakefield and the recorded attendance 9,525. In looking for a hat-trick, Castleford had, on the way to the final, already disposed of Keighley, Leeds and Warrington. With a full-strength side, they were in confident mood. Leigh too, though, fancied their chances even if, as Kevin explains: 'Traditionally, Headingley was a bit of a bad ground for Leigh. In finals, though, you must accept what comes your way. We were confident as we set off for the ground. We had the knowledge that Castleford may well be more afraid of Murph than we were of any of their players.'

The teams that day lined up as follows - Castleford: Derek Edwards; David Harris, Tony Thomas, Ian Stenton, Ron Willett; Alan Hardisty, Keith Hepworth; Dennis Hartley, Johnny Ward, Doug Walton, Bill Bryant, Mick Redfearn, Mal Reilly. Sub: Clive Dickinson. Wearing Leigh colours, meanwhile, were Tommy Grainey; Rod Tickle, Geoff Lewis, Mick Collins, Joe Walsh; Terry Entwistle, Alex Murphy; Alan Whitworth, Kevin Ashcroft, Harry Major, Bob Welding, Mick Murphy and Laurie Gilfedder.

Of that Castleford team, five had played in the previous two finals, Edwards, Willett, Hardisty, Dickinson and Bryant. The club was nicknamed 'Classy Cas' and for very good reason. The half-backs, Hardisty and Hepworth, would become as well known in the rugby league world as eggs and bacon. Castleford also had two tremendous ball winners in their front row, big Dennis Hartley at prop and the ball-playing international Johnny Ward at hooker. At loose forward was the up-and-coming Malcolm Reilly, who would go on to become a legend both in England and Australia.

In short, blessed with the confidence that all consistently successful sides have, Castleford would be a hard mob to clean out. Even so, many Leigh supporters crossed the Pennines that day as the Lancastrians too were playing with a new found confidence, since Alex Murphy had woven his own will to win into the Leigh fabric.

With the game underway, Ron Willett kicked a penalty goal, as Castleford soon began to test the mettle of Leigh's will power. Gamely, Murphy and his men withstood the early barrage and came into their own ensuring that Castleford needed to find a strong will of their own to blunt some swift, skilful attacks instigated by Kevin from dummy-half. Eventually, one of his guided missile passes set up a half-break by Murphy who, with perfect timing, sent out a long pass to Rod Tickle and he hared over for an unconverted try. When Laurie Gilfedder landed a penalty goal, Leigh were ahead by 5 points to 2. Willett's accurate boot, though, landed two further penalties as Castleford closed ranks and the teams went in at the break with the Yorkshire side ahead by 6 points to 5.

In the second half, Leigh dominated without being able to breach the tough Castleford defence. The territorial advantage gained was due to Kevin's overwhelming ball-winning ability. He shovelled the ball out and this gave the strong and fast threequarters of Leigh ample scope to find a way through the tight tacklers from 'down t' lane', but to no avail. Then, suddenly, Murphy tore through a gap and was heading for the posts when a Castleford tackler flattened him with a head-high shot. Gilfedder teed up the ball in front of the offending team's posts for an attempt that would have given Leigh the lead, but tonight was not to be one of Laurie's better ones with the boot and he drove the ball wide. As the game came to a close, Willett sealed it for Castleford with a late penalty goal as Leigh were denied any further chances.

Beaten but unbowed, the men from Hilton Park had to be satisfied with the consolation that, as a team, they had come on well and would certainly get even better. The renowned cup fighters from Castleford had been made to fight all the way to hold on to their trophy. In Kevin Ashcroft and Gordon Lewis, Leigh had two of the best men on the field. Certainly, Kevin had done himself no harm at all before the international selectors. They took note and would watch this quickly improving hooker again before very long.

* * *

Always the innovator, Kevin would note how his opponent worked in the scrum and use his knowledge of what various other hookers did to improve his own game. Like all great players, he never stopped learning about rugby league and its players. Kevin also developed the in-built knack of playing well in big matches. One of his season's best was against Warrington at Hilton Park in the aforementioned first round of the Challenge Cup.

On a raw February afternoon, it was a tie played out in a typical Wembley-or-bust manner. A hard encounter, with tough tackling from the first whistle, suited Kevin's robust style. Apart from bossing the dummy-half area, he won the ball hands down in the set scrums and he led the way on defence. As a result, an 11 points to 5 win gave Leigh a plum tie in round two against the old enemy, Wigan, at Hilton Park. That result, though, was a disaster for Leigh, with Wigan winning by 20 points to 2. Kevin's deflation didn't last long. For early in the next week he received a long hoped for letter asking whether he would be available to represent Great Britain in the World Cup, beginning in May 1968 in Australia and New Zealand. Understandably, this perked Kevin up no end and his remaining season ended on a high note in form. Leigh had emerged as one of the league's most improved teams and, from the position of thirteenth the previous season, they attained a heady elevation to seventh. This allowed them a play-off against a strong Hull Kingston Rovers side at Craven Park where, less happily, they received a 22-3 drubbing.

So, while Kevin's Leigh team-mates took the summer off to relax and overhaul the machinery for next season's onslaught, he found himself packing for a trip down under. But beforehand, the Rugby League boss Bill Fallowfield informed every squad member who was not involved in the Championship play-offs that a friendly match had been arranged between a World Cup side and Halifax at Thrum Hall. It was to be played on a Friday evening, 3rd May 1968, and billed as a 'warm-up' game. Kevin snorts: 'A warm up game! We had just ended a forty-three game season, did we need a warm up game? I think not. We found out that some guest players had been invited to play and great players they were... Billy Boston, Geoff Wrigglesworth, Arthur Keegan, Tom Van Vollenhoven, Keith Hepworth and Rob Valentine.'

The starting line-up was: Arthur Keegan (Hull); Billy Boston (Wigan), Geoff Wrigglesworth (Bradford Northern), David Watkins (Salford), Clive Sullivan (Hull); Derek Edwards (Castleford), Tommy Bishop (St. Helens); John Warlow (St. Helens), Kevin Ashcroft (Leigh), Cliff Watson (St. Helens), Ray French (Widnes), Arnie Morgan (Featherstone Rovers) and Charlie Renilson (Halifax). The game was won easily enough by the World Cup squad, the touring members of which, in order to be measured up for the international blazer and trousers, then travelled over to Hepworths the Tailors in Leeds, claiming second class rail fare from RLHQ for the privilege. 'There was a Hepworth's in Leigh,' recalls Kevin. 'I could have just as easily called in there to get measured.' The touring party was asked to assemble at Manchester Airport early and, in those days, the players' families usually came to see them off.

On paper, the nineteen-man squad that flew off to the World Cup down under looked good enough to do well. It consisted of: Bev Risman (Leeds, captain), Kevin Ashcroft (Leigh), John Atkinson (Leeds), Tommy Bishop (St. Helens), Ian Brooke (Wakefield Trinity), Alan Burwell (Hull Kingston Rovers), Mick Clark (Leeds), Derek Edwards (Castleford), Peter 'Flash' Flanagan (Hull Kingston Rovers), Ray French (Widnes), Bob Haigh (Wakefield Trinity), Roger Millward (Hull Kingston Rovers), Arnie Morgan (Featherstone

Rovers), Charlie Renilson (Halifax), Mick Shoebottom (Leeds), Clive Sullivan (Hull), John Warlow (St. Helens), Cliff Watson (St. Helens) and Chris Young (Hull Kingston Rovers). The team manager was Bill Fallowfield and the coach-assistant manager was Colin Hutton (Hull Kingston Rovers). Upon arrival, the squad was based in Sydney and trained well in preparation for the first game against Australia at the Sydney Cricket Ground, scheduled for 25th May.

Kevin was roomed with Cliff Watson and found him to be a great room-mate who could sleep through anything. During the training sessions prior to the first match, 'Flash' Flanagan, another great bloke, had complained about a stomach bug. During a lull in training 'Flash' asked Kevin what he was going to do with his contract money for tour selection. When Kevin told him that he had to PLAY in an international match before he received anything 'Flash' was amazed. He thought for a moment, then said to Kevin, 'Don't say anything Kevin, but you will get your money.' Now, Flanagan had been named as the hooker for the first game and he went over to Colin Hutton, his club coach, and said that he was feeling ill with stomach pains. Throughout the training sessions, Flanagan had been the team's dummy-half and play-maker around the ruck. Kevin, as reserve hooker, had also run through the moves and plays, so he knew what was expected. Colin Hutton sent 'Flash' to see the doctor and immediately brought Kevin into the hooking role for the match. Kevin says: 'The late Flash Flanagan was one great guy. What he did for me in that instant showed what a man he was. A wonderful hooker and a gentleman.'

When the big day arrived, it was a beautifully sunny Australian winter's day. The crowd at the Sydney Cricket Ground was 62,256 and the referee was Mr. J. Percival of New Zealand. The Great Britain team was: Risman; Brooke,

Shoebottom, Burwell, Sullivan; Millward, Bishop; Clark, Ashcroft, Watson, French, Haigh and Renilson. The subs were Edwards and Warlow. The Australian side, meanwhile, was equally tough, containing many battle-hardened Test veterans. It read: Eric Simms; Johnny Rhodes, Johnny Greaves, Graeme Langlands, Johnny King; Tony Branson, Billy Smith; Arthur Beetson, Fred Jones, John Wittenberg, Ron Coote, Dick Thornett and Johnny Raper. Subs, Bobby Fulton and Dennis Manteit.

Kevin takes up the story of the tour: 'Australia came at us from the kick-off. Their plan was to knock us off our game. The tackling from both sides was hurtful and awesome. The Aussie game was always forward dominated. Batter down the middle, using only a couple of passes either side of the play-the-ball, then when on the opposing line, zip the ball wide very quickly, usually with Thornett, Coote, Raper or Beetson running headlong into our half-backs and centres.

'They came on strong in the scrum too. John Wittenberg came at me with his head, so I beat him to the punch and stuck my head into his. It was like nutting a wall. Cliff Watson, as one would expect, had a go at Wittenberg. I had a go at Freddy Jones who was a hard bugger and Mick Clark stuck to his guns against Artie Beetson, but was badly out-weighed. Shortly after, the rugged Watson damaged his leg and, whilst he went off for treatment, we played with twelve men.

'Our pack was disrupted and the Aussies took advantage. In they charged at one scrum, their front row like three raging buffalos. They hit us with a devastating crunch and my two props buckled. I pulled loose from them and Beetson hit me with what I thought was a sledge hammer but, I was told later, was a right cross. As I came back into the light, I fully expected at least my two props to be having a go at Beetson and Wittenberg. Without the ultra-tough

Watson, though, I had a bit of a shock. One prop was having a laugh with Beetson and the other was stood twenty yards away pulling his shorts up. I often wondered what Stan Owen and Peter Birchall would have done.

'As it happened, we were beaten 25-10. Mr. Percival was too kind to the Aussies, giving them a hatful of penalty kicks, the majority of which we knew nothing about. The huge difference in the points was due to the boot of Eric Simms, South Sydney's aboriginal full-back, who kicked eight goals. Smith, Coote and Raper scored tries for Australia and, for us, Ian Brooke and Clive Sullivan scored tries, while Bev Risman kicked two goals.'

Whilst over there during the World Cup, Kevin was impressed by the strength and overall fitness of every Australian player. 'Speaking to them after games and noticing the training methods at various clubs we visited, I was totally surprised at the amount of weight training they all did,' he says. 'I had often heard about this type of training but hardly anyone back home used it. I had often talked about the tough weight training Vince Karalius did in his career and it dawned on me that this was the only way forward, for me at least. I decided there and then to start a weights programme when I arrived back home, which I did by converting our garage into a weights room that I used throughout the remainder of my playing career.

'I was satisfied with my performance in that first game and was eternally grateful to Flash Flanagan for being such a great bloke. I knew that he was the first-choice hooker and that, when recovered from his stomach problem, he would be back in the side. So I concentrated on becoming a good tourist, helping out all I could on match days and maintaining my enthusiasm. The competition ended with Australia and France playing in the final at Sydney Cricket Ground on 10th June, the final positions in the table being

Australia first, France second, Great Britain third and New Zealand fourth.

'In time, John Wittenberg and I became good mates and he always made his way to see me when next I was in Australia, so too did Arthur Beetson. Both these men were great blokes to meet, have a drink with and good company, vastly different to their presence in a Test match.'

Three days after the World Cup final, Great Britain played Toowoomba and Kevin was selected. The side was Derek Edwards; Chris Young, Ian Brooke, Alan Burwell, John Atkinson; Mick Shoebottom, Tommy Bishop; Mick Clark, himself, Cliff Watson, Arnie Morgan, John Warlow and Charlie Renilson. The subs were Roger Millward (for Bishop) and 'Flash' Flanagan (for Renilson). The tourists won by 28 points to 10 and Kevin scored one of his side's six tries. John Atkinson (2), Chris Young, Alan Burwell and Roger Millward scored the others, while Mick Shoebottom (3) and Roger Millward (2) kicked the goals.

'We knew what to expect up there in Queensland,' recalls Kevin. 'Biff, bang and wallop from the word go. Their international centre, John McDonald, was a classy player and a good goal-kicker and he had a great game against us. I certainly could pick 'em. Opposite me was a hooker called Brown who was straight from the cane fields. Strong and fit, all he wanted to do was fight me. I had a couple of goes with him and he was a tough lad. Gradually he quietened down and he took some beating in the scrum.

'Our final game in Australia was against Queensland, up in Brisbane, two days after the Toowoomba game. They put a big, strong pack out against us and two excellent centres. The two middle backs were McDonald and Lionel Williamson, who played with distinction for Bradford Northern. Their pack contained Col Weiss (Bundaberg), Dennis Manteit (Brisbane Brothers) and Brian Fitzsimons

(Townsville), all of whom had played or would play for Australia. The Great Britain side for the final game had Risman in at full-back for Edwards, Sullivan in for Young on the wing, Millward in for Shoebottom at stand-off, Flanagan in for me at hooker and French in for Warlow in the second row. Another tough game ended in a 33-18 win for us. Clive Sullivan (4), Alan Burwell, John Atkinson and Roger Millward scored tries, and Bev Risman added six goals.

'So my first tour ended. I was a little disappointed that I had only played in two matches but that is the way of tours. The trip did give me greater confidence in my ability as now I was a full international player and I was delighted with my form in the games I did play in. I was pleased that I was considered a good tourist, that meant a lot. I had also picked up what was required to help me in my individual game, that of the weight training programmes.'

* * *

Back in England and the 1968/69 season began in great style for Leigh. Kevin recalls: 'We started like a house on fire with Alex driving us on. We travelled to Hull Kingston Rovers, always a dodgy trip for Leigh, and won a real good and open game 27-15. That was followed by two cracking wins at home, Leeds by 22-19 and Barrow by 23-13, which really got the spectators buzzing. Then we had a bad home defeat by Castleford, who beat us by taking us on in the pack, keeping the ball tight and relying on the half-backs supporting the forward breaks. This led to a tight game won by Castleford, 10-5. A good win at Rochdale lifted our spirits for the next match which was against Wigan at home and drew a crowd of nearly 17,000. Wigan stole it by 12 points to 10. That one hurt because we could so easily have won it convincingly, but we failed to take our chances. Murph was in great form, slicing the Wigan defence to pieces, but we didn't convert the chances into points.'

The Lancashire Cup then came around and Leigh drew Blackpool Borough at home. 'We went into it a wee bit complacently,' recalls Kevin, 'and struggled to get a 15-15 draw.' The replay at Blackpool the following Wednesday gave Borough their best gate of the season. It also saw Murphy at his brilliant best, as he registered four sparkling tries. 'They put my solitary try in the shade,' smiles Kevin, 'but it was still part of the 32-15 win. The stats for the six games in September made poor reading, played six, won one, drawn one, lost four. We needed a shot to liven us up as, after a bright start, we were now looking none too good. No matter what we tried we were still hit and miss. A drubbing at Saints by 27 points to 2 hurt a lot. As we went into October things got better and, although we lost to Saints again in round two of the Lancashire Cup, wins against Widnes, Swinton, and a great win at Hull Kingston Rovers in the BBC Floodlit trophy by 27-19 had us thinking that our form was coming back. A couple of draws, 2-2 at Castleford and 7-7 at home to Wigan, then a good win up in Cumbria against Whitehaven 19-8, had us in good spirits to face Leeds at Hilton Park, in round two of the Floodlit Trophy, where again we were on song. Murph had missed a few games, but he was back for Leeds and again at his best. We won 25-11.

'Then, in the week of the draw with Wigan, I received a letter from the Rugby Football League advising me that I had been selected to play against France for Great Britain on 30th November 1968. Great news, as the game was at Knowsley Road and it would be nice to play in this country at that level. Domestically, I missed the game against Salford at Leigh, which we lost, but the international match compensated for that.'

The international in question took place on a cold and dull afternoon against a big, tough French outfit. A talented British line-up read: Arthur Keegan (Hull FC); Bill Burgess (Barrow), Neil Fox (Wakefield Trinity), Dick Gemmell (Hull FC), Alan Burwell (Hull Kingston Rovers); 'Daz' Davies (Swinton), Tommy Bishop (St. Helens); Dennis Hartley (Castleford), Kevin Ashcroft (Leigh), John Warlow (St. Helens), Colin Dixon (Halifax), Kenny Parr (Warrington) and Charlie Renilson (Halifax). The subs were Roger Millward (Hull Kingston Rovers) and John Stephens (Wigan). The French were their usual selves, quick, elusive and, according to Kevin, 'buggers for coming in second tackle with the knees. The referee, G. Jameau of Marseille, allowed one or two high-shots and a lot of the knees to occur without taking any action. One or two French forwards learned quite a lot of the English language not in any dictionary.'

The French team featured: Yves Chabert (Cavaillon); Serge Marsolan (St, Gaudens), Pierre Saboureau (Catalan), Claude Mantoulan (Perpignan), Andre Ferren (Avignon); José Calle (St. Esteve), Marius Frattini (Cavaillon); Henri Maracq (St. Gaudens), Raymond Rebujent (Catalan), Jacques Cabero (Catalan), Francis De Nadaï (Limoux), Adolphe Alesina (Carcassonne) and Jean-Marie Armand (Bordeaux). Bill Burgess was too strong and fast for his opposite number and scored a hat-trick of tries. Dick Gemmell scored twice. Kevin himself managed another try as did Alan Burwell and Colin Dixon, while Neil Fox kicked five goals. In a final scoreline of Great Britain 34 France 10, Calle and Cabero scored the visitors' tries and Chabert added two goals. 'That was just about right on the day,' says Kevin, 'although in the return game in Toulouse we knew it would be a lot tougher. Their front row, as usual, had tried the strong-arm stuff, but against Dennis Hartley and John Warlow they couldn't win.

Our overall pace in the backs proved too much for them and a few kicks and punches were coming through as the game ended.'

The game on Kevin's return to Leigh was the semi-final of the Floodlit Trophy against Wigan at Central Park. 'After our 12-10 defeat in the league at Wigan, then our 7-7 draw at home with them, we expected another tight and rough game,' he continues. 'That's exactly what happened but the result read 9 points to 7 in Wigan's favour. Despite being on the box, there were over 12,000 spectators in the ground. After the disappointment of losing in the semi-final, we then went on a four-game winning run until we played Salford at home and Warrington away. These games were drawn, 6-6 with Salford and 2-2 at Wilderspool. The stalemate at Warrington was as hard a game as I had ever played in up to then, including the Test match in Australia. It was a real man-eater of a game that sapped one's strength. Our dressing room was like a casualty ward, stitches being put in, ice packs on knees, necks and backs, players laid on the seats being bandaged. It was like the battle of Balaklava.'

Those latest two draws added to an unusual number of drawn matches played in that season. Leigh had drawn against Blackpool Borough in September, 15-15, Castleford away in October, 2-2, Wigan 7-7 at home in November, then 6-6 with Salford and 2-2 at Warrington. 'Five draws in one season,' reflects Kevin. 'Some players go through their entire career without playing in a drawn game. Draws were very unusual indeed then. Close scores, yes, but draws were very scarce. Of course, in those days a draw at home meant losing pay and the draw away gave you winning pay.' Another bad result came with the loss to Rochdale Hornets in the Challenge Cup first round at Hilton Park, where over 6,000 people watched Leigh go out 13-4.

Then came that return international clash with France on

2nd February 1969. 'On Saturday morning we flew out of Manchester to Toulouse,' remembers Kevin. 'I was beginning to become Jack the Lad with all this air travel. We had four changes from the side that beat the French in St. Helens. The great, tough Mick Shoebottom of Leeds came in at stand-off for 'Daz' Davies; my old mate Cliff Watson came in at blind-side prop for the St. Helens forward John Warlow; John Mantle, the big Saints forward, came into the second row for Kenny Parr; and the ball-playing loose forward from Leeds, Ray Batten, was in for Charlie Renilson. The substitutes, Roger Millward (Hull Kingston Rovers) and John Stephens (Wigan), stayed the same.'

The French, meanwhile, disturbed by the heavy defeat in England, made wholesale changes. In fact, only four men retained their places, Marsolan, Mantoulan, De Nadaï and Marracq, who subbed. The revised French team read: Jean-Pierre Cros (Albi), Serge Marsolan (St. Gaudens), Claude Mantoulan (Perpignan), Guy Andrieu (Limoux), Louis Bonnery (Limoux), Jean Capdouze (Perpignan), Roger Garrigue (St. Gaudens), Georges Ailleres (Toulouse), Yves Begou (Toulouse), Patrick Carrias (Avignon), Francis De Nadaï (Limoux), Hervé Mazard (Lezignan) and Jean-Pierre Clar (Villeneuve). The referee was England's own Mr. Fred Lindop of Wakefield and the attendance, 7,536. 'It had been pointed out to us that this French side contained eight of the players who beat Great Britain in the 1968 World Cup round in the mud of Carlaw Park, Auckland,' recalls Kevin, 'and that was only seven months ago. We knew their danger men, Capdouze at stand-off, Mantoulan in the centre and the back three in their pack, De Nadaï, Mazard and Clar. The two big props too would cause trouble if we gave them space to run.

'Jean-Pierre Clar was a superb international loose forward. He could handle the ball, tackle and was as tough as old boots. He led from the front and would target a tough

British forward and take him on. An excellent leader, he took the game by the scruff of the neck and dictated every move. Most of us tried to get to him and rattle him, but he was a good footballer and getting to him was almost impossible.'

In front at half-time by 7 points to 4, the French were geed up by their fanatical supporters, as the strains of La Marseillaise rang around the Toulouse stadium. Neil Fox landed three goals and Colin Dixon crashed over for Britain's only try. France's try scorers, meanwhile, were Mantoulan, Bonnery and De Nadaï, while Capdouze kicked two goals. It was enough to earn the French an unexpected but fully deserved 13-9 win. 'We had no complaints,' admits Kevin. 'The French came at us early and never stopped. In Jean-Pierre Clar they had a superb general and a hard working forward. A month later, this French side, with only one change, defeated an equally strong Welsh side at the Parc des Princes, Paris, by 17 points to 13, to show just how good they were.'

CHAPTER FOUR

At home in Leigh, the club had been active in the buying of players and snapped up two forwards who would make a huge difference to their pack strength, both from rugby union. Derek Watts was a tough lad and solid scrummager from Tenbury Wells, while his soon-to-be-colleague, Paul Grimes, was a giant second-rower signed from the Gateshead Fell RU club, who took to the 13-a-side code like a fish to water.

Although now a full international hooker, Kevin was still gaining experience all the time. His ability in the set scrums could be seen in his consistent winning of position, despite having to play with several different half-backs. With Alex Murphy feeding the scrum, Kevin says, he could have worn a sleeping mask and still won more than his share: 'Alex was bloody brilliant. His timing and feeding of the ball made it possible for me to have a smoke and a cup of tea in the pack and still win it!' When 'Murph' didn't play or moved out to stand-off, Kevin had various other good scrum-halves feeding for him, such as the former Wigan half-back Terry Entwistle, Ian Jones, signed from the Pilkington Recs junior side, Kevin's old mate Tommy Grainey and David Eckersley, who would also go on to play international football. His props changed a bit too. Mick Murphy, Alan Whitworth, Dave Chisnall, Derek Watts, Harry Major, Laurie Gilfedder, Derek Higgs and Alan Harrison all held Kevin up at some time or other that season.

The year had been a fine one for Kevin. 'It was good,' he says. 'I played twice against the French; Leigh won nineteen games and drew four; we had a great spirit at the club and we actually thought we could go on and win something big, no kidding. We had finished the season well, winning six of the final nine games which gave us a tough trip up to Workington Town in the play-offs. We could and should have won this one, but lost it by 11 points to 9. We made several good chances but failed to take them.'

Just as disappointing was Leigh's final league position - two places lower than last season. Although ninth place was still acceptable, it was well below where the players thought they should have been. On the plus side, Kevin's try-scoring rate had improved; he had scored five tries to the previous season's four. And, by now, he was into his new weights regime, which he maintained throughout the close-season. With the arrival of pre-season training, however, little did Kevin or the rest of the Leigh players know that they were about to embark upon the most successful couple of seasons in the history of their famous old club.

At home, Kevin and Janet's son Gary was now four years old and he had noticed that various teams allowed young mascots to lead out the teams on matchday. Gary pestered his dad to see if he could be Leigh's mascot and Kevin said he would ask. The club agreed and young Gary Ashcroft went on to gain a record that possibly will never be beaten, but more of this true and almost unbelievable story later.

As the 1969/70 season kicked-off, having particularly targeted the Challenge Cup, Alex Murphy set about his quest to build a side capable of winning at Wembley. His biggest problem was the lack of a top class goal-kicker. Not since the days of Brian Fallon had Leigh had anyone who could knock over one hundred-plus goals a season. If Leigh were to win a major trophy then finding such a player was crucial. So, the search was on. Another priority was the acquisition of a good and experienced loose forward. This problem, though, was overcome almost immediately when Wigan's excellent back-rower, Geoff Lyon, moved from Central to Hilton Park.

The season began with a Lancashire Cup first-round tie at home to Warrington. 'We had a tough start but it would show just what we had in the locker,' remembers Kevin. 'In the previous season, we had to fight like hell to hang onto a 2-2 draw at home to Warrington and, although we had gone on to do better at the back end of the campaign, we figured that this would be another hard game.' It was too; a real cup tie from the start that, thanks largely to Kevin's domination in the set scrum, Leigh won 15-12. Five days later, though, a trip to Central Park brought about a devastating 24-8 defeat. Although a bad loss, it can have only served to induce a new flow of enthusiasm among Kevin's team-mates, because Leigh then went on a thirteen-match winning run.

During this time, news was also coming in from Rugby League headquarters that, owing to what was seen as a plague of untidy scrums, the powers-that-be were to bring in a new rule, whereby if a hooker was penalised three times in a match he would be sent off and receive a mandatory one-match suspension. As Kevin recalls it: 'Most times, it was the two open-side props, plus the blind-side props not binding properly, that gave the hooker a bad name.' Either way, for a time, the hooking fraternity played it fair in the hope that this rather silly instruction would go away.

During their winning run, Leigh again played Wigan, this time at Hilton Park. Before that game, Kevin had received a letter from the Lancashire Rugby League telling him he was selected to play for his county on 24th September against Cumberland at Workington. So, when he turned out against Wigan, with the county game only three matches away, Kevin, who had always seemed a target for abuse when playing Wigan, thought he had better keep his nose clean. Some hope. As the game got underway, several nuts came flying in at the early scrums. Then, a punch into Kevin's face and a knee into his groin. That's it, he thought. Anything goes. And come the middle of the second half, Kevin and his opposite number, the Wigan hooker, were rolling around punching and kicking one another. The referee, Huddersfield's Billy Thompson, had had enough. 'Off! The pair of you, for fighting!' he said. And the two rakes trudged away through the mud, disconsolately. Disaster, thought Kevin: 'I had been sent off three times the previous season, so I expected them to come down heavily on me.'

As usual, the disciplinary committee met at the Rugby League's old Chapeltown Road HQ on the Monday, where both Kevin and his nemesis made a personal appearance. As they waited to be called, Billy Thompson, the referee, went in first to give his version of what had taken place. Then the two hookers were ushered in. Unknown to the committee, while waiting outside, the pair had worked out a plan and both agreed to support each other's testimony. The chairman was Mr. Jack Grindrod of Rochdale Hornets.

'Well, Kevin, what have you to say?' Mr. Grindrod asked. Kevin described the toughness of the game and the circumstances in which he had arrived at the incident in which he and his Wigan counterpart were dismissed. Mr.

Thompson, with all due respect, had been mistaken. 'We weren't fighting,' Kevin said. '[He] had just passed the ball and I was trying to avoid him, when I slipped due to the slippery conditions. I fell into him and we both fell to the ground. He sort of caught me in mid-air and we rolled across the ground. We weren't fighting at all.' The Wigan hooker agreed with every word. Jack Grindrod, a very streetwise director, retorted: 'If it happened as you say, how on earth did you get those cut eye brows, split lips and bruises?' 'Oh, we got those during the game. It was a hard one,' Kevin replied. At which the referee, Billy Thompson, stood up, looked at the two hookers, and turned to the committee. 'Gentlemen,' he said. 'I was not at the match described by Mr. Ashcroft. I must have been somewhere else completely. Good evening.' And with that, he simply walked out of the meeting.

With Billy Thompson gone, the chairman asked both hookers to leave the room whist the committee discussed the case further. As Kevin walked passed Mr. Grindrod, the chairman whispered to him: 'Have you received your letter about the county game?' Kevin nodded. He knew that a four-match ban would deny him his first county cap. About ten minutes later, the two were called back to face the committee. The chairman spoke: 'Two men of your experience should be ashamed of yourselves. The committee has decided to make an example of you. You are both suspended for three games,' and he winked at Kevin. He was clear to play for Lancashire.

* * *

Kevin missed Blackpool Borough, Rochdale Hornets, both away, and Swinton at home, all won in the big run. The situation in the county game was that Lancashire had already beaten Yorkshire and needed to defeat Cumberland to be crowned County Champions. So, not only would Kevin Ashcroft receive his first county cap, there was a chance of him being presented with the most beautiful of all the gold medals - the County Championship winners medal.

Lancashire's team that day was a strong one. It read: Ray Dutton (Widnes); Bill Burgess (Salford), Chris Hesketh (Salford), Frank Myler (St. Helens), Mike Murray (Barrow); Alex Murphy (Leigh), Parry Gordon (Warrington); John Stephens (Wigan), Kevin Ashcroft (Leigh), Mike Sanderson (Barrow), Bob Welding (Leigh), Dave Robinson (Swinton), Doug Laughton (Wigan). Subs: Dave Hill (Wigan) and George Nicholls (Widnes). The Cumberland team was: Paul Charlton (Workington Town); Keith Davies (Workington Town), Bob Wear (Warrington), Tony Colloby (Blackpool Borough), Ian Wright (Workington Town); Bobby Ryan (Whitehaven), Harry Maddison (Whitehaven); Harold McCourt (Workington Town), Howard 'Smiler' Allen (Workington Town), Dennis Martin (Workington Town), Eddie Bowman (Whitehaven), Tom Gainford (Whitehaven), Bill Pattinson (Warrington). Subs: John Shimmings (Whitehaven) and John 'Spanky' McFarlane (Workington Town). The referee was Mr. Eric Clay of Rothwell.

Lancashire won the game and the County Championship by a resounding 30 points to 10. Alex Murphy scored three tries and Parry Gordon, Dave Robinson and Doug Laughton a try apiece, with Ray Dutton kicking six goals. The Cumberland reply was a try each to Ryan and Maddison, while Tony Colloby kicked two goals. Kevin did enough to be pleased with his county debut. He was up against a tough, cagey character in 'Smiler' Allen, who by then was a seasoned campaigner and a strong scrummager. Murphy was by far the most skilful player on view, though, and his pace was unbelievable on a heavy pitch. Kevin still cherishes that first County Championship medal and rates it as the most beautiful in his vast collection. It also gave him his first piece of winner's gold to go with his two runners-up medals.

This was a busy time for each and every Leigh player, but particularly so for Kevin, a key player in a most important and high-pressure position. The hooker was a crucial member of the side because of the vital jobs he had to complete within the set plans of the team. Firstly, he had to win the ball at the scrum. Equally important was his job at dummy-half, where every move began. One bad pass and the move was over. Choosing the best way to start an attack was also vital. Kevin had to think about all of these things during every minute of every game. And it wasn't even that the life of a hooker was glamorous, either. It wasn't. Your star players could usually be found at stand-off half, centre or loose forward. Even so, a hooker who did the job correctly was worth his weight in gold.

Leigh, then, were already on the trail of two trophies - the Lancashire Cup, which had begun with the win at Warrington in the season's first game, and the ever-popular BBC Floodlit Trophy. In the first of those competitions, beating the Wire was followed - during the great thirteen-game winning run - by an 11-10 win over Rochdale Hornets away in round two, and a solid 15-4 victory in the semi-final at home to Widnes. Also in that successful run was a Floodlit Trophy first-round win over Wakefield Trinity, but that was to come later. The Lancashire Cup was the immediate concern as Leigh fought their way to the final against Swinton at Central Park. The Lions, meanwhile, had taken an equally hard route having beaten Oldham, Blackpool Borough and Wigan.

The 1969 Lancashire Cup final was played on a sunny afternoon with a stiff breeze blowing. Kevin remembers:

'The feeling at Leigh was that if we could only win a cup competition, then the big time was just around the corner. We had beaten Swinton at home in the league, 12-2, and although they had taken us all the way, we really fancied our chances.' Swinton's side was the same one that had won the semi-final. It read: Ken Gowers; John Gomersall, Bobby Fleet, Alan Buckley, Mike Philbin; Billy 'Daz' Davies, Peter Kenny; Harold Bate, Derek Clarke, Graham Mackay, Bill Holliday, Rodney Smith and Dave Robinson. Leigh also stood by the men who had taken them through. Their team was Tommy Grainey; Rod Tickle, Tommy Warburton, Mick Collins, Harold Stringer; Dave Eckersley, Alex Murphy; Dave Chisnall, Kevin Ashcroft, Derek Watts, Bob Welding, Jimmy Fiddler, Geoff Lyon. Leigh's sub was Dennis Brown, who came on for Harold Stringer.

Unfortunately, in this final, the expected fast-flowing football between sides who loved to throw the ball about never materialised. It was a dour, forward-orientated bash with a few deft touches from the evergreen Alex Murphy. The player who stole the show, though, was a half-back not normally noted for his kicking expertise. Out of the blue, Peter Kenny kicked four drop-goals in a perfect exhibition of the skill. His eight points were added to by a Mick Philbin try, crafted by the excellent loose forward Dave Robinson. Philbin's try plus one drop-goal by Kenny gave Swinton the edge, 5-2, at half-time, with Leigh's only score an Alex Murphy drop-goal.

Still, playing with the aid of sun and wind, it looked as if Leigh would come good in the second half. But with Kenny successfully firing over drop-goals at regular intervals, Swinton adopted a gameplan that bottled their opponents up. Murphy tried all he knew to change that, but his plans misfired as Kevin began to lose out in the scrums and Derek Clarke, the Swinton hooker, virtually won the game for

Swinton with the ball he won in the tight. This was a game for forwards and kickers, with both open-side props, Dave Chisnall for Leigh and Harold Bate for Swinton, having great games.

'We were outplayed on the day,' says Kevin. 'Clarkey hooked very well and Harold Bate did a good job in the pack, as well as the loose. There were times I didn't see the ball being put into the scrum, so well did Swinton scrummage.' Nor did Leigh have any complaints about Yorkshire referee Eric Clay. 'He kept a tight hold on the game as one would expect in a cup final, and did a good job,' confirms Kevin. Even so, Alex Murphy was knocked out by an elbow that everyone missed, and he was helped from the field to the dressing room for treatment. But the game was lost by then and, apart from the brilliant breaks by Murphy that came to nothing, the most memorable moment was when Kenny hit his fourth and final drop-kick from a good thirty yards out. It soared over the crossbar and between the posts at a huge height. Leigh had failed again at the final hurdle, but the spirit was not dampened and the old feeling of determination to do better at the next opportunity was still within the players.

With their season far from over, Leigh continued to strengthen an already very strong squad. Stan Dorrington was signed from junior football. Les Chisnall was bought from Huyton to add experience to various back positions. Most crucially, Stuart Ferguson was signed from Swansea rugby union. As hoped, Ferguson's ability to kick goals took Leigh from being a good side to a very good side, capable of beating anyone in the league. The defeat in the County Cup final became the spur that drove the Leigh side onward and upward.

'We had said all along that if we could find a good, reliable goal-kicker who could knock over one hundred-plus goals in a season, then we had the tools to win something big regularly,' says Kevin. 'Losing in finals and big league games by a only few points made it obvious where our weakness was. Stuart Ferguson put that right. In his first twenty games he kicked fifty-six goals.'

While the Lancashire Cup was lost, the BBC2 Floodlit Trophy remained a possibility, especially when Hull Kingston Rovers were beaten at Craven Park, 12-6, in round two. However, one of the best wins of the season was in the semi-final, when Leigh travelled to Castleford, three-time winners of this prestigious competition. This time, in an absolutely brilliant match played on a nerve-tingling night in Yorkshire, Leigh took the honours with a superb display of controlled football to win by 12 points to 11. Major reasons for the victory were Kevin's domination of the scrums and Ferguson's three long-range goals.

Only eight games since the defeat by Swinton in the County Cup final, Leigh had regained a lot of kudos with their supporters and now, having reached the Floodlit final, they would face their oldest enemy, Wigan. Central Park was the venue and the meetings in the league between the two clubs so far this season were level at one win each. It wouldn't be easy. Leigh had not won any major trophy since they beat Widnes, 26-9, at Wigan, in the County Cup final of 1955. Wigan, meanwhile, could boast last season's Floodlit Trophy final as their most recent success, when they had beaten St. Helens. This latest crop of Wigan finalists read: Cliff Hill; Stuart Wright, Bill Francis, Peter Rowe, Kevin O'Loughlin; Dave Hill, Johnny Jackson; John Stephens, Colin Clarke, Keith Ashcroft, Bill Ashhurst, Keith Mills and Doug Laughton. Leigh, meanwhile, fielded: Stuart Ferguson; Rod Tickle, Stan Dorrington, Mick Collins, Joe Walsh; Dave Eckersley, Alex Murphy; Dave Chisnall, Kevin Ashcroft, Derek Watts, Bob Welding, Paul Grimes and Geoff

Lyon. Leigh's substitute was Gordon Lewis, who replaced Ferguson.

Early on, Leigh looked the more confident side. Their defence blotted out all of Wigan's carefully prepared moves with a desperate tackling performance that was their best of the season. Nothing could pass as Kevin, Derek Watts and Dave Chisnall blocked the ruck area and Geoff Lyon, Bob Welding and big Paul Grimes snuffed out any danger in a tight radius around the play-the-ball. Such solid unshakable defence began to frustrate the Wigan attackers, which allowed Stuart Ferguson, stepping up to the mark in his first big rugby league game, to kick a superb touchline penalty goal and give Leigh the lead. Ferguson, signed only a few weeks before, showed the nerve of a veteran as he slotted his memorable kick over. Shortly afterwards, Ferguson landed another cracking penalty from fifty yards, and then another mammoth touchline effort, to take Leigh into a 6-0 lead. When Ferguson was then helped off the field with a shoulder injury, it was Murphy's turn to drop a good goal and extend the margin to eight points.

Dave Hill reduced that deficit with a neat drop-goal, as Wigan seemed to get their second wind with the arrival of half-time. And early in the second half, Bill Francis landed a penalty goal as the home side began to smell a victory. With the scoreline now 8-4, Wigan attacked furiously. The Leigh defence, with Kevin and Geoff Lyon to the fore, withstood a battering as Wigan's big pack started to get the better of the more mobile Leigh six. Kevin, though, was still winning the ball from the scrum, and had several 'dust-ups' with Colin Clarke in the process. With the Wigan pack going so well, they seemed to ignore their quick and very effective backs and, as the Leigh forwards gradually regained the initiative, the effect of not using their threequarters was seen to have been a mistake. During a period of superiority, they had failed to score points. The midfield battle was won, almost lost, and then won again by the gallant Leigh pack, who were now finishing strongest.

Alex Murphy was at his best as his forwards regained their lost ground. And it was Murphy who had the final say when he broke brilliantly in midfield, veered out towards the very quick Rod Tickle, and sent the flying wingman over with a superb long pass for the only try of this tough-tackling game. The 11-4 lead was shortened by a Francis penalty goal, but that was still an 11-6 winning margin. For the first time in fourteen years, Alex Murphy, Kevin and their team-mates could take a trophy back to Leigh. And to make victory even sweeter, this was also the first time that any Leigh team had beaten a Wigan side in any sort of final. Heady stuff indeed.

* * *

In the first round of the grand old Challenge Cup, meanwhile, Leigh made the trip up to Derwent Park, Workington, where they were again victorious, 17-6. There was a hiccup in round two, however, when a tough Huyton side almost pulled off a famous win, before eventually having to settle for an 8-8 draw. Three days later, came the replay at Hilton Park. 'People used to ridicule Huyton,' remembers Kevin, 'but on their day they were a dangerous side. The result at Alt Park could have gone their way but for Stuart Ferguson's goal-kicking. He scored all our points with four long-range goals. The replay was unbelievably hard on a glue pot pitch. We won through, 2-0, again thanks to Stuart Ferguson kicking a great goal out of the Hilton Park mud. That meant we faced another huge game in the third round against our old mates from Wigan. This time, though, we were at home and 19,000 spectators crushed into the old ground to see it. It was another huge struggle. In heavy going, we faced another forward-orientated slog.'

The feeling between the two clubs was most unsportsmanlike. 'Not only on the field with the players, but on the terraces between the two factions of supporters,' recalls Kevin. 'The old deep-rooted emotions of tribal warfare are still there even today in what we call our derby games. To the hard core of supporters, and players too, to beat or lose to Wigan either made or sometimes destroyed your season. On this bitterly-fought occasion, Wigan destroyed our Wembley hopes, 6-4. It could not have been closer. We were even in the scrums and the heavy conditions suited my style of play. I suppose that both teams had their chances, but the pitch conditions ruled out any form of copybook rugby.'

Around this time, Dave Chisnall was given the nod for Great Britain's 1970 tour of Australia and New Zealand, and it was well deserved. Along with Les Chisnall, meanwhile, Leigh brought in the grand half-back Tom Canning from Oldham, thereby giving Alex Murphy more options in team selection. The league position improved too, Leigh attaining seventh place in the table, a step up of two places from the previous season. Twenty-one games were won out of thirty-four played and three drawn. The league position gave Leigh a home-tie in the play-offs against Widnes, which was won, 21-10. That meant a trip to St. Helens where a 16-5 defeat ended their Floodlit Trophy-winning season.

Even better, though, was still to come. For Leigh, the 1970/71 season would prove to be the most successful in the club's long and proud history. An already impressive squad was to be strengthened still further by key signings. Robust forward Geoff Clarkson was signed from Bradford Northern, adding to the pack's size and mobility. Mick Mooney arrived from Rochdale Hornets, Tony Barrow came in from Saints and the supreme enthusiast, Peter Smethurst - an inspired buy - joined Leigh from Salford. In the first twenty-one games of this season, Leigh lost only three.

'There was a feeling within the club,' says Kevin. 'No one could explain it. We had a confidence that we could take on anyone and that was without being big-headed. You looked around the dressing room at your team-mates and it came to you that here was a side that could beat the whole league. The other wonderful feeling was that you couldn't wait to go to training. Your mates were there and they felt the same. The training nights were great, as were the Saturday nights after a good win. Our winning sequences had proved that we were at last consistent and a team has to be consistent to win anything big.'

The Lancashire Cup took Leigh to Wilderspool in the first round and Warrington, as they always did, attacked their opponents with a vengeance. 'Tommy Canning was at half-back with Murph,' Kevin remembers. 'They both scored super tries which, along with a sneaky one from me and Stuart Ferguson's four goals, to go with Murph's two drop-goals, gave us a comfortable enough win in the end, 21-9. Of our three defeats during the great spell to come, we lost to Saints, 26-7, and Featherstone Rovers, 23-17, both away games. Once back on the winning track, we had a cracking win over Leeds at home by 36-8 and an equally good win, again at home, over Hull Kingston Rovers, 23-5. Then came another rock-hard home match in round two of the County Cup against Workington Town.'

For this one, Leigh had to get to grips with the powerful Cumbrian forwards. 'It was brutal to say the least,' says Kevin. 'We had to fight tooth and nail to overcome them. In the end, though, we ran out winners by 12 points to 8, with Murph and Tommy Canning getting the tries again, Ferguson one goal, and Murph dropping two belting goals.'

September 1970 then ended in a flourish, with Salford beaten home and away, 20-14 at Hilton Park and 19-7 at the Willows. In between, Bradford Northern were beaten 23-12, again at Hilton Park.

To a modern rugby league audience, just how many games were played in those days may, perhaps, be surprising. In that particular month, for example, Leigh played eight games in twenty-five days. And these games, let us not forget, were played on muddy pitches too. Every player worked full-time, between 8-00am until 5-30pm at least, and had a life away from football.

Into this gruelling mix fell the semi-final of the Lancashire Cup, an away tie at Naughton Park, against ultra-tough Widnes. As expected, the major battle was up front. In a thrilling game, though, it was Leigh who came out on top 13-10, with Ferguson kicking three goals, Dave Eckersley and Kevin each dropping a goal apiece and Dave Chisnall barging over for a popular try. The side chosen to play Widnes shows exactly the strength-in-depth that Alex Murphy had been looking for when he first took on the Leigh job. A most unusual looking team on paper, it read: Stuart Ferguson; Rod Tickle, Harold Stringer, Les Chisnall, Joe Walsh; Dave Eckersley, Tommy Canning; Dave Chisnall, Kevin Ashcroft, Derek Watts, Roy Lester, Geoff Clarkson and Mick Mooney.

Appearing in a major final was becoming a habit with Leigh. This time, the big event would be played out on the wide-open spaces of Swinton's huge Station Road ground. 'I think it was Hunslet in the league that we beat after the semi- final and by a big score,' muses Kevin. 'Then we drew Swinton at home in the preliminary round of the Floodlit Trophy. Another win. Then it was Widnes in the league by 18-7. I was sent off in that one for persistent feet up in the scrum but the wins kept on coming.' Indeed they did.

Rochdale Hornets were dumped out of the Floodlit Trophy's round one proper at Leigh, 14-5. Kevin, though, missed that game on account of a one-match suspension for the dismissal against Widnes.

* * *

In October, the conventional league season switched off in order to accommodate the 1970 Rugby League World Cup. Great Britain's squad was mainly made up of the Ashes-winning side that had toured successfully in the summer. Kevin had been disappointed not to travel to Australia and New Zealand. The two hookers taken were Peter 'Flash' Flanagan (Hull KR) and no-nonsense Tony Fisher (Bradford Northern). Flanagan was a quick mover across the ground and suited the hard, unyielding pitches that the Aussies played on. Fisher was a respected, hard hitting hooker who could mix it with the best.

For the World Cup, though, Kevin was included on the back of a run of good seasons and his ability to turn it on in big games. Also, he had previously been on World Cup duty in 1968. In this latest nineteen-man squad he was joined by his touring Leigh team-mate Dave Chisnall. In alphabetical order, it read: Frank Myler (St. Helens - captain), Kevin Ashcroft (Leigh), John Atkinson (Leeds), Paul Charlton (Salford), Dave Chisnall (Leigh), Ray Dutton (Widnes), Tony Fisher (Bradford Northern), Bob Haigh (Leeds), Dennis Hartley (Castleford), Keith Hepworth (Castleford), Chris Hesketh (Salford), Syd Hynes (Leeds), Kerry Jones (Wigan), Doug Laughton (Wigan), Mal Reilly (Castleford), Mick Shoebottom (Leeds), Alan Smith (Leeds), Jimmy Thompson (Featherstone) and Cliff Watson (St. Helens).

The opening game of the tournament for Great Britain was against Australia at Headingley on 24th October. By then, the Aussies had already scored a resounding 47-11 win over New Zealand at Central Park, Wigan. They knew, however, that their second game against the home country would be far tougher. Not surprisingly, the British selectors opted for a team made from players who had done so well down under. It read: Dutton, Smith, Hynes, Myler, Atkinson, Shoebottom, Hepworth, Hartley, Fisher, Watson, Thompson, Laughton and Reilly. The subs were Hesketh and Haigh. Determined to erase the summer's bad memories, the Aussies too fielded a strong side: Eric Simms; Mark Harris, Ray Brannighan, Bobby Fulton, Lionel Williamson; Dennis Pittard, Billy Smith; John O'Neill, Elwyn Walters, Bob O'Reilly, Bob McCarthy, Paul Sait and Gary Sullivan. The Australian subs were Johnny Brown and Ron Turner. In the event, the British boys got away to a flyer, beating the Aussies by 11 points to 4, with Syd Hynes the only tryscorer. The following day, New Zealand beat France at the Boulevard, 16-15, before Great Britain too faced the Frenchmen at Wheldon Road, Castleford. Happily for Kevin, he was one of the two changes made from the team that had beaten Australia. Kerry Jones came in on the wing for Alan Smith and Kevin was in for Tony Fisher.

The French were at their best for this one and Kevin came up against his old sparring partner, Jacques Cabero, in a match refereed by Fred Lindop of Wakefield. It was another fight-after-fight game, as the French attempted strong-arm stuff but, against a full-strength British pack, all those tactics did was keep down the score. Ray Dutton kicked three goals in a 6-0 win for the Brits. Three days later, at Station Road, Swinton, Great Britain took on New Zealand and needed to win to go top of the World Cup league table in a game again refereed by Lindop. That they duly did, 27-17, to finish with a more than acceptable played three, won three. The home side that day was: Dutton; Jones, Hynes, Hesketh, Atkinson;

Shoebottom, Hepworth; Chisnall, Ashcroft, Watson, Thompson, Haigh, and Laughton. Subs: Charlton and Reilly.

Even though France then defeated Australia at Odsal, Bradford, 17-15, the Aussies still managed to secure second place in the table as a result of superior points difference. That set up a Great Britain versus Australia final at Headingley, Leeds, on 7th November. The Great Britain team reverted to the one used in that opening encounter, with Fisher coming back in for Kevin and Smith replacing Kerry Jones.

This time, it was always going to be about pay-back, and the British boys allowed the Aussies to dictate the pace and just what type of game it would turn out to be. Instead of playing them at football, running battles were the order of the day as the Aussies both captured the world crown and outsmarted their opponents to boot. Lindop was once more the referee and did his home nation no favours, with many claiming that the Aussies had pulled the wool over his eyes too. In any case, the result was a shock win for Australia, by 12 points to 7.

* * *

With the World Cup over, things soon got back to normal in England's domestic competition. For Kevin and Leigh, St. Helens were next to visit Hilton park in the league, where Leigh won a thriller, 15-13, with a real gutsy performance. Back in the side after his suspension, Kevin won the scrum count by a huge margin and that, at least partly, earned him a call-up for more county duty.

On 11th November, Lancashire faced Cumberland at Craven Park, Barrow, in the County Championship, where Kevin registered a try in a 28-5 win for the red rose team. The Lancashire side that day was: John Walsh (St. Helens),

Stuart Wright (Wigan), Billy Benyon (St. Helens), Chris Hesketh (Salford), Joe Walsh (Leigh), Frank Myler (St. Helens), Jimmy Boylan (Widnes), Dave Chisnall (Leigh), Kevin Ashcroft (Leigh), Eddie Brown (Rochdale Hornets), Eric Prescott (St. Helens), Eric Chisnall (St. Helens), Doug Laughton (Wigan). Subs: George Nicholls (Widnes) and Martin Murphy (Oldham). Along with Kevin's try, Stuart Wright, Chris Hesketh, Frank Myler (2) and Eric Prescott scored tries too, while John Walsh kicked five goals. The Cumberland side read: Paul Charlton (Salford), Keith Davies (Workington Town), Ian Wright (Workington Town), Tony Colloby (Blackpool Borough), Rodney Morris (Whitehaven), Bobby Nicholson (Workington Town), Joe Bonner (Wakefield Trinity), Les Moore (Workington Town), Howard Allen (Workington Town), Frank Foster (Barrow), Harold McCourt (Workington Town), Eddie Bowman (Workington Town), John McFarlane (Barrow). Sub: Dennis Martin (Whitehaven). Martin scored Cumberland's try and Tony Colloby kicked a goal, while the referee was Mr. Ronnie Jackson of Halifax.

Against Cumberland, Kevin maintained his knack of playing well in representative games and his performance earned him high praise from the Lancashire committee. After all, the Cumbrians had earlier beaten Yorkshire in Whitehaven, so the Championship would go to Lancashire if they could beat Yorkshire in January 1971.

Meanwhile, back at Leigh, and Whitehaven were beaten 23-11 at Hilton Park one week before the County Cup final showdown with St. Helens at Swinton on 28th November. Just two days after that prestigious Lancashire Cup final, Leigh and Saints were then scheduled to face their third such showdown in a month, this time in the second round of the BBC2 Floodlit Trophy on the 30th. Nevertheless, with their club now in brilliant form, the Leigh supporters felt sure that this was to be their year. The County Cup, they knew, was the big one and Alex Murphy's men were determined to lift it as winners for the first time in 15 years.

Swinton, the current holders, who had defeated Leigh in the previous year's final, had already fallen to Saints in the second round of this season's competition. Huyton and Wigan were also beaten by Leigh's opponents in the run-up to the final. Saints were in impressive form and had recently hammered the touring Australians, 37-10. Indeed, their only loss in eleven games had been to Leigh earlier in the month. After eleven straight wins of their own, no wonder Leigh came into the final cock-a-hoop.

Again, the playing conditions were dreadful and not helped by a heavy downpour immediately prior to the match. Beforehand, the purists had expected a free-flowing game, and why wouldn't they with the superb skills of Alex Murphy, Dave Eckersley, Rod Tickle and Kevin Ashcroft on display, not to mention the expertise of Frank Myler, Kel Coslett, Billy Benyon and Tony Karalius. The heavy pitch, though, ruled out any hope of fast, flamboyant football. What the crowd of 10,735 witnessed instead was a hard, no nonsense, battle of wills. The two packs were big, tough professional forwards whose sole object was to win that Cup both for the prestige and the winning pay packet. The backs had little chance to excel on the quagmire of a pitch. Lining up for Saints were: Frank Barrow; Les Jones, Billy Benyon, John Walsh, Frank Wilson; Frank Myler, Alan Whittle; Albert Halsall, Tony Karalius, Graham Rees, John Mantle, Eric Chisnall and Kel Coslett, with Eric Prescott subbing. The Leigh side read: Stuart Ferguson; Rod Tickle, Mick Collins, Les Chisnall, Joe Walsh; Dave Eckersley, Alex Murphy; Dave Chisnall, Kevin Ashcroft, Derek Watts, Paul Grimes, Geoff Clarkson and Mick Mooney, with Tommy Canning as sub. The referee: Mr. Billy Thompson of Huddersfield.

The inability to play open football because of the heavy going led to the odd squabble, which more often than not then turned into a fight. The tight tackling of the forwards saw even more fighting break out and before very long tempers got the better of several players. One unusual fact about this game is that there were three brothers playing. Les and Dave Chisnall were in Leigh's team and Eric Chisnall played for St. Helens. Something had to happen and, sure enough, when Dave Chisnall was dismissed from the field by Mr. Thompson, it was for having a go at their kid. Then Les Chisnall and Alan Whittle received their marching orders, reducing the teams further, but giving Saints the distinct advantage of one player extra.

After the opening forty minutes the score was still 0-0, as sound defence from both sides nullified any attacking ideas. Coslett then opened the scoring with a neat penalty goal, which was matched by Ferguson ten minutes later. As Coslett's accurate boot sent another penalty soaring over the crossbar to put Saints 4-2 up, it looked as though the weather would a major factor in the contest. Suddenly, Leigh had begun to look a spent force. They needed to find some inspiration, desperately. Step forward, Alex Murphy. Always a champion whenever touches of brilliance were required, as the game ticked into its final minutes Murphy hoisted a towering spiral kick just over the head of the otherwise excellent Frank Barrow, who had to turn and run back towards his own line, the very worst position for a full-back to be in.

As Kevin tells it: 'Murph had told us to chase this kick, as he had spotted a gap between Frank and the try line. He turned Frank around to attempt the most difficult of catches, running back and catching the ball coming down over your shoulder. Me, Mick Collins and Geoff Clarkson converged on Frank and the ball hit him on the shoulder, bounced away and landed on its point on the only bit of dry grass on Station Road. As only a rugby ball can, it then bounced back on itself right into the path of the supporting Dave Eckersley, who dived on the ball for a try, before disappearing under a mass of team-mates, who all dived on him in celebration. Ferguson added the conversion and Billy Thompson blew for time.'

The grand old County Cup was back in Leigh hands at last. It had not been a pretty victory but a win is a win, especially when it earns a club a major trophy. The victory also fulfilled Alex Murphy's promise made after the BBC Floodlit Trophy win some eleven months before, that 'there are more cups on their way'. It had been a brutal contest - indeed one critic called it 'a sordid struggle of flying fists and three dismissals'. The truth was that Leigh had done the job that they wanted and built it on a never-say-die spirit and one second of 'Murphy Magic'. A sign of their achievement was that, two days later, St. Helens went to Hilton Park as planned and won 4-0 in the Floodlit Trophy.

At a Civic Reception in honour of the victory, Alex made another promise to the people of Leigh, when he said that he would take the team on their first ever trip to Wembley.

The good league form continued into the new year with wins against Featherstone, Warrington and Hull FC, a game which saw the debut of the superb Peter Smethurst. On 24th January, the first round of the Challenge Cup brought Bradford Northern to Hilton Park, with Leigh having to dig deep to scratch out a 9-2 win. Then, back in the league, Castleford were beaten at home 12-3 and Whitehaven away - another rough, tough game - with Leigh victorious again, 12-5. The draw for the second round of the Challenge Cup, meanwhile, gave Leigh a tricky away tie at Widnes. The renowned cup-fighting Chemics made a real grandstand attempt to stop their visitors in the tracks, and the Widnes forwards gave the Leigh pack a real working over until Kevin, a try-scorer, Peter Smethurst and Dave Chisnall came good late on in a hard-fought 14-11 win.

On 24th February, Kevin was again called up to take part in the County Championship. Back in January, Yorkshire had beaten Lancashire in the normal inter-county game, meaning that all three counties had one win each. Points differential meant that Yorkshire and Lancashire were above Cumberland, so the red rose and white rose now faced a play-off at Wheldon Road, Castleford. Kevin had missed the first Yorkshire game and Colin Clarke had hooked that evening. But now he was back and a strong Lancashire outfit read: Colin Tyrer (Wigan); Joe Walsh (Leigh), Alan Buckley (Swinton), Chris Hesketh (Salford), Les Jones (St. Helens); Dennis O'Neill (Widnes), Jim Boylan (Widnes); John Stephens (St. Helens), Kevin Ashcroft (Leigh), Brian Hogan (Wigan), George Nicholls (Widnes), Terry Cranmant (Swinton), Dave Robinson (Wigan). Subs: Colin Clarke (Wigan) and Dave Eckersley (Leigh). The Yorkshire line-up ran: Brian Jefferson (Keighley); Keith Slater (Wakefield Trinity), Ian Stanton (Castleford), Nigel Stephenson (Dewsbury), Chris Young (York); Alan Hardisty (Castleford), Keith Hepworth (Castleford); Terry Clawson (Hull KR), Clive Dickinson (Castleford), David Jeanes (Wakefield Trinity), Brian Lockwood (Castleford), Bob Irving (Oldham), Tony Halmshaw (Halifax). Subs: Dave Topliss (Wakefield Trinity) and Mick Stephenson (Dewsbury).

In the end, Yorkshire won the contest rather easily, 34-8, with tries from Jefferson, Slater (2), Nigel Stephenson (2), Jeans, Irving and Topliss, while Hardisty, N. Stephenson (3) and Jefferson kicked their goals. For Lancashire, Les Jones and George Nicholls scored tries and Colin Tyrer landed a goal. Kevin was beaten for the ball by the underestimated

Clive Dickinson of Castleford, as Lancashire's hulking pack could not get to grips with the lighter and faster Yorkshire forwards.

* * *

Meanwhile, the regular club season continued and in March came the next round of the Challenge Cup, when Leigh were given a plum home tie with Hull FC. Kevin recalls that: 'Murph was looking to play the right men in the right places again, depending on who we were playing. Tony Barrow, always an honest player, had hit some good form in the centre, but there were men waiting to take over if that form dipped. Dave Eckersley had been the regular stand-off half but Murph moved him to full-back and he was outstanding there. So, for this major Cup tie, Murph selected Eckersley, Ferguson, Barrow, Collins, Walsh, himself, Canning, Chisnall, me, Watts, Clarkson, Grimes and Smethurst. It was another typical Challenge Cup tie with no holds barred. Though not a try was scored, we won through by 8-4 with almost 16,000 in.'

Alex Murphy could not only run extremely fast and score tries for fun, he was also one of the best kickers of a ball out of hand in rugby league. His touch-kicking was long and accurate and his drop-kicking was a huge gift. 'Murph dropped three beautiful goals to go with Ferguson's penalty, to give us our eight points,' says Kevin. 'The tackling was cup-tie stuff and there were plenty of bruises being iced in the dressing room after that game.' With Hull safely dispatched, Leigh went on another seven-match run of victories including a super home win against Wigan, 15-3, only three days after the Cup tie.

That Wigan game drew 13,000 spectators, giving Leigh a combined total of 29,000 people in the ground over three days. The seven games won also included victories over Bradford Northern, Hull, Swinton and Hunslet, all away, and Workington Town at home. However, it was the seventh match which was most special. 'It was against Huddersfield in the semi-final of the Rugby League Challenge Cup, at Central Park before 15,000 people' remembers Kevin. 'The other semi-final was played at Odsal, between Castleford and Leeds, both good sides.'

Whatever the entertainment value in that fixture, Leigh's semi-final with Huddersfield produced eighty dour minutes of struggle, stamina and will-power. Wearing Leigh colours that day were: Eckersley; Ferguson, Barrow, Collins, Walsh, Murphy, Canning, D. Chisnall, Ashcroft, Fiddler, Grimes, Clarkson and Smethurst. And Leigh it was who enjoyed the greatest territorial advantage, but only slightly, mainly due to Kevin's pull in the scrums. On attacks into Huddersfield's half, Ferguson managed to kick three penalty goals, while Jimmy Fiddler and Kevin chipped in with a drop-goal each. The end result was a 10 points to 4 win for Leigh and a first-ever appearance for the club in a Wembley Challenge Cup final.

Not surprisingly, the town went mad with delight. The streets around Hilton Park were trimmed with red and white bunting, much of it hanging between houses on opposite sides of the street. Red and white flags were flown out of house windows to celebrate this momentous occasion. When the Leigh team left Central Park, their bus was surrounded by delirious supporters, as the players inside basked in the deserved sunlight of stardom. Alex, meanwhile, made his plans early for both the Wembley trip and the week proceeding the final.

As a player at St. Helens, Alex's mentor had been the great Jim Sullivan, the doyen of international full-backs and a brilliantly successful coach. Big Jim always did his pre-final training at Southport and Alex was not going to change a winning formula. But there was still around seven weeks to go and plenty of football to be played before the trip to London.

Their excellent form in the league had given Leigh a great chance of completing the golden treble: the Lancashire Cup, the Challenge Cup and the league Championship. No wonder the proud Leigh public were ecstatic. Ominously, in the first two games after the semi-final, Leigh suffered two of the worst defeats of the season; a 20 points to 7 loss to Wigan away, then a 32-5 hammering by Huddersfield at Fartown. A couple of wins over Dewsbury and Warrington soon put the wheels back on, but the final away trip to Hull KR ended in a loss, 34-15. Wembley on the mind? Maybe. Either way, the play-offs gave Leigh an early chance of revenge, as Hull KR were the visitors to Hilton Park six days later. On that occasion, Leigh won a nail-biter in which Ferguson kicked five goals in a 10-5 victory. Eight days later, the Championship dream went out of the window when Wakefield Trinity came to Hilton Park and beat Leigh 8-5. Poignantly, during the run-up to Wembley, the ever-reliable Dave Chisnall was sent off against Hull KR in the play-off game and received a two-match ban, which denied the side-stepping prop an appearance at the Empire Stadium.

Only thirteen days away from the final and the newspapers and television crews began beating on the door for stories and interviews. Alex organised a film shoot at Hilton Park. 'There was a bookie who lived in Leigh,' recalls Kevin, 'and this bloke owned a cracking greyhound which was winning every race he entered. Murph challenged the dog to a race over twenty yards against Rod Tickle, the fastest man on the club's books. All the newspapers turned up and BBC local television. The race would be started by an athletics gun - on your marks, get set, bang!

'Now, make no mistake, Alex was quick over twenty yards, electric even, so as ever on the look out to make a few quid, he pulled Rod Tickle out at the last minute and moved the finishing marker to 15 yards from the start. "Rod can't run, he is injured," he told the bookie. "We can't let the TV down so I will take his place and, to make it interesting, I will back myself for a straight £100." The bookie was a bit hesitant, knowing Alex and his tricks. "First past that pole?" he checked as he stood on the starting line. "That's right," said Murph, "and pay up straight after the race." The bookie smiled but Alex had one more thing to tell him. "The television is here to witness it and so are my players. If there is no one hundred quid, you will have one hundred bruises." The bookie swallowed and said okay.

'The players were a bit apprehensive as their team-mate and coach lined up with this canine running machine, but Alex winked at them and took his stance. The gun went off and so did Murph, like a rocket. Now, the lads had seen him run before but never as quick as this, and Alex flashed past the post first by inches. He hardly stopped as he jogged around and up to the bookie. "That'll be a long 'un you owe me," he said, and held out a hand for his money.'

* * *

The squad for Wembley was named and each Leigh player was asked to take a week off work, as they would be travelling on the club bus to training at Southport on Monday, Tuesday and Wednesday, before coming home early to rest each evening. The work they did was a carbon copy of the drills Jim Sullivan put his Saints team through, up and down those huge sand dunes by the sea. On Monday and Tuesday, that is. On Wednesday they played golf at the famous links near the resort.

The Widnes lads in the squad made their own way to the course and, as the main body waited whilst they changed, suddenly, over the crest of a small hill, came a sight they never expected to see. It was Joe Walsh, complete with one of those huge flat caps worn by golfers, plus fours, checked pullover and matching socks. He also wore golf shoes with the buckle across the top and had a set of new clubs worthy of Arnold Palmer. The squad was in stitches of laughter, because they all thought Joe had been to a fancy dress shop for the outfit. But, on inspection, it was the real thing. In the end, Joe sold the clubs to a complete stranger in the changing rooms.

Later that evening, Kevin and Janet were watching television at home when on came *Police File*, a regular programme in those days in which news of recent crimes was broadcast in the hope that someone might be able to help the police in solving them. Kevin sat bolt upright when the presenter suddenly informed the nation that they were going over to an outfitters in Runcorn, where a complete golfing outfit, including a magnificent set of expensive golf clubs, had disappeared overnight. What a coincidence, thought Kevin.

Besides making their first appearance at Wembley, another Leigh first around this time concerned Kevin's four-year-old son, Gary, who had now been the official mascot for the club for almost a full season. Upon reaching the Challenge Cup final, Leigh wrote to the Rugby Football League and mentioned in their letter that they had a mascot. Sorry, they were told, no mascots are allowed at Wembley. Understandably, Gary was broken-hearted and so Kevin said he would do what he could for his son. In tandem with Alex, a plan was concocted to outwit the authorities and somehow smuggle Gary into the dressing rooms, thence onto the hallowed turf.

Up against the might of Leeds, Leigh went into the 1971 Challenge Cup final as long outsiders with the bookies. Paul Grimes, who played in the second row that day, reflects: 'I couldn't understand why nobody gave us a chance. We had finished the league run in fourth position, only four points behind Leeds, who were in third. We were a good team in our own right. We were fit and superbly motivated. We never once considered getting beat.' Mick Collins, too, was superbly confident before the game. 'With Alex in our side, we were a team in every way,' he says, 'and our pre-match preparations went superbly. Our thoughts were that we can beat anybody on the day and we were completely relaxed in everything we did.'

In London, the team stayed at the Hendon Hall Hotel. Up early on Friday morning, Murphy took his team out onto the grass of Hyde Park for a few stretching exercises and an impromptu game of touch and pass, for which a row of tracksuit tops acted as a try-line. They had only been playing for around three minutes when up rode two mounted policemen. 'Excuse me, sir,' said one of the bobbies to Murphy. 'Do you see that sign? It says no ball games.' Alex tried to explain. 'We play at Wembley tomorrow and we are only having a loosen-up,' he said. To which the policeman replied: 'I don't care if you are Real *&^%$ Madrid. No ball games.' So off they all trotted back to the hotel.

* * *

Soon it was time to go and have a look at the pitch and stadium. On the toss of a coin, Leeds went first, supposedly between 12 noon and 1-00pm. The Leigh walkabout was then scheduled to take place between 2-00pm and 3-00pm. Kevin smiles as he relates the story. 'We went in directly on 2-00pm,' he says. 'Leeds were still having a last look around.

The Wembley groundstaff were all working on the pitch and they did an unusual thing. Knowing we were the absolute underdogs, and us dressed to the nines in our new blazers and flannels, looking a million dollars, to a man, they applauded as we walked out onto the turf. Leeds, on the other hand, were dressed casually, some without coats on. When we found out later that they hadn't got the wonderful reception that the Wembley men gave us, we felt great. As we were passing the Royal Box, one of our players shouted, "Look at their body language, they are beaten before we start." Immediately, Joe Walsh, never without a word, ran over to one of the groundstaff, who was watering some flowers, and borrowed his watering can. He called out to the Leeds team, who all turned around. "Here lads," he shouted, holding up the watering can. "This is the only *&^%$ cup you'll win this weekend." While we all fell about laughing, the Leeds team walked off dejectedly.'

Leigh's specialised training that afternoon was a couple of pints and off to the Hendon dog track. 'Murph had a couple of sure things, and they both won so we were quids in,' remembers Kevin. 'Only a few of our lads had ever been to London before so, after the dogs, Murph ordered the bus to take a short landmark tour around the city. Afterwards, we went back to the hotel for a bedtime cuppa. Then, with Murph and me being the last two sitting in the lounge, he dropped a bombshell. "I am going to Warrington as player-coach-manager after tomorrow's game," he told me. "I want you, Dave Chisnall and Geoff Clarkson to come with me." I was dumbstruck, especially when I realised that Murph was deadly serious. "Think it over after the game tomorrow and I will talk to you then," he said.

'None of the lads could sleep, so we met in Murph's room for a chat and a game of cards. Our rooms were all at the front of the hotel and, at about 12 midnight, some Leeds supporters who were staying there suddenly turned up outside, on the pavement below our rooms, singing and chanting with a drum and a couple of trumpets. Joe Walsh was having none of this, so he filled a wastepaper basket with water from the bathroom and, peeping out of the window to get his aim right, tipped the contents over the drunken supporters. Now, by some quirk of fate, a gleaming Rolls Royce limousine pulled up right where Joe was aiming. The revellers stopped their singing and made way for a Sheik to enter the hotel. Joe's aim was perfect. But unfortunately his bomb didn't land on the Yorkies, it hit the Sheik, who was blathered in water. The card party quickly dispersed back to their rooms and went off to sleep.'

Next morning, the players rose at ten, took a shower, ate breakfast and tried to relax with the newspapers before their wives and girlfriends arrived at the hotel. The team bus then set off at 1-00pm for the stadium, with young Gary Ashcroft sat at the back of the bus between Peter Smethurst and Kevin, with a blanket draped around his shoulders.

Kevin remembers: 'I just told Gary to be quiet and sit still until we were in the dressing room.' Fortunately, Ashcroft junior was no stranger to publicity as his debut as team mascot had been published - along with photographs - in the national newspapers, so he knew how to behave. On arrival at Wembley, the team alighted from the bus with Gary under his dad's arm and the Leigh players milling around him. The Leigh dressing room staff were also in on the plot, so a big wicker skip containing the playing gear was swiftly opened and Gary deposited quickly into it, with the lid firmly closed. Eagle-eyed security guards checked everybody into the changing area as the skip was innocently wheeled through and into the security of the dressing room. So far, so good. Alex stationed a man at the door with the instruction that no one should enter.

When news of the Leeds team was relayed through to the Leigh inner-circle, it emerged that the brilliant ball-playing loose forward Ray Batten, the mainspring of the Leeds midfield attack, and free-scoring wingman Alan Smith were both out of the side through injury. This was a tremendous boost to the Leigh team as Batten and Smith were very much key players for the Yorkshiremen.

As kick-off approached, Peter Smethurst and Kevin helped Gary into his replica gear for the presentation ceremony, and he looked the part in his brilliant pristine cherry and white hooped jersey, complete with the Leigh coat of arms on the Wembley Cup Final badge over the left breast. Kevin recalls: 'We all said that the strip looked superb with those startling cherry bands against a spotless white background. A few words from Murph, a knock on the door by a touch judge and a call of "Come on lads, it's time" brought us all to our feet. I had a final word to our Gary to be still until we were walking out and, with the little lad tight to my side nearest the wall so that he was hidden from the security guards, we moved out into the high, airy corridor leading to the pitch. Mr. Jack Harding, our chairman, led out the team and, as we received the call to go, Gary was ushered to the front carrying a ball. He took hold of Mr. Harding's hand and walked out across the sand from the tunnel and onto the beautiful green acre of the Wembley turf as the first-ever mascot to lead his team out onto the actual playing area of the stadium.

'We had been advised to walk out in order of numbers behind the captain, but Murph said that he wanted his vice-captain next to him so I did that and the remainder of the Leigh side followed us in order. My everlasting memory will be seeing all those thousands of cherry and white scarves and banners at the far end of the ground. The Leeds team looked tense and rather dull in their new blue and amber jerseys, compared to our sparkling gear. I have never ever been with a team so laid back and confident before a big game. Leeds looked nervous but our lads were unbelievable. Dave Eckersley, right behind me, whispered: "&^%$* hell, Ash, will you look at that," as he took in the stadium and all the Leigh colours. It seemed as if the whole ground was full of cherry and white. Joe Walsh was singing a little tune to himself and there was not one sign of nerves anywhere in our line-up.'

Gary Ashcroft, meanwhile, stood between Mr. Harding and Alex Murphy at the front of the line, ready to be presented to Lady Derby and Britain's then-Home Secretary Mr. Reginald Maudling. The youngster shook hands with confidence and both dignitaries were impressed by him.

Leigh had arrived at Wembley via wins against Bradford Northern, Widnes, Hull FC and Huddersfield, a hard road indeed. Nor had Leeds had it easy. Their wins were against Oldham, Bramley, St. Helens and Castleford. As usual, the rugby league writers had their own opinions on how this game would figure and one billed it 'the battle of pace and finesse against brawn and power.' Most said that all Leeds had to do was stop Murphy, as Leigh were a one-man team. Balderdash! Alex had gone to town as only he could in answer to the theory that this would be one game too far for the brave Leigh side, and that it could well be the most one-sided final in the history of Wembley. This Leeds team, they said, would be too strong and fast for Leigh to handle. To which Alex replied: 'From number one to number thirteen, Leeds are a great side, but that does not mean that they can't be beaten. The bigger they are the harder they fall and Leeds are going to fall at Wembley. We are going to hit them like a ton of bricks. We have no thoughts of defeat. We are geared to win!'

The teams on that famous day lined up as follows. Leeds:

John Holmes; John Langley, Syd Hynes, Ron Cowen, John Atkinson; Tony Wainwright, Barry Seaborne; John Burke, Tony Fisher, Ted Barnard, Dave Hick, Bob Haigh and Bill Ramsey. Their substitute was Les Dyl. Leigh's solid and determined outfit read: Dave Eckersley; Stuart Ferguson, Stan Dorrington, Mick Collins, Joe Walsh; Tony Barrow, Alex Murphy; Derek Watts, Kevin Ashcroft, Jim Fiddler, Paul Grimes, Geoff Clarkson and Peter Smethurst, with Les Chisnall as substitute. The referee was Billy Thompson.

As it happened, the game did indeed turn out to be a one-sided affair but not in the way that the pundits had predicted. It was Leigh who dictated and controlled the match from the kick-off. Leeds were certainly shell-shocked when Jimmy Fiddler dropped a neat goal to open Leigh's account, and this was followed soon after by a Stuart Ferguson penalty goal. Leigh were on the scoreboard again when Alex Murphy drew the Leeds loose forward onto him and Stan Dorrington stepped into a gap in the Leeds defensive line, with a call to his captain, 'My ball, short', before Murph obliged with a peach of a pass that sent Dorrington speeding over for a perfect try, to which Ferguson added the extra two points.

Stan Dorrington had, pre-match, been quoted as saying, 'I'm happy just to be in the nineteen-man Wembley squad', and now here he was striding over the whitewash. That's the magic of Wembley. Kevin's own display inspired several great reports on his game. One such was written by Jack Bentley in the Daily Express the following Monday morning. It called him: 'the non-stop hooker.' Alex Murphy hammered another nail in the Leeds coffin with a thirty-five yard drop-goal and Ferguson added a further penalty to send Leigh in 13-0 ahead at half-time.

The second half of this memorable Challenge Cup final had all the hallmarks of a London stage play, as incidents occurred at a rate of knots. John Holmes opened the Leeds account with a penalty, then Murphy again dropped a superb goal before Stuart Ferguson, treating the crowd of 84,514 to a masterclass of goal-kicking, fired over another long-range penalty. Then the shock of shocks, Leigh player-coach Murphy appeared to be pole-axed by a head-butt from the Leeds captain, Syd Hynes, in an off-the-ball incident. It is a moment that has endured throughout the years as a real mystery. Did Murphy dive, or didn't he? No one but Alex will ever know for sure but, in a split second, he went down as if hit by a sniper's bullet and entered rugby league folklore.

From as far back as the very first Wembley Challenge Cup final in 1929, it had been accepted as an unwritten law that all players must be on their best behaviour at the Empire Stadium. The Rugby Football League would not stand for any nonsense regarding anyone being sent off. The powers-that-be wanted our game, in those days on its biggest stage, to be whiter-than-white. No thuggery should be seen whatsoever. Many within the game believed that 'no one will ever be sent off at Wembley.' Others said that referees in charge of finals were briefed beforehand that no-one should be dismissed. It was a long-standing tradition that players behaved themselves under the Twin Towers.

Around twenty past four in the afternoon on 15th May, 1971, that tradition was knocked into a cocked hat. Billy Thompson blew his whistle, pointed to the dressing rooms and told the Leeds skipper: 'Off you go Syd, you are dismissed'. Hynes proclaimed his innocence. 'Billy, I never touched him,' he told the official. But Thompson was adamant. 'Off Syd,' he repeated and Syd Hynes began the longest walk of his career.

Meanwhile, paramedics rushed onto the field to tend to the fallen Murphy who, after several minutes, was dramatically carried off on a stretcher, amid booing from the partisan Leeds supporters. Most dramatically, the television cameras appeared to catch Alex in the act of cheekily winking, although Murphy was later to tell the BBC that: 'People said that I feigned injury and that I winked when I was on the stretcher. Well, I can honestly say that I might have blinked but I didn't wink! I really did take a knock and woke up in the dressing room being attended to by the Wembley doctor.'

Whatever the case, ten minutes later David Eckersley dropped a great goal and then, five minutes from time, the full-back supported a break by Kevin before racing over for a superb try, which Ferguson converted. Alex Murphy was confirmed as the Lance Todd Trophy winner just as Tony Wainwright, the Leeds stand-off, was awarded a penalty try and John Holmes kicked the goal. The final scoreline of 24-7 shook the rugby league world to its bootstraps.

'Murph had warned the Leeds board that Leigh would surprise everyone and beat them with football played at the highest level,' remembers Kevin. 'That's what we did. We were all mystified that no one gave us a chance. Not only were we the Lancashire Cup winners, we had finished next to Leeds in the league table and had slaughtered them at Hilton Park by 36 points to 8. We were a very good side on our day. Even at the end of the game it was like a magnificent dream.' Not so for the Leeds players, for whom the defeat felt more like a nightmare. John Holmes, the Leeds full-back, told a reporter: 'It was an awful afternoon for us. All I seemed to do was stand under the posts and watch the goals fly over.'

When Murphy received the Challenge Cup from Reginald Maudling MP, the Leigh faithful went wild. Young Gary Ashcroft was carried shoulder high around the pitch in the lap of honour, and the players felt the elation of possibly the greatest match they would ever play in. Roy Lester was the unfortunate Leigh substitute not called upon to participate in the actual game, as it was Les Chisnall who went on when Murphy left the field after the Hynes incident. Even so, he was as excited as anyone and told reporters: 'The atmosphere on the bench was red hot. In fact all week at home it was up to boiling point, with the spectators stopping us in the street and wishing us luck. It seemed that the supporters and the players had a common aim and one aim only, to bring the big Cup back home to Leigh. It was like a non-stop carnival and there was this special bond between the great supporters and the team. People will remember this day forever. It [winning the Cup] was based on confidence, team spirit and a group of lads who pulled together superbly.' No one was in any doubt that this had been the greatest single display ever given by any team representing the Leigh club.

No surprise then that the team, directors, staff, wives and girlfriends celebrated long into the night when the Leigh party returned to its London hotel. On the negative side, the only shadow hanging over proceedings was the imminent departure of Alex Murphy to Warrington. On the positive side, the welcome home to Leigh was still to come. The Sunday newspapers were full of this unique story of a small Lancashire coalmining town breaking the hearts of big-time, big-spending and big-city Leeds.

One elder statesman of the rugby league writers fraternity wrote that: 'In past finals, I have seen players get away with more than Hynes was accused of, indeed another Leeds player sailed perilously close to the dismissal wind with his second and sometimes third tackles. Although well beaten, Leeds appeared to lack spirit, a commodity Leigh had in spades and gave no indication of ever producing a fightback of any kind. Having the slightest pull in scrum possession, Leeds were let down by poor handling in the face of a fierce defence by Leigh and gave only the briefest of glimpses of their normally wonderful fluency. Only full-back John Holmes and half-backs Barry Seabourne and Tony Wainwright came anywhere near normal form.'

Writers claimed a hat-trick of history-making events during the build-up and playing of this dramatic final. Firstly, there was little Gary Ashcroft, striding out as the first-ever mascot to tread the famous turf. Secondly, there was the dismissal of a player, Syd Hynes, for foul play. And thirdly, there was the carrying off of Alex Murphy, and his miraculous recovery in time to collect the Lance Todd Trophy.

As expected, the reception back in Leigh was no less unbelievable, as the team bus staggered towards the Town Hall. Despite the entire population of Leigh being no more than 46,100, an estimated crowd of 100,000 people turned out to cheer the Leigh side home. From Boothstown to Leigh, some ten miles in distance, folk gathered from miles around to hail Leigh's first Challenge Cup final win since the 13-0 win over Halifax in the pre-Wembley days of 1921. The Mayor admitted that it was even better than the victory celebrations after the Second World War.

The team bus was more than two hours late, inching a way through thousands of people straining to catch sight of their favourites and the famous old Challenge Cup itself. Mounted police struggled to control the heaving throng, as it pressed forward to witness the homecoming. The police barrier was stretched to its limit as extra policemen dashed from their motorbikes and patrol cars to reinforce the barrier. The foyer of the Town Hall became a casualty station as fans, mostly teenage girls, were treated for shock and fainting. For one elderly lady, it was the bonus of a lifetime. She had seen the 1921 team bring the Cup home and said it was like 'a wonderful dream'. Young Gary Ashcroft too was welcomed by a huge cheer when he was carried shoulder high by player-coach Murphy.

'I had never seen as many people in the town of Leigh before,' recalls Kevin. 'They were climbing up lamp posts, hung out of windows, stood on the top of cars and buses. There were young kids, millions of them it seemed, all brought by their dads, older brothers or anyone who would look after them safely. There were old men and women, crying with joy, it was wonderful to be amongst them all. Everybody wanted to touch the Challenge Cup. Dads held their kids in their out-stretched arms, just to let them touch it. It was moving to think such a gesture meant so much to them. In years to come, the dads would say, "You touched the Cup when you were a little 'un".

'We went into the inner sanctum of the Town Hall and jokers like Joe Walsh were saying things like, "The last time I was in here I was under arrest". It must have cost the council a small fortune and Joe was telling everyone, "Your rates will be going up to pay for this little lot". Murph arranged for the team to take a week off work and we went around the Leigh area every day with the Cup, showing it to schools, factories, old folks homes, wherever people wanted to see it. But Murph himself didn't show. He was at Warrington sorting out his move. It was great to see the people's faces when the old Cup came around. It was a tonic to them.'

Many years later, Kevin was asked by the Manchester Evening News if he could explain how much that Challenge Cup win against Leeds in 1971 meant. His account of his feelings still carry the pride of achievement that every Leigh player must have felt that day.

He wrote:

'So the long awaited day was finally here and off to the hotel in London we went. It was a different world. Eighty per cent of the team had never been to London before, let alone stay in an hotel which had lights and carpets. We could have beaten anybody in the world that day. It was just the way it was, nobody felt any pressure. To us it was just a great weekend out with a game of rugby chucked in. We had nothing to lose. We even backed ourselves to win, we were that confident. At 2-45pm, we took this relaxed approach onto the field with us. Leeds were lined up next to us looking straight ahead and tense. Our lot were laughing and joking, with Joe Walsh somewhere behind me singing his head off.

'If we needed a lift, which we didn't, we got it when we entered the Stadium from the tunnel and saw the huge bank of red and white at the opposite end of the ground. It was one of the most moving experiences of my life and a moment I will take to my grave.

'From the first tackle, when Alex Murphy flattened someone, it set the tone of the game. It was one of the most niggling matches I ever played in. The ferocity of our tackling knocked Leeds for six and they kept on dropping the ball and played into our hands. We packed twenty years of rugby into the eighty minutes of that game. At no stage did we look like losing. The tide was already flowing our way when one of Wembley's most famous incidents happened, the Leeds skipper, Syd Hynes, was sent off for flattening Murphy. Alex was stretchered off but later returned to guide us through the final six minutes. By the time I had laid on a try for Dave Eckersley the Cup was on its way to Leigh.

'We had done it and earned a few bob in the process

although nobody mentioned money as this wasn't a day about money. We would have played for nowt. You can't put a price on those memories. We were all proud to have played a part in a piece of rugby history and succeed in bringing the cup home to Leigh.'

Says it all, really.

CHAPTER FIVE

Shortly after the great weekend in London, a terrible tragedy took place in the Ashcroft household. Donna, Janet and Kevin's little daughter, died. As with most tragedies of this kind, nothing of much use could be said, but everyone who knew Donna's parents had heartfelt sympathy for them in their plight. Such devastating sorrow far outweighed any on-field glory. Somehow, the slow recovery back to some sort of normality began for Janet, Kevin and Gary.

At Hilton Park, meanwhile, the 1971/72 season kicked off against the background of Alex Murphy and Dave Chisnall's joint-departure for Warrington. Moves were afoot to take Geoff Clarkson to Wilderspool too. Murphy had also enquired about Kevin, but was told categorically that he was not for sale. So Kevin stayed at Leigh, under the new coach Peter Smethurst and his assistant, Derek Hurt. St. Helens were taken on at Knowsley Road in round one of the Lancashire Cup and, although the team played its heart out, Saints just edged a thrilling game, 11-10. Eight days later,

Leigh were at St. Helens again to play Saints in the league winners versus Challenge Cup winners annual play-off.

The previous game had shown that there was not much between the teams, but Leigh were still reeling from the sudden move away by Murphy and Dave Chisnall, who had been a cornerstone of the pack, plus Geoff Clarkson was now playing in his final game before moving on too. The side missed the magic that Murphy brought to the table; his presence alone on the pitch was worth several points start over other teams. But the great man had gone and it was left to the amiable and still tremendously enthusiastic Peter Smethurst to 'follow that'. To do so, of course, would have needed a magic wand. Peter did his utmost to rally the troops that Alex had left behind, but a repeat of the success enjoyed under Murphy was virtually impossible.

The Leigh side that contested the Champions versus Cup winners was a very good one, make no mistake. Rod Tickle came in on the wing for the injured Joe Walsh. Jimmy Boylan - signed from Widnes - was in at scrum-half for Alex, and Roy Lester, who had subbed at Wembley, was in the second row for Geoff Clarkson, who sat on the bench. The side, then, read: Eckersley; Tickle, Dorrington, Les Chisnall, Ferguson; Barrow, Boylan; Fiddler, Ashcroft, Watts, Grimes, Lester and Smethurst, with Clarkson subbing. Saints too were a very strong side, especially at home, and they were represented by: Geoff Pimblett: Leslie Jones, Alan Whittle, David Taylor, Frank Wilson; Ken Kelly, Jeff Heaton; John Stephens, Tony Karalius, Ray Hughes, Bobby Wanbon, Eric Chisnall and Kel Coslett, with the two Erics, Hughes and Woodyer, as substitutes. The referee was the experienced Mr. Sam Shepherd.

Despite the apparent importance of the fixture, only 3,612 people attended what turned out to be a very close encounter. Just one try was scored and this by the tough

Bobby Wanbon, with Kel Coslett kicking three goals and Ken Kelly landing a drop-goal. For Leigh, Stuart Ferguson kicked two goals, as Saints won the bragging rights, 11-4. In those days, of course, because of the importance of possession of the ball from the competitive set scrum, the ability of the hooker was possibly more significant than today. The clash of the regular hookers, both in the tight and in the loose, was a mouthwatering feature of any game. The battle for supremacy between Kevin and Tony Karalius was one of the things that spectators paid to see. These battles, for that is what they were, continued over eighty minutes and covered every aspect from intelligent dummy-half play, through good defence, to continuous support play and inspirational team leadership, usually as pack leader.

Kevin Ashcroft and Tony Karalius possessed each of those qualities in abundance. Both were international and county class hookers, who gained many awards in their careers. Kevin, always man enough to give credit where due says: 'Tony was a strong player. He carried the Karalius family trait of being a winner and one always had a hard afternoon when playing against him. You never came across any hooker who was a pushover. The position of hooker itself demanded a toughness unique to the pack. You were there as a target, the bulls eye on the hit list and to show anything other than a completely fearless attitude would attract a barrage of physical abuse.'

Yet there was another emotion that being a regular hooker brought. 'That of respect of the man opposite you in the set scrum,' says Kevin. 'Sure, you nutted him and knee-ed him and punched him when you could, because that was part and parcel of the ritual of getting on top. In the bar after the game, though, you would have a laugh and joke about the strokes you had just pulled on each other and, nine times out of ten, would be the best of buddies, at least until you met again during a match, then it was back to square one.'

Gradually, the Leigh team settled down without Alex Murphy, but the consistency of the previous season was missing. Kevin was contacted regularly by his former coach, who told him that Warrington were constantly making enquiries about his availability for transfer and suggested that he should start chipping away at the Leigh board to put him on the transfer list. So, Kevin went through the correct procedure but the directors simply said: 'No'. This irritated Kevin and, with Murphy prodding him into action behind the scenes and telling him about his plans at Wilderspool, he continued to pester Leigh with further requests for a move. Indeed, things got so bad that Kevin was asked by Murphy if he fancied staying away from Hilton Park in an effort to force the board's hand into letting him go. An arrangement could be forthcoming in which lost revenue could be paid to Kevin, so that he would lose nothing by his absence. Kevin, though, preferred to carry on playing and keep chipping away to be put on the transfer list.

Feelings were running high on both sides, as shown by the position of Tommy Sale. A great worker for the Leigh club, as a player and committee man over very many years, Tommy had first signed for Leigh in December 1938 and given ten seasons' service to the club on the field. No man was more respected at Leigh than he. Tommy had taken to Kevin, both as a player and a man, since his arrival from Rochdale. So determined was he not to let another international player leave the club that Tommy said he would resign from the board should Kevin be allowed to leave.

Kevin was absent for at least two games though, after being sent off at home to Featherstone Rovers for persistent feet up in the scrum. Then, as the season drew on, one particular victory brought some relief of tension, a 10-5 win over the touring Kiwis on 20th October. Mick Collins and Stuart Ferguson scored tries, while Ferguson kicked two goals. Leigh's side read: Eckersley; Ferguson, Stringer, Collins, Walsh; Barrow, Boylan; Alan Ogden (signed from Oldham), Ashcroft, Barry Simpson (signed from Swinton), Grimes, Lester and Tommy Martyn (signed from Batley).

Eventually, one of Kevin's meetings with the Leigh board bore fruit. They agreed to transfer him to Warrington, but only at the end of the season. Kevin agreed to that as, although he wanted to move to Warrington, he also wanted to leave Leigh in the correct manner. He was also finding it difficult to get time off work. Kevin missed a few training nights and, after the defeat at Salford by 10 points to 9 on 2nd January, he missed every game until 12th February, when he played in the second row in a 20-7 loss at Saints.

In the Challenge Cup, Kevin was back at hooker for the 4-3 defeat to Swinton at Hilton Park, as any hope of retaining the silverware went up in smoke. And he was forward sub against Keighley, away, on 12th March, before missing a week and returning to the second row on 26th March in a 10 points to 5 defeat to Dewsbury. He had another run in the second row against Batley at home in a 17-12 win and, in yet another change of position, was chosen at open-side prop against Castleford, away, in an excellent 14 points to 7 win. After that, it was back to forward sub against Leeds at Leigh, which ended in a 22-15 Leeds win. If nothing else this season, Kevin was certainly showing his versatility, a point reinforced when he then played at loose forward in a 21-12 win at Thrum Hall, Halifax, before moving back to hooker for the top-sixteen Championship play-off at Headingley, where Leeds triumphed 40-2, with Kevin dropping the goal that registered Leigh's points.

* * *

When the news broke that Kevin was being transferred to Warrington, Tommy Sale was true to his word and resigned from the workings of Leigh Rugby League Football Club. It was a bad time all around.

Kevin had been very happy at Leigh, but the promise of bigger and better things would have interested anyone. A big problem for Kevin, for quite a few years, was his place of work. He was now working shifts at the Elkington Northern Brass Stamping Company. This shift work played havoc with his training, most times he had to sneak away early and get his mates to clock off for him. Occasionally, he had to work nights, which meant he was always late at the start of that shift even after leaving training early. So, when Alex Murphy phoned Kevin to arrange a meeting at Warrington with the vice-chairman of the club, Mr. Brian Pitchford, to negotiate a deal that would take Kevin to Wilderspool, he knew that a job which allowed him to train was a priority.

A wealthy man in his own right, Brian Pitchford was the chairman of the huge Thomas Locker Holdings Company in Warrington. The chairman of the club, though, was the powerful Mr. Ossie Davies. Mr. Davies was the chairman of the giant civil engineering company, Leonard Fairclough Ltd and he sent his apologies to Kevin as he was away on business when the meeting was called. Kevin went along with Murphy to the meeting and found Brian Pitchford a charming and down-to-earth man. The two gelled immediately.

'Right, Kevin, what are you looking for to join us here at Warrington?' Brian asked. 'There are two things I would need Brian,' he replied. 'One is a job which allows me to work and still get to my training and playing appointments. Secondly, I would need the use of a car to get me to and from

Warrington and home.' Brian Pitchford thought for a second and asked: 'Who are you working for now, Kevin?' 'The Brass Stamping Company in Leigh,' Kevin told him. Again Brian considered his options and said: 'OK, you can start for me at Thomas Lockers in the wire shop. That will allow you to get off for training. Start whenever you have worked your notice in Leigh. Just give me a call and I will arrange everything. Your transport, a new Hillman Husky, will be here for you next Wednesday. Just ring my secretary and she will tell you where to pick it up.'

Brian then produced the official transfer forms. Kevin signed and he was a Warrington player. He worked for Brian Pitchford at Thomas Lockers for nine years and climbed quickly to be a foreman fitter. Of the many interesting jobs he undertook was the fitting of new heat shields on two of the North Sea oil rigs, the Claymore and Piper Alpha, whose construction began in 1973, before the first oil production in 1976.

Kevin recalls: 'The first thing I knew about it was when the manager called me into his office and told me that he had a special job for me to do. "I want you to take your team out to an oil rig in the middle of the North Sea," he said, "and fit a couple of heat shields." I asked him: "How far out in the *&^%$ North Sea? And how the *&^%$ do we get there?" The manager laughed and explained that we would be flown up to Aberdeen, then a short hop by helicopter out to the rig. Short hop! It took us over an hour. In huge seas, the rig was a pin point of light when we first saw it and my mates, and me, were a bit dubious about landing on the pin point in this storm. The co-pilot told us there was no problem as the rig would get bigger as we neared it. It certainly did and the bloody thing was immense. It was still a bit hairy as we tilted and turned on landing but we did the job and were back on the mainland in a couple of days. We did another oil rig and the weather was much better. The oil workers were great blokes, living with danger all the time. They were all solid, tough kids doing a frightening job, especially in those heavy seas.'

Tragically, just how perilous their job could be was to become obvious over a decade later on 6th July 1988 when, amid the devastation of explosions, fire and toxic fumes, 167 Piper Alpha workers lost their lives, with just fifty-nine survivors, in the world's worst offshore oil disaster.

* * *

Back in 1972, and pre-season training began at Wilderspool and Kevin had the added problem of fitting into a new set-up, although he knew most of the players through playing against them and, of course, he was joining up again with Murphy, Dave Chisnall and Geoff Clarkson.

Unlike the time he joined either Rochdale Hornets or Leigh, this time Kevin was arriving as a current Great Britain player and a big signing for the club. Meeting up with the chairman, Ossie Davies, was a red letter day for Kevin, as both Mr. Davies and Brian Pitchford would become good friends to Kevin and his family. Kevin found Ossie Davies a great bloke. There was no edge to him whatsoever. The players too were all good lads and welcomed Kevin with open arms.

One who became a staunch mate was Parry Gordon, who actually played twenty-one seasons for Warrington, a truly admirable one-club man. Others who joined the club a little after Kevin included Brian Brady who, Kevin reckons, could have eaten for Great Britain, the tough Aussie forward Dave Wright, the two rock hard Welshmen, Bobby Wanbon and Mike Nicholas, Dennis Curling, Tommy Conroy, Derek Whitehead, Wilf Briggs, Frank Reynolds, Brian Gregory,

Barry Briggs, Derek Noonan, Joe Price, John Lowe, Billy Pickup, that great finisher and former Wales international wingman John Bevan, Wayne Gaskell and the two Philbin brothers, Barry and Mick. Alex Murphy, meanwhile, hadn't changed much regarding patterns of play or his fitness training from his very successful days at Leigh. He believed in leaving things if they were going right and never changed anything for change's sake.

Kevin showed his durability in his first season at Warrington by appearing in forty-one of the forty-four games played. The three he missed were the result of one-match suspensions for scrummaging offences. These were Widnes away in a Floodlit Trophy defeat on 14th November, a loss at Leigh away on the 23rd April 1973, and a bad loss at home in the semi-final of the Championship to Dewsbury on 6th May. Kevin scored thirteen tries in all and dropped six goals. His tries were built on a mixture of astute dummy-half play and splendid support work and, although Alex Murphy only figured in twenty games that first season, Kevin was totally in contact mentally with the Warrington coach. Indeed, the pair displayed the same brand of telepathy that had worked so well at Hilton Park.

In fact, this telepathy seemed to rub off on rest of the footballers in the squad, too. It is said that good teams always know what their key players are thinking about doing next and this was certainly the case at Warrington. Another bonus for the side was that there were so many natural match-winners in the team. Whenever they were in a spot of bother, one or other of these great players would come up with a winning move, a try or a drop-goal, which would put the team back on track. Things also turned around with the influx of one or two new signings, and Alex Murphy made a huge difference whenever he played, every time.

Kevin takes up the story. 'We felt as if we were on the verge of a new adventure,' he says. 'The great Warrington team of the Bath, Bevan, Fleming and Helme era had gone and, as most clubs do, they found the return to greatness very hard indeed. The board, led by Ossie Davies and Brian Pitchford, saw in Alex Murphy the way back to a successful and Cup-winning period. They knew that Murph had the know-how to build a powerful squad and also regain the confidence of the thousands of Warrington supporters who were starved of success. New faces were a must, but they had to be better than the ones there already and they would cost money on the transfer market.

'That is where Mr. Davies came in, with his business acumen and strong personality. His vice-chairman too, Mr. Pitchford, was very astute in the business world. Between them, they would provide the money and the knowledge to introduce the Alex Murphy-suggested players into the club. This was achieved within two seasons of Murph's introduction as coach. With the influx of cash to buy players and the usual publicity that accompanied Murph wherever he went, Ossie Davies saw the need to see a fairly quick improvement in form to justify his spending on players and his head-hunting of Alex from Leigh.'

* * *

By now, Kevin Ashcroft had developed a deep respect and admiration for Alex Murphy. He explains: 'I could sit and listen for hours as Murph talked about the game. He was a great assessor of people, particularly players. He had a computer brain where rugby league was concerned. He would tell us in team talks how a particular player would react if put under pressure, or which player would lose his rag and get sent off. He knew ways of keeping the ball away from the opposition match-winners and starving them of possession. His presence in the dressing room was awesome. When he spoke, you listened.

'He also made you feel that you mattered. If he had seen a good forward, he would pull me and ask what I thought about him. Is he tough enough? What's his pace like? Is he a strong runner? Then, after he had taken another look at him, he would say again: "Would he be good for us, Ashy?" I remember him telling me to be patient when I first went to Wilderspool. He explained how he wanted to build a big, rough side that could play football as well. "It can't be done overnight Ashy," he had said. "I have some weeding out to do before I bring in the men we want." His in-bred football knowledge allowed him to see if a player considered past it could be brought back by playing in a great side. Bobby Wanbon was a case in point. Saints considered he was about done, but Murph signed him and gave the big Welshman a new lease of life. He was brilliant for us.'

The new season started well with a big win at home to Hull FC, by 31 points to 20. Four really tough fixtures came next - St. Helens away, Swinton away, Widnes at home, and then Saints again at home in the Lancashire Cup. The scores in these early games show the closeness of the competition. Although Saints won the game at Knowsley Road 15-11, Warrington beat Swinton 17-14 and Widnes 13-4, both at Wilderspool, then lost to Saints again at Warrington by 18-16 in the County Cup. The Warrington side then began to pay back Ossie Davies with some good results, including a 26-7 win at home over Wigan. The only loss in an eleven-match run was at Fartown, where Huddersfield won in the John Player Trophy, 23-15. Six days later, Warrington went back to Fartown and won in the League, 24-10. On 31st October, Widnes came to Warrington in the first round of the Floodlit Trophy and drew 18-18. Two weeks later, Widnes won the replay at Naughton Park 14-11, they had all been tough games too. So, despite Warrington holding on well to a good league position, they were out of the Lancashire Cup, John Player Trophy and the Floodlit Trophy already. Two major trophies were left to play for; the Challenge Cup and the league Championship. Position in the league table would dictate home or away games in the Championship play-offs, but any team needed a bit of luck with the draw in the Challenge Cup.

As it happened, Halifax were drawn away in round one of the Challenge Cup, another hard team to beat, but a good solid performance saw Kevin's team through by 7 points to 4. Widnes visited Warrington in round two and were beaten 20-8, before Featherstone Rovers came to Wilderspool and took part in a real Cup thriller. The Yorkshiremen played the game brilliantly and yet, even at the death, Warrington could have pulled it out of the fire, before Featherstone held on to win 18-14 on their way to beating Bradford Northern in the 1973 Wembley final.

Back in the league, and in the final eleven games to the play-offs, Warrington won seven, drew one and lost three. The play-offs brought Wigan to Wilderspool and the Wire won by 30 points to 15. Four days later, they beat Rochdale Hornets at Wilderspool, 16-9. Unfortunately, Kevin was sent off in that game and missed the semi-final play-off in which the outsiders Dewsbury came to Warrington and outplayed the home side by 12 points to 7, to gain a monumental victory. Dewsbury had built up a very good side on the quiet and they went on to beat Leeds convincingly at Odsal in the Championship Trophy final.

So, Kevin's first season at Warrington had produced some great money in league victories, but no silverware in the club's trophy cabinet. Another point to bear in mind is that Alex Murphy had only played in twenty of the forty-

Above: Earlestown District
School team. Kevin is seated
front row, second from right
Below: A proud Kevin Ashcroft
shows off the Lancashire
Schools Junior Cup

Above: The young Kevin in ABA semi-final action
Below: The Newton Sea Cadets boxing team

Kevin in action early in his career with his self-professed favourite club - Rochdale Hornets. *Above*: Kevin gets on the end of a training move with (from front) Liatia Ravouvou, Appi Toga, Peter Birchall & Stan Owen at the Athletic Grounds.

Below: The team lines up. Back row, left to right - Mike Hope, Jack Gregory, Tony Pratt, Stan Owen, Kenny Parr, Appi Toga. Front row - Peter Birchall, Joe Chamberlain, Syd Miller, Johnny Noon, Johnny Fishwick, Graham Starkey, Kevin Ashcroft (standing)

Above: Kevin gets involved in a tackle for Rochdale against Keighley, in inimitable style.

Right: Peter Birchall & Kevin Ashcroft pose for the camera whilst on international duty with the under-24s in Toulouse, France

Left: Leigh chairman Jack Harding presents Kevin with his first Great Britain cap on the field at Hilton Park in the 1968-69 season.

Above: Kevin takes tips from Roger Millward, Cliff Watson & Dennis Hartley before the 1968 World Cup

Below & left: Kevin in the action - as usual - during a competitive tournament

Below right: Kevin & furry friend get close in Brisbane

Above: Kevin - ripped shirt & all - celebrates the final hooter, as Leigh famously shock Leeds in the 1971 Challenge Cup Final at London's Wembley Stadium

Left: The match programme & other items of paraphernalia from one of the biggest days in Leigh RLFC's history

Bottom: Leigh's soon-to-be conquering heroes take a pre-final stroll up a garlanded Navigation Street in the town

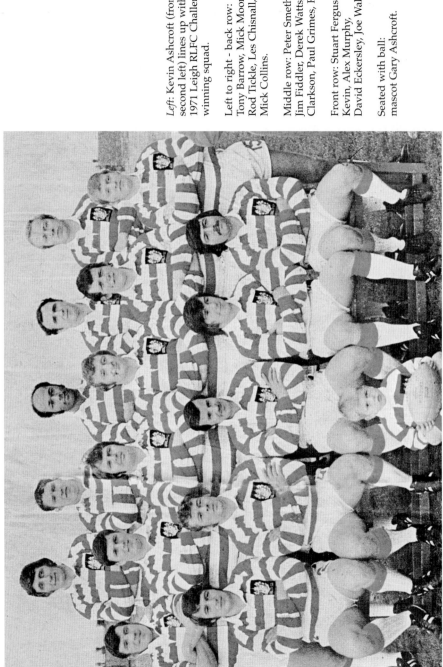

Left: Kevin Ashcroft (front row, second left) lines up with the 1971 Leigh RLFC Challenge Cup winning squad.

Left to right - back row:
Tony Barrow, Mick Mooney, Rod Tickle, Les Chisnall, Mick Collins.

Middle row: Peter Smethurst, Jim Fiddler, Derek Watts, Geoff Clarkson, Paul Grimes, Roy Lester.

Front row: Stuart Ferguson, Kevin, Alex Murphy, David Eckersley, Joe Walsh.

Seated with ball: mascot Gary Ashcroft.

Above: Warrington's 1974 Challenge Cup-winning team. Left to right - back row: Derek Noonan, Brian Brady, Derek Whitehead, Billy Pickup. Middle row: Mike Nicholas, Barry Philbin, Dave Wright, Bobby Wanbon, Dave Chisnall, Derek Clarke (trainer). Front row: Alan Whittle, Parry Gordon, Kevin Ashcroft, Alex Murphy, Mike Philbin, John Bevan.

Below: Kevin prepares to pack down with Bobby Wanbon & Dave Chisnall

Above: The Wire walk out at Wembley
Below: Parry Gordon and Mike Philbin dive for the ball while beach training in Southport

Above: Coach Murphy & Co drink to success. *Below*: Kevin Ashcroft lifts the Championship Cup after the 1973-74 season

Above: Kevin scores the matchwinning try at Wembley in 1974. *Below*: Another scrum breaks up in chaos, as Warrington meet St. Helens in the Lancashire Cup

one games in the season. Both Ossie Davies and Brian Pitchford had been involved with Warrington as sponsors for many years and both realised that the side was developing into something special. To reach the semi-final of the Championship and earn a high place in the league table showed that the bigger Cup-winning results were just around the corner.

Kevin remembers well the start of what turned out to be a momentous 1973-74 season. 'We had three hard games on the trot,' he says. 'Rochdale Hornets, who were a very tough side, were beaten at the Athletic Ground 7-6, Leeds were beaten at Warrington courtesy of two Whitehead penalty goals and three drop-goals by Alex, to give us a 10 points to 4 margin, and we had a good win at Widnes, the day after beating Leeds, which allowed us to leave Naughton Park with a 19-9 win. My old club Leigh came to Wilderspool in the Lancashire Cup and I managed a drop-goal in a 20-15 win. A 6-6 draw at Hull Kingston Rovers put us in good spirits for a tough Lancashire Cup second round game at Whitehaven. But we threw chance after chance away and dug ourselves a huge hole up there at the Recreation Ground. The result was a fine 19-8 win for them. Alex was furious. "We gave that *&^%$£ game away and that won't do at all," he stormed. "Get a cup of tea and we are straight back down home." Onto the bus we trooped in utter silence. I had seen Murph like this only a couple of times and I knew we had better do exactly as he said.

'After about an hour and a half, some of the lads wanted to go to the toilet and gently asked Alex if we could stop by the side of the road. "Make it quick," he growled, and I knew he meant quick. So out we all jumped in the middle of nowhere in the pitch dark. I finished and was back on the bus as I knew what he would do. "Right driver, off you go, now," Alex ordered. "What about the lads?" the driver enquired. "*&^%$ the lads, I said off, now," and the driver set off as ordered, leaving about six players still relieving themselves into the ditch. On we drove and the lads left were certain we would come back for them, but I knew differently when he was this way out. The lads started walking when a police car drew up, full of cones from a road repair. "I can't get you in here, lads, but I will catch the bus up and get him to wait for you," the bobby said. Thinking the bus would be just over the next brow, the lads walked and walked for miles. Then the bus was spotted waiting for them. They boarded and the bus was again quiet until we reached Warrington. You did as you were told with the man.'

* * *

Bundled out of the Lancashire Cup, Leigh's next game was in the John Player Trophy at home to Oldham, which was won, 31-14. 'The feeling we had at Leigh returned at Warrington,' says Kevin. 'The feeling that we were on the brink of a big success. We thought that it may have been the Floodlit Trophy, but the touch of poor form that affects all clubs at some time during the season hit us and, between the first-round win and the second-round tie at the Willows, Salford, we beat Castleford 22-5 and Bramley 9-0 and lost to Wakefield Trinity at home, 13-10. Then we went down to Featherstone Rovers away, 18-8, and Saints away, 25-6.'

A player made his debut in the Castleford game who was set to become a big star at Wilderspool, John Bevan the former Welsh rugby union international wingman, who was big, fast and had a hand-off like a steam hammer. 'In this game, too, I was dismissed for scrum infringements,' remembers Kevin, 'and I missed the next four matches. Charlie Middlehurst deputised for me. I was back to play at

Salford, but they proved too much for us on the day and we lost the Floodlit cup game, 26-4. Five days later, we played Salford again, this time at Wilderspool in the league, and won 20-13.'

Revenge - but three days later Warrington had to travel to Central Park where they would face Wigan in a new cup competition, the Captain Morgan Trophy. This competition was for the round-one winners of both County Cup competitions, plus Widnes, who had lost by one point in the first round of the Lancashire Cup. This turned out to be a real test for a team that was just finding its feet in cup-ties. Both defences were miserly and a lot of time was spent between the two twenty-five yard lines. But the golden boot of Derek Whitehead, with three penalties and two drop-goals, plus a Murphy special drop-goal, saw Warrington through a brutal game in which many punches were swapped. The following two games were then lost, Bramley away, 18-10, and Saints at home, 11-5. Kevin remembers the Captain Morgan Cup game well. 'We drew Castleford at home and the team was: Whitehead; Bevan, Noonan, Cunliffe, Pickup; Murphy, Gordon; Chisnall, Ashcroft, Brady, Mike Nicholas, Gaskell and Conroy, with Curling and Bobby Wanbon as subs. Our pack laid the foundation for the win and Conroy, Brady and Cunliffe scored our tries, while Whitehead landed three goals.'

The cup-ties were now coming thick and fast, but before the Captain Morgan semi-final at Headingley, Warrington had a league game against the dreaded Whitehaven at home. 'They certainly had the jinx over us,' admits Kevin. Taking into account how Murphy rested two or three key players, the Cumbrians beat Warrington fair and square by 18 points to 8.

The semi-final, meanwhile, was played under a first-out-of-the-hat system and Leeds had home advantage. Selecting horses for courses, Murphy put out a physically huge team to crush the Leeds pack first, and then his tough threequarters could handle the footballing backs that the Leeds public loved to watch. The Warrington team that day read: Whitehead; Bevan, Reynolds, Noonan, Pickup; Murphy, Gordon; Chisnall, Ashcroft, Brady, Nicholas, Dave Wright and Ian Mather. The subs were Mick Philbin and Wayne Gaskell. 'We had a tough team,' recalls Kevin. 'And Alex's plan worked a treat. Our big mobile pack out-gunned the Leeds six with myself and Parry Gordon scoring our tries and Whitehead landing four goals. Murph always believed in taking something from a good position and Whitehead, Murph and myself all dropped goals from positions grafted for by the pack. We came away from Headingley with one of our best victories of the season, winning by 20 points to 13.'

Ossie Davies and Brian Pitchford were delighted. Their hand-picked team had marched on to a final, just what they wanted. However, there was another key match seven days later, when Castleford were the visitors to Wilderspool in round two of the John Player Trophy. New signing Alan Whittle from St. Helens made his debut at stand-off half in place of Murphy and the centres switched over, otherwise it was the same team which had won so well at Headingley. Another fine win followed, by 18 points to 9, with tries by Gordon and Nicholas, five goals by Whitehead and a neat drop-goal by Kevin making up Warrington's points.

An away loss to Wakefield Trinity, 26-15, and then a good away win over Leigh, 29-7, followed, before Warrington met Dewsbury at Wilderspool in the third round of the John Player Trophy. As Kevin recalls: 'My first professional team and the first meeting since they came to Wilderspool in last season's play-off and beat us fair and square. They had lost Mick Stephenson to Penrith in Australia and had never replaced him at hooker. A youngster called Keith Voyce who was a good prospect got the job, but he lacked the vital experience needed against blokes like myself, Keith Bridges, Clive Dickinson, Colin Clarke and the other older hookers. I managed to win the ball around three to one, which gave our backs ample scope to run.' Mike Nicholas, Derek Noonan, Alan Whittle and John Bevan scored the tries, and Derek Whitehead kicked four goals in a 20-12 win.

Within eight days of the Dewsbury tie, Warrington had played another two games. Wigan won at Wilderspool 17-12 in Warrington's fourth game in nine days, and there was another defeat by Whitehaven up in Cumbria, 9-5. Again, a perfect indication of just how arduous and competitive the league was back then. The semi-final of the John Player Trophy gave Warrington a plum tie at home to St. Helens on 12th January 1974. In it, a full house at Wilderspool saw Warrington give a masterclass of rugby league football. Mick Philbin, Derek Whitehead, Derek Noonan and John Bevan scored tries, Whitehead kicked three goals and Kevin dropped a goal in a superb 20 points to 9 win. Cock-a-hoop now, on 20th January Kevin and his team travelled to the Watersheddings to take on Oldham, where they registered a great 22-15 win. In the next seven games, Warrington played five cup-ties and two of those were finals.

* * *

The Captain Morgan Trophy final came first, at the Willows, Salford, against those tough, doughty cup fighters, Featherstone Rovers. So far, Rovers had been fortunate with the draw, having played all their games at Post Office Road and beating Keighley, Wakefield Trinity and Workington Town. Warrington had taken a harder road; Wigan away, Castleford at home and Leeds away. The Featherstone team for the final read: Harold Box; Paul Coventry, Mike Smith, David Hartley, Graham Bray; Mel Mason, Chris Wood; Les Tonks, Keith Bridges, Billy Harris, Mick Gibbins, Alan Rhodes and Keith Bell, with Richard 'Charlie' Stone the sub. Warrington were without the maestro Alex Murphy, but still looked a formidable side. That team read: Derek Whitehead; Mick Philbin, Derek Noonan, Frank Reynolds, John Bevan; Alan Whittle, Parry Gordon; Dave Chisnall, Kevin Ashcroft, Brian Brady, Bobby Wanbon, Dave Wright and Ian Mather, with Billy Pickup and Joe Price subbing. Before a gate of 5,259, the referee was Mr. Fred Lindop of Wakefield.

The two teams were so evenly matched that without the genius of Murphy it could easily have been a draw. The battle up front between Tonks and Bridges against Chisnall and Ashcroft finished equal, breaking even in the scrum. On a very heavy late January pitch, the chances of fast, open play were non-existent. It was a slog with fierce tackling and no holds barred. Derek Whitehead was adjudged man of the match because of his magnificent fielding of high kicks near his own line, together with two superbly struck penalty goals that won the first Cup for Ossie Davies and Brian Pitchford. The 4-0 win gave an indication of the heavy conditions, as the ultra-tough Warrington pack stood its ground against the very respected Featherstone Rovers six.

Kevin remembers: 'We were all delighted to get that first trophy under our belts and in the reception after the game Ossie Davies was relishing the hard-fought win. The game coincided with his wife's birthday celebrations and Mrs. Davies had missed the game because of supervising her party to be held early evening, with a large number of guests invited. Ossie Davies's son, Neville, was at the game and, as the Warrington celebrations got underway, Mr. Davies junior approached his dad to remind him of his wife's soiree. He said that they would be late if they stayed at Salford any longer. Enjoying his champagne, Ossie turned to his son and said: "Go to the party and tell your mother that she has had fifty-three of these parties, but this is the first cup I have ever won. I will be along shortly." At which he turned to down another glass of the fizzy stuff.

For the players, it was back to business immediately. The following week, Warrington travelled to Thrum Hall to take on Halifax in the first round of the Challenge Cup. 'Halifax, once one of the strongest teams in the league, had hit hard times,' says Kevin. 'Caught in the bottom half of the old single division, Halifax were relegated into the new Division Two for season '73/74, when the game went to two divisions of sixteen teams each. Halifax were still a hard nut to crack though, up there near the snow line.' Though a final score of 34-4 looks like a runaway, it was only in the last twenty minutes that Warrington took full control of the game, Kevin scoring one of the Wire's six tries, with Whittle, Dave Wright, Brady, Gordon and Nicholas scoring the other touchdowns, and Whitehead kicking eight goals.

* * *

Next up for Warrington was yet another cup final, when they took on Rochdale Hornets in the John Player decider at Central Park, Wigan. Though a the middle of the table team, Kevin's old club were nevertheless still a very dangerous outfit. The weather had been atrocious all week with torrential rain almost non-stop. It eased on Friday morning, one day before the match, but the game still looked doomed as there was water standing on the pitch, like a swimming pool. The Wigan groundsman, Billy Mitchell worked wonders in those twenty-four hours to produce a surface that, though very heavy, was playable come kick-off time.

Even so, journalists were predicting that the game may

not be finished. They forecast that the players would be unrecognisable and said that conditions were downright dangerous. But, after a very long look at the pitch, the referee, Mr. Gerry Kershaw of York, declared the game on. Hornets had arrived at the final via Huddersfield, York, Leeds and Bramley, all at home, while Warrington too had found the luck of the draw in that all their ties had been at Wilderspool, against Oldham, Castleford, Dewsbury and St. Helens.

The Rochdale Hornets side that day was: Jim Crelin; Norman Brelsford, Tom Brophy, David Taylor, Willie Aspinall; John Butler, Peter Gartland; Bill Holliday, Ray Harris, Stewart Whitehead, Terry Fogerty, Bill Sheffield and Tony Halmshaw. The absence of Alex Murphy apart, Warrington were at full-strength. The Wire team read: Whitehead; Philbin, Noonan, Reynolds, Bevan; Whittle, Gordon; Chisnall, Ashcroft, Brady, Wright, Wanbon and Barry Philbin. Warrington used two substitutes, Billy Pickup and Mike Nicholas. A low attendance of 9,347 was at least partly explained by the inclement weather.

Glowing reports suggested that both teams were a credit to the game in the way they tried to play open football despite the atrocious conditions. The reports told of nine sparkling tries and also of honest endeavour, in which superb fitness, enthusiasm and endurance was on display from both sides. The Warrington pack opened strongly with their captain, Kevin Ashcroft, leading the way with his powerful runs from the play-the-ball. Kevin also held a first-half advantage of a 10-3 lead in the scrum over Hornets' very able hooker, Ray Harris. The big four in the Wire pack, Ashcroft, Chisnall, Wanbon and Barry Philbin, ably supported by Brian Brady and Dave Wright, made ground with strong cohesive forward attacks, supplemented by excellent support work. Platforms were set from which the

Warrington backs looked dangerous each time the ball was fanned out to them. Chisnall suffered a damaged ear and was replaced in the pack by Nicholas, who scored the Wire's first try on twenty-seven minutes when he latched onto an Ashcroft break, took the hooker's pass and stormed over. Derek Noonan followed suit on the stroke of half-time, when he supported another Ashcroft break to accept the skipper's inside pass and romp over. These tries, together with three Derek Whitehead conversions, sent Warrington in at the break with a 12-0 lead.

The Warrington pack had been magnificent in that first half. The forwards' defence against a strong, skilful and brave Rochdale pack that had Fogerty, Halmshaw, Sheffield and Holliday to the fore, was excellent and one huge tackle by Bobby Wanbon on Stewart Whitehead, right on the Wire line, was indeed a notable one. The Rochdale coach Frank Myler must have said the correct things at half-time, though, as the Hornets came out all guns blazing.

The ball travelled like lightning through the hands of Gartland, Taylor and Halmshaw to Brophy, who sent his threequarter partner Brelsford hurtling to the corner flag for a great try. At the other end, a rush by Wanbon supported by Ashcroft and then Wright allowed Noonan to cross for his second try, converted by Whitehead. Soon, it was 17-8 to Warrington, as Hornets, showing tenacity, exploited a hole in the Wire defence and Taylor crossed by the flag. Holliday then converted with a magnificent touchline conversion. In the end, though, a devastating six-minute spell finished brave Rochdale's chances of a first major cup win since 1922. Firstly, Bevan intercepted a high pass and strode to the line, and then Derek Whitehead side-stepped his way over for a brilliant solo score. Both tries were converted by Whitehead. Even then, Hornets, game to the end replied with a 40-yard interception try by the powerful Brelsford and a gifted consolation try to Brophy one minute from time. It had been a super game played in very trying conditions.

So, Kevin Ashcroft climbed the steps in the Central Park best stand to receive the John Player Trophy and also the man of the match award of a silver salver and a cheque for £25. Kevin immediately donated the money to Billy Mitchell, in appreciation of his efforts to have the pitch ready to play. A celebration dinner was held at Wilderspool stadium and a cash prize cheque for £5,000 was presented to the club as winners of the competition. Within a mere fourteen days, Warrington had won two major trophies and there were still two more to play for.

* * *

Traditionally, in the sport's earliest days, there were four major trophies to be won in a season: the Lancashire or Yorkshire Cup, the Lancashire or Yorkshire League, the Challenge Cup and the Championship trophy. The Lancashire or Yorkshire League was decided by the number of victories a team had produced in the season against teams from their own county. In the history of the game, only Hunslet, Huddersfield and Swinton had ever performed the illustrious feat of winning the lot. This time, Warrington had missed out on the traditional 'All Four Cups' because of that defeat at Whitehaven. But if they had the stamina to maintain their terrific form, they could still win four of the five major trophies in 1974, and that in itself would surely put them on the roll of honour at Rugby League HQ.

Halifax had been beaten in round one of the Challenge Cup - and Hull KR beaten 20-7 at Wilderspool - before it was time to embark on another strength-sapping Challenge Cup tie against the tough, under-estimated Huyton at home in the second round. As it turned out, only a concerted effort enabled Warrington to overcome the underdogs from Merseyside, 21-6. Derek Whitehead's six goals made a big difference to the scoreline. Back in the league, Dewsbury were beaten 26-10 at home, before another huge Challenge Cup tie, in the third round against Wigan at Central Park. This was the archetypal test of stamina, fitness and courage that is required in every record-breaking run by any club.

If Warrington's major ambition was to be achieved this particular season, one game in all the crucial games had to stand out; the one about which the players still say: 'That was one of our best wins'. The Wigan cup-tie was just that match. Meetings between the two clubs had always caught the imagination of supporters and press alike, as Kevin explains. 'As a champion team, you must keep up your champion's image,' he points out. 'So we knew that to beat Wigan on their own patch we would have to tackle like demons and take every chance that came our way. We also knew that we were now playing without the genius of Alex Murphy, so one huge option was missing for us; his ability.'

Warrington trained extra hard for this latest challenge. 'As Central Park had not totally recovered from the dreadful rain of John Player final day and the wet weather since, we set our stall out for one of the toughest games of the season and we were not wrong,' Kevin recalls. 'Try as we may we couldn't break down the Wigan defence which was awesome on the day. We had talked before the game about getting points, if not by scoring tries. We knew Derek would kick the goals for us, but we needed a back-up plan besides his great goal-kicking. I had knocked over five drop-goals this season, so we worked on the plan that I should have a pot at dropping goals if in the right area for me. I practiced having a pop from dummy-half and from just behind our line of attack. As I said, tries were at a premium, so I worked to our plan and managed three drop-goals to go with

Derek's two penalties to give us a 10-6 win in what was an absolute thriller of a cup-tie.'

Another semi-final to play, then, and the biggest yet. The four teams left in were Warrington, Dewsbury, Leigh and Featherstone Rovers. The draw was made and the Wire drew last season's beaten semi-finalists, Dewsbury, in a game to be played at Central Park. The Leigh versus Featherstone game was to be played at Headingley.

Two days after the Wigan quarter-final, Warrington had to travel to play Leeds, where they were forced to make a few changes due to bumps and bruises. Kevin was suspended for two weeks, because of offences in the scrum against Huyton in the cup-tie. Barry Philbin was out, as was Parry Gordon. Dennis Curling was on the wing for John Bevan and, on the bench, were two excellent players as substitutes in Wilf Briggs and the tough Welshman, Clive Jones. The team was: Whitehead; Mick Philbin, Noonan, Reynolds, Curling; Whittle, Lowe; Chisnall, Middlehurst, Brady, Wanbon, Wright and Tommy Conroy. Playing superb football, Warrington shocked Leeds, 18-6. Wanbon and Briggs scored the tries and Whitehead landed three goals and a drop-goal, while Middlehurst dropped two goals. Five days later, Warrington were away to Castleford again with an odd-looking back division in Derek Finnigan, Dennis Curling, Dave Cunliffe, Billy Pickup, Dave Sutton, Wilf Briggs and Johnny Lowe at scrum-half. Charlie Middlehurst kicked a goal and two drop-goals in a 14-6 win.

The semi-final at Wigan against Dewsbury, this writer remembers vividly. I was the assistant coach at Dewsbury at the time and our senior coach, Tommy Smales, was a great believer in set moves, both from tap-penalties and the play-the-ball. We went to Wigan that day full of confidence as the team thought that they had let a Wembley appearance slip out of their hands the previous season, when beaten by

Bradford Northern at Headingley. It was 23rd March and a dull afternoon. The Warrington side was back to strength, with Kevin off suspension and Mike Nicholas also back after being sent off against Wigan in the cup-tie and getting a two-match ban. Dewsbury had played all season without Mick Stephenson, who was now playing in Australia, and their team was: Adrian Rushton; Greg Ashcroft, John Clarke, Nigel Stephenson, Gary Mitchell; Allan Agar, Alan Bates; Harry Beverley, Keith Voyce, Dick Lowe, John Bates, Jeff Grayshon and Joe Whittington. Warrington fielded: Whitehead; Mick Philbin, Noonan, Reynolds, Bevan; Whittle, Gordon; Chisnall, Ashcroft, Wanbon, Wright, Nicholas and Barry Philbin. The attendance was 11,789.

The truth is that Dewsbury were never at the races. Warrington were too powerful, too big, too fast and too good for a Dewsbury team that had peaked the previous season when they won the league Championship, beating Warrington at Wilderspool in the semi-final. This time it was Warrington with eyes on the Twin Towers. Playing behind a dominant pack, their backs ran in three tries to Reynolds, Whittle and Bevan, with Whitehead kicking two goals and Kevin two cracking drop-goals. A result of 17-7 flattered the Yorkshiremen who were way behind for most of the match.

Warrington were on their way to Wembley. The genius Alex Murphy had done it again, albeit this time as a coach, as he did not play in any of the rounds. Not surprisingly, the two men who backed him to do just this, Ossie Davies and Brian Pitchford, were delighted. The players too were beside themselves with joy, as a Wembley appearance became a reality. Even so, Murph continued to drive his charges on. The consummate professional, he would only be pleased if the Challenge Cup was won. Then and only then would he think about the league Championship final, and a possible four-cup haul in an already productive season.

* * *

Come the big day, Featherstone would be Warrington's opponents, after having beaten Leigh in the other semi at Headingley, 21-14. The sides had faced each other three times already that season. 'Rovers were the typical hard knock Yorkshire side,' says Kevin. 'They beat us 18-8 at Post Office Road in early October and that was a tight game. Then we beat them in the Captain Morgan final in January by 4-0, in an unbelievably rock hard contest. The final match of the three was in April, on a firm ground at Wilderspool. What a game that was. We were fighting in lumps, with everybody in, a real rough-house, but we came through 9 -7. We talked it over with Murph and he advised us that if it looked as if things were going the same way at Wembley, then we had to get the first ones in.'

On Tuesday 5th March, a letter from Rugby League HQ had arrived at Kevin and Janet's home, advising Kevin that he had been selected for the 1974 tour of Australia and New Zealand. Of course, Kevin had been out there for the 1968 World Cup and been a member of the 1970 World Cup squad over here as well, along with playing international football off and on since his call up to the under-24s while at Rochdale Hornets. But this was extra special. He would be a full-blown British Lion. John Bevan and Mike Nicholas were also in the touring party, so Warrington were well represented.

Just about everyone in the game expected Parry Gordon to claim one of the half-back places, his pace would surely be ideal on those hard Australian grounds. Steve Nash, of Featherstone Rovers, was red-hot favourite for the first choice number seven and the nearest challenger to Parry was Alan Bates, the tough Dewsbury scrum-half. On the

Sunday before Kevin's letter arrived, Dewsbury had played Warrington at Wilderspool and the two fancied half-backs were in opposition. To say Parry Gordon came out on top would be an understatement. In a 26-10 Warrington win that day, Gordon scored five, yes five, superb tries and had his best game of the season. This writer remembers going back to Dewsbury with Alan Bates on the team bus and he was very upset that he had left himself down. But stranger things happen at sea, as they say, and the following Tuesday morning a letter was pushed through the letter box of Alan Bates while Parry Gordon received none.

Warrington's league position, fourth behind Saints, Leeds and Featherstone, would ensure them a home draw in the play-offs, if it was maintained. And the results following the semi-final win certainly helped that league placing as Rochdale Hornets and Oldham were beaten at Wilderspool. 'We struggled against a good Rochdale outfit and were a bit fortunate to win by 16-13,' remembers Kevin. 'The tough games all season and the pressures of so many cup finals, and the runs we had in them, may well have knocked the edge off us bit, so Alex brought us around by switching certain players in selected games and giving a deserved rest to others to light the fires again. He was brilliant at this, always choosing the correct games to rest his key players in.

'Four days before the key game against Featherstone, which we won 9-7, we played at Dewsbury and Alex needed a fresh squad for the Featherstone set-to. The side that was beaten 31-18 at Crown Flatt bore little resemblance to our strongest team, but the reserves played their hearts out against the durable Yorkshiremen. The next three games were all away and we lost them all. Wigan wanted pay-back for the three defeats inflicted and won another rousing battle by 10 points to 2. This was followed by a heavy defeat at Salford, 21-3, with Warrington sporting a very unusual pack.' The third defeat was to Widnes in another tight game, 18-11. Then, one week before the play-offs, Warrington beat Leigh in the last league game of this monumental season. The 27-16 victory cemented a home tie in the play-offs.

'To win both the Challenge Cup and the Championship we would have to win five games on the trot, and these five games were against the best teams in the land,' recalls Kevin. 'Another problem was that, in the Championship play-offs, the games got harder each round. There was no easy ride. Hull FC came to us first and Murph fielded the strongest side possible, other than including himself.' It read: Whitehead; Mick Philbin, Noonan, Pickup, Bevan; Whittle, Lowe; Chisnall, Ashcroft, Brady, Wright, Nicholas and Barry Philbin, with Dave Cunliffe and Wayne Gaskell as subs. The Warrington forwards did their stuff, leading to tries for Bevan (2), Mick Philbin and the half-backs Whittle and Lowe. Brian Brady, in scoring mood all season, notched the sixth while Derek Whitehead landed eight goals.

The following week, the psychological strain was even greater. 'When we played Bradford Northern in the next play-off, the pressure was almost overpowering,' says Kevin. 'We were, in one sense, afraid to be beaten, so fiercely did we want to win the two remaining major cups. Alex tried all his magic and used his experience to calm us down, easing up on the tough training and pinning his faith in our sky high team spirit. The biggest problem was that not even the great team that Alex Murphy had played with at Saints had won four major cups in one season, so no one knew how to eliminate the tension. In the end, though, the saunas and massage treatment that Alex used to relax us that week must have done the trick, because were at our best against a Bradford team who figured we might have had Wembley on our minds. They came at us snarling and wanting to draw us into a fight, but we maintained our discipline, moved the ball wide at the correct time, and Bevan, Noonan and Whittle all raced over for tries. Whitehead converted them all and put us into the Championship semi-final with a 15-9 win.'

The conventional wisdom was that it could not be done. 'They can't reach another final this season,' everyone said. 'One game away from the big Wembley final, they will be looking after themselves and won't be doing much tackling.' The people who said that didn't know the Kevin Ashcrofts, Alex Murphys and Parry Gordons of this world. The honour and personal prestige of the whole Warrington team was at stake. 'Hard luck lads' was no good to them. They were hungry for records and were burning to say that they were members of a team that won four cups in one season.

A massive psychological boost as they entered this period was the news that Alex Murphy would partner Derek Noonan at centre in the Championship semi-final. Such was Murphy's aura that, although he had only played once in the past twenty-six matches (in the win over Leigh at home), he was welcomed back by all the team, who felt that with him in the side they were virtually unbeatable.

The game in question would be against Wakefield Trinity and Warrington were at home again being, with Saints, one of the two highest-placed league teams left in the competition. Kevin has crystal clear memories of the match that followed. 'In a season of tough games this was one of the toughest,' he says. 'Again, with Wembley being only seven days away, Wakefield Trinity were rough and tough from the kick-off. Thinking we may capitulate under pressure, Wakefield played it tight in the forwards, hoping to draw us in but, with Murph on the pitch, we played to our strengths. We did take on the Wakefield pack but, when the time was right, we also moved the ball wide. Mick Philbin showed his strength by holding off two tacklers and scoring a try wide out. Murph dazzled his opposing centre and wingman, drew them both onto him and unleashed John Bevan, who scorched over for our second try. Derek Whitehead kicked both the conversions and I managed another drop-goal. Wakefield went at us to the end, but we held out to win by 12 points to 7. The spectators went berserk. Their beloved team were in yet another final.'

* * *

Two games to play and the two biggest prizes to lift. The first, of course, was the following Saturday at Wembley. The preparations for this game were the same as Alex had used at Leigh. The players took Wembley week off work and on Monday, Tuesday and Wednesday it was out to Southport to run the dunes. During a brief lull in the running, the team's rest was shattered by a heavy drumming beat that could be heard from a long distance away. As the players dashed to the end of the dunes to see what was going on, they were nearly run over by a huge horse, galloping along the flat sand. What a great and beautiful animal he was. Alex shouted: 'It's Red Rum' and the Warrington team gave the big horse a cheer as he went about his usual Grand National type of training. There was some banter as the forwards shouted remarks to Alex like, 'Are you entering us for the *&^%$ National?' and 'Are we on the same winning money as Red Rum?'. Alex was giving his squad a very hard three days, and had earmarked the recovery period as Thursday, Friday and Saturday morning.

The Southport training went well and the spirit in the side was, as usual, awesome. The team's hotel was right in the centre of London, at the Kensington Palace. 'We set off on Thursday lunchtime and arrived at the hotel in time for a bite to eat and a stroll around the big city,' remembers Kevin.

'Our time for a look at Wembley was on Friday morning and the place looked superb. On my first trip, everything had seemed to go so fast, especially the actual game, we all missed things with Leigh that were obvious on the second visit. Soaking up the atmosphere even in the empty stadium was almost as emotional as walking out in front of 80,000-plus spectators. The old stadium was a wonderful place. Our Gary also played his part in this super occasion as he did the double with a second appearance as the mascot, only this time it was accepted by both the Wembley authorities and The Rugby Football League.

'He walked proudly out with the teams, three years older than his first time, when we smuggled him in the kit skip. At the end of the game, there was an attempt to stop the youngster going up with us for our medals, but Murph dug his heels in and that meant that he got his way. Our Gary went up between Alex and me to the presentation, another first!

'On the Friday evening before the match, Murph kept to the same routine as he had before, and we went to the Hendon dogs. Alex knew his way around and, before any of the races, he sidled down to the barrier and called one of the handlers over to him. He had a short chat, bunged this handler a tenner, and came away with the winners of four of the races. We all had a good touch and made a few bob. So the spirit again was sky high. Alex Murphy was, and still to this day is, a great dressing room personality. If I was still coaching, I would welcome him into my dressing room any time, if I wanted to liven my team up. He has a magnetism about him that stirs up the blood. Call it what you will, luck of the Irish, a gift of God or whatever, but he has it still, in spades.

'People who don't know Alex usually consider him to be too confident and slightly arrogant, but I can assure people that, most of the time, that opinion is brought on by simply being jealous of his success and ability. Alex has a heart of gold. He has given up - and still gives up - his time, free of charge, for anything that assists the ill, or children, or any worthwhile event. He is the people's champion. He was as volatile as nitroglycerine, though. We secretly laughed at Leigh one day, when our first-half's play had been chronic. Alex was going barmy. "Nobody goes for a piss until I have had my say, so sit down and listen." We did, because we had seen him before like this. "Now," he said, but stopped as Roy Lester walked passed the door. "Hey!" Alex shouted. And Roy came back, looking sheepish. "You soft bastard, you haven't tackled a man this half." Roy looked bemused. "Er, Alex. I'm on reserve duty today," he said. "I'm not even playing." Alex said, "alright, then" and turned to get onto some other poor bastard.'

The day of the final arrived and the usual slight delays occurred, as the team bus gently eased its way down the famous Wembley Way. The place was a colourful ocean of fans, all determined to do what they could to help their favourites bring the grand old Cup back to Wilderspool or Post Office Road. On the Warrington bus, Murphy's pack knew that the onus would be on them to give a crucial momentum to the side. Their go-forward style would be tested to the full by an outstanding Featherstone team of mostly local lads who had grown up in the pit village and been blooded into rugby league football as soon as they could walk.

In the event, the 1974 Challenge Cup final made history as one of the most brutal ever to be seen at Wembley. Lots of theories were proposed later on why this game was so tough and bruising, and why so many apparent acts of vengeance were carried out. Looking at the evidence now, a number of things may have culminated in this confrontation between two iron-hard teams, both sharing a philosophy of 'what is in front of me will be knocked down hard, either in attack or defence' (or, as they say in the ultra-professional world of American gridiron football: 'If it moves, crush it'). These two teams were recognised as being the toughest in their county, boasting big, strong and mobile packs of forwards. It was also a fact that the clubs had met three times this season already, with Warrington's 2-1 aggregate advantage and the closeness of the scorelines showing just how evenly matched they were; 18-8 to Featherstone at Post Office Road; a 4-0 win for Warrington in the Captain Morgan at Salford; and a 9-7 victory at Wilderspool just over a month before this final. Also, the men in charge were possibly the most aggressive, competitive and successful coaches in the league at that time, Alex Murphy and Peter Fox, great motivators and thinkers alike. On top of all that, these were simply two very good sides aching to get their hands on the Cup.

Upon taking the Warrington job, Alex Murphy had predicted that the club would be at the top within three seasons. This was now his third season in charge and, here he was, on the threshold of yet another tremendous period destined to reiterate his position as the most successful player and coach of the modern era. The referee for this mighty affair was the gentlemanly Mr. Sam Shepherd of Oldham. Mr. Shepherd was a very experienced referee who appeared to specialise in officiating fast, free-flowing and entertaining games. The attendance was just over 80,000 and the receipts were £132,000, a world record for a rugby league game, beating by over £7,000 the previous record established at last season's Featherstone versus Bradford finale, won by Rovers.

As it turned out, most journalists agreed that this was not one of Sam Shepherd's usual fast-flowing games, but none could honestly claim that it failed to stir the blood and set the pulses racing. Watching from the stand, one could feel the bumps and fierce collisions as if one were actually involved in the tackles, so determined were the players of each side to be the victors. Amongst the dignitaries in attendance was his Excellency, the Australian High Commissioner, The Hon. John Armstrong, who presented the cup and medals. The Featherstone Rovers team that day was: Harold Box; Dave Dias, Mick Smith, David Hartley, Graham Bray; John Newlove, Steve Nash; Les Tonks, John 'Keith' Bridges, Billy Harris, Alan Rhodes, Jimmy Thompson and Keith Bell. The Rovers substitutes were Dave Busfield and Richard 'Charlie' Stone. Warrington fielded: Derek Whitehead; Mike Philbin, Derek Noonan, Alan Whittle, John Bevan; Alex Murphy, Parry Gordon; Dave Chisnall, Kevin Ashcroft, Brian Brady, Dave Wright, Mike Nicholas and Barry Philbin. Their substitutes were Billy Pickup and Bobby Wanbon.

The much-respected rugby league journalist, Jack Winstanley, reporting on this final, compared it to an 'Alex Murphy stage-managed show'. Kevin agrees. 'Murph wanted to become the first man to have captained three winning clubs in this competition,' he says, 'Saints, Leigh and Warrington. He was pushing thirty-five years old at the time and this could be the last-chance saloon. Alex was not the kind of bloke to let a chance like this slip. He did what he always did, he led from the front.'

Murphy told his charges that he wanted them to impose themselves upon Featherstone from the very first whistle. 'Coaches from that era would often advise their players to introduce themselves early,' continues Kevin. 'That was the statement Murph made in making his first tackle of the game, after only two minutes, on the big centre David Hartley. Alex banjo-ed him good and proper. He was in at everything and took some stick himself. Harold Box nailed him with a beauty stiff arm in retaliation for Murph's big hit on Hartley, but he never cried, just got on with his game. As one reporter said at the time, the only thing Murph lost that day was the toss.'

There were niggles going on at most tackles, plus one or two real bust-ups. 'Sam Shepherd never bothered about the odd smack, so long as it wasn't too obvious,' says Kevin. 'He would talk to the player who received the smack first and say: "Now, I saw that and I will talk to him. Don't go taking the law into your own hands, leave it to me." Then Sam would quietly tell the offender to stop or next time he would remove him. It usually worked. Sam Shepherd was aware of the tough play going on in this final and I suppose he thought, well it is a cup-tie after all. Box opened the scoring with a penalty goal, Derek Whitehead replied with two for us, then Box made it 4-4. Two more Whitehead goals took us into a 8-4 lead before Alex had to leave the field with rib and dead-leg problems. Billy Pickup came into the centres and Alan Whittle moved to stand-off half.'

On the stoke of half-time, Featherstone were awarded a penalty and kicked the ball into touch. From the tap-kick to restart the game, Nash feigned a run to the open but instead dropped Thompson back down the short side and, although Warrington seemed to have it covered, the second-row forward found the supporting Newlove, who suddenly stepped off his right foot, sliced between Nicholas, Noonan and Chisnall, and went over near the posts for a cracking try. Box converted and Warrington went in for their oranges 9-8 down and looking shaded. The game, though, was far from over.

'Alex came back on after 50 minutes, having had five pain-killing injections,' remembers Kevin. 'Parry Gordon retired to the bench, with Alex working the scrums. There was a scrum about ten yards into our half. The ball shot in and shot out to us; I was still standing. I saw Alex run across Alan Whittle and drop him off into a huge gap. I was out of the upright scrum quickly and tucked in behind Alan as he sprinted away, to be confronted by Harold Box. Alan was a great stepper and put in a big step to beat Box who flung out his arm in desperation. The force of his hand dislodged the ball from Alan's grasp and the ball bounced backwards right into my path and into my arms. I had about fifteen yards to run and could feel the presence of a defender behind me. I gritted my teeth and went into a dive for the line from two yards out, just as the tackler grabbed me from the back. It was the Featherstone centre Mick Smith, but my momentum carried me over. Derek kicked the goal, and then two further penalty goals, to take us out to 17-9 in front.

'A few minutes later, I was hit on the side of my head by a king-hit from Billy Harris. I walloped him back and he went down but, out of the corner of my eye, I then spotted a Featherstone player coming for me at a fair rate of knots. Just before the impact, a Warrington jersey dashed in front of me and the Featherstone man never arrived. It was Keith Bridges, who was on his way to do me no good whatsoever. He was intercepted by Bobby Wanbon, who caught him full on the chin with a right cross. A melée began, with Barry Philbin, no mug at that game, picking out the biggest man on the field, Les Tonks, and knocking him down. Barry sat astride Les battering his face. Sam Shepherd settled the trouble down and Bridges was assisted to the sideline, as was big Les with blood pouring out of a badly-gashed cheekbone. Peter Fox had lost his two key scrummagers in one incident. The subs were sent on but it was no contest and we won every ball from the tight, whilst Bridges and Tonks were gone. There was commotion on the touchline as Tonks was led to the dressing room, with Peter Fox calling him back. But he would not return until his eye was patched up correctly. Bridges was revived with smelling salts, a cold sponge down his back and massage on his chin and neck. He bravely tottered back on unsteady legs, as the touch judge attracted Sam Shepherd to allow him on.

'Alex said to me, "What the *&^%$ hell are they doing with him? They're sending him back on! Do your stuff Ashy." The first scrum, I dropped the nut on Bridges and he was off for good. This was dog-eat-dog Challenge Cup final football. We all knew the dangers and we all took the chance. No doubt, today, with the clear legislation in place regarding injuries, neither player would have been allowed back on the field and rightfully so.'

Alex Murphy dropped two more goals and then, in the 75th-minute, Mike Nicholas put the game to bed with an excellent solo try. With a score of 24-9, Warrington had won the Challenge Cup for the first time in twenty years. The first time, in fact, since the drawn final against Halifax at Wembley in 1954, after which the Wire went on to win the replay at Odsal, 8-4, before a then-world record crowd for a rugby match in either code of 102,569. Warrington, though, did collect injuries to Murphy, Gordon, Brady, and the unlucky Mike Nicholas, whose injury, in scoring the final try, caused him to pull out of Great Britain's 1974 tour of Australia and New Zealand.

Kevin continues: 'Our lucky mascot, our Gary, went up with us to collect the Challenge Cup. The thousands of Warrington fans went barmy, singing and chanting, and those two great blokes, Ossie Davies and Brian Pitchford, were in the dressing room ecstatic with joy. Two very wealthy men in their own right, yet they were so totally committed to our winning the Cup. There were tears of absolute satisfaction. Their gamble to bring success back to Warrington had paid off.'

In the tea room at Wembley, one of the first faces Kevin

saw after the game was his old Art teacher from Manchester Road school, Mr. Colin Williams, subsequently to become better known as Colin Welland, the actor in Z Cars, writer of Chariots of Fire and co-founder of Fulham RLFC - nowadays Harlequins RLFC. The club, it seemed, was back in the big time. Alex had said from the outset that he would produce something big within three years and he had come up with the goods. At the Kensington Palace hotel, the celebrations went throughout the night and the squad set off in great spirits, if a wee bit tired, on the journey back to Warrington.

'The crowds were again enormous as we approached Warrington Town Hall,' recalls Kevin. 'Thousands thronged the roads and there were great cheers as we hoisted the grand old Cup high in the air for the supporters to see it. Inside this very ornate building we were toasted time and time again by the various city fathers. The Lady Mayor was delighted with the parading of the Cup and Parry Gordon and I were stood back allowing the lads to soak up the atmosphere. "Have you ever been in the Mayor's parlour?" she asked us. We replied that we never had and the Lady Mayor advised one of her footmen to open up the room. We had never seen anything as beautiful before - gold and polished silver everywhere. Presentations were made to Warrington from all over the world.

'Parry, though, noticed the Lady Mayor's well-stocked bar and, immediately, she was behind it pouring doubles for the three of us. About half an hour later, a footman came in and told us that the whole parade of dignitaries were waiting on the coach to go to the official reception and banquet at Wilderspool. Parry and I walked out amid cheers from the lads and scowls from Murph. "Where the *&^%$ hell have you two been," he whispered to us. Parry, as cheeky as ever, said: "With the Lady Mayor, Alex" and out she came, with her hat to one side, tottering like Hylda Baker. We arrived at Wilderspool to further wild scenes of supporters and, finally, found our way to the tables. The Lady Mayor was sat next to Ossie Davies and Brian Pitchford, but was fast asleep before the soup came out.'

* * *

Seven days after the Wembley final, Kevin and the Warrington team had the chance to be the first team since 1927/28 to win all four major cups in one season. Swinton were the last club to perform the feat, winning the Challenge Cup, Lancashire Cup, Lancashire League Cup and the Championship Cup. Although Warrington could not win the same competitions as Swinton, in place of the Lancashire Cup and Lancashire League Cup, they had the equally-prestigious Captain Morgan Trophy and the John Player Trophy instead. However, the Championship Cup remained very much within their reach.

The Championship was originally played for in a top-four club play-off, very similar to today's play-offs and Super League Grand Final. The top team in the league table played the fourth, while second played third. Later, it was changed to a top-sixteen play-off. In effect, to win the Championship, a club now had to beat four teams instead of two. Warrington's opponents in this year's Championship final were St. Helens. The Saints had beaten Workington Town and Castleford at home and Leeds away, en route to the big day at Central Park, Wigan, where a healthy crowd of around 20,000 people attended. The referee was Mr. Peter Geraghty from York.

Always the last game of the season, the Championship final was seen as a football showpiece, played on firm ground with a fast, exciting spectacle usually guaranteed.

Lining up for Warrington were: Derek Whitehead; Mike Philbin, Derek Noonan, Billy Pickup, John Bevan; Alan Whittle, Alex Murphy; David Chisnall, Kevin Ashcroft, Brian Brady, Bobby Wanbon, Ian Mather and Barry Philbin. Subs: John Lowe and Wayne Gaskell. With speedy backs and a big mobile pack, St. Helens were the ideal team to take on a highly confident Warrington outfit. Their side read: Geoff Pimblett; Dave Brown, John Wills, Frank Wilson, Roy Mathias; David Eckersley, Jeff Heaton; John Mantle, Graham Liptrot, Mick Murphy, Eric Chisnall, George Nicholls and Kel Coslett. Sub: John Warlow. Gary Ashcroft was again the mascot and he, like the players, was presented to the President of the Rugby Football League, Lord Derby.

As we have seen, in any key game of rugby league in those days, possession of the ball from the set scrum was crucial. Kevin's dominance, therefore, proved vital, as the younger and less experienced Graham Liptrot found out. The Warrington hooker won ball from almost every major scrum, whether near the Saints line or the danger area of his own 25-yard line. Kevin states: 'My props, Dave Chisnall and Brian Brady, were both shorter in height and more compact in build compared to the two really tall Saints props, John Mantle and Mick Murphy. Dave and Brian were able to pack lower and drive upwards in the scrum, enabling them to unbalance the Saints front row. Statistics gave us a thirteen-to-six advantage in the scrums, but there seemed more scrums than nineteen, because Dave and Brian caused upset every time we packed down with their scrummaging technique. The scribes questioned Murph's and my tactics of attempting a few drop-goals when Saints looked almost gone, but if one had gone over it well may have finished them there and then. That was our plan.'

The weather, too, was most un-May-like. It poured down throughout and, again, this suited Warrington whose strong forwards carried the ball up superbly in the wet and slippery conditions. Kel Coslett opened Saints' account with a penalty goal, but this was cancelled out almost immediately by a masterful long pass by Alex Murphy that allowed Mick Philbin to race over for an unconverted try. Barry Philbin, revelling in the damp conditions with his hard, straight running and his penetrative bursts, kept St. Helens on the back foot. Lack of possession hampered the Saints style. They knew that if they lost the ball in broken play, Warrington would surely win it back from the scrum. Even so, the elusive running of Frank Wilson earned Saints a try and Coslett's conversion took the men from Knowsley Road out to a 7-3 lead. Then, Dave Chisnall ran onto a pass from Kevin and looked as if he was about to steamroller through the first tackle. Instead, the prop side-stepped like a wingman and went clear through the hole. Brian Brady, looming up at his side, took the pass and blasted his way over, before Derek Whitehead kicked the goal that gave the Wire an 8-7 lead at the break.

Warrington were halfway towards completing a memorable four cups season. Worryingly, though, early in the second half, Billy Pickup took a knock and was forced to leave the field. But Alex Murphy simply swapped the backs around and brought John Bevan into the centre. Almost immediately, Bevan received the ball, beat the first tackler with a hand-off, swerved outside the second and went past the third with superb acceleration before sending Derek Noonan slicing over for a great try, Whitehead adding the conversion. In front now by 13 points to 7, with almost thirty minutes to play, the game was still by no means won, especially when Wilson brought the crowd to its feet with a good try, converted by Coslett. With sixteen minutes to play, there was once again only a single point in it, 13-12 to Warrington. As the minutes ticked away, Murphy attempted several drops at goal, for a score for Saints now would most likely win them the Championship, shattering the hopes of all the players, directors and staff at Wilderspool.

Realising this only too well, St. Helens got their second wind. With the clock ticking down, they hammered their way upfield and, in one of the most exciting finishes for years, were close enough for a drop at goal by their expert marksman, Kel Coslett. Somehow, the ball found its way back to Kel, who took a steadying second and, bang, a super kick was winging its way towards the posts. The crowd hushed. On the field, twenty-six pairs of eyes looked to the heavens, watching the spiralling ball in total silence as it sailed overhead, apparently on target. Then, in its last few yards of flight, the ball suddenly veered away, to the outside of the posts. Peter Geraghty, the referee, blew for time and Warrington had achieved the impossible. They had won four cups in one season. As one writer put it: 'The winning of the four cups signalled the end of one of the most successful seasons, not only in the Warrington club's history, but that of any club in the game,' before adding that, 'it also carried one of the biggest wage bills.'

Again, wild scenes welcomed the Warrington team as they arrived back at Wilderspool. 'The crowd was immense around the ground but all behaving themselves,' says Kevin. 'They just wanted to be part of this great, record season for the club. We had in fact won five cups this season, as we had won the Locker Cup by beating Wigan in a pre-season annual charity match. That old Cup looked well stood in the company of the four major trophies we brought home.'

* * *

So ended Warrington's fabulous 1973/74 fairytale. On the family front, the Ashcroft's had celebrated the birth of their second son, Craig, on 10th April. And as a player, these were Kevin's halcyon days. He'd had the great early experience at Rochdale Hornets; the wonderful times at Leigh; his move to Warrington and then this unbelievable season just passed. Nor was it yet over. On top of this most recent record-breaking success, he had cemented a place on the Lions tour of Australia and New Zealand, flying out in this particular month of May.

Of course, Kevin had toured down under before, but that was a short World Cup event some six years earlier when, as we have seen, the competition only lasted for around three weeks. This time, he would be there much longer and events were already moving quickly. Five days after the Championship final, he was in Sydney.

An international tour is - or should be - the zenith of any player's career. On this occasion, Great Britain's tourists were treated like gods and welcomed warmly everywhere they went. But also still fresh in Kevin's mind were those two recent major games and the return to Wilderspool with the third and fourth cups of the season. The Warrington fans had never had so much to take in, even in the successful 1950s, when their favourite team was without doubt one of the strongest, toughest and most skilful teams around. This current side had played and beaten the best. They had tasted defeat only once in the season's many cup competitions - at Whitehaven in the Lancashire Cup - and won the rest.

Kevin reflects: 'Warrington Town Hall is absolutely beautiful. The entrance is very much like Buckingham Palace and, when we arrived, we never expected the lavish food and drink waiting for us, especially as we had already been really well received after bringing back the Challenge Cup. To be given another huge Civic Reception so soon was a real treat for the club. We were ushered onto the balcony and the crowd below us stood cheering and chanting. It was like something out of an American movie. The microphone was passed around the players and each man received a tremendous cheer as he spoke a few words.

'I took the mike and, as the crowd hushed, I said: "Have some of you been here all week?" This brought a cheer and, as it died down, I said: "You won't be bloody cheering when you get next year's rates bill for all this grub and booze we have lined up!" This brought another round of laughter and cheering. Sadly, this time Parry and I were not invited into the Mayor's parlour. What a pity.'

So, another great party was had at Wilderspool. All the Cups were on show and everyone felt very proud of their club and their team-mates. In situations such as these, strong bonds of friendship and respect are made that last forever. As, in fact, is also the case whenever a touring team heads down under.

CHAPTER SIX

With the eyes of a nation's entire rugby league community upon it, the Great Britain touring side of 1974 bore a huge weight of expectancy upon its shoulders.

Four years earlier, the 1970 tourists had recaptured the Ashes from the Aussies in a stirringly successful two Tests to one series victory. Everyone in the United Kingdom yearned for more of the same. When the squad was announced, as usual, it contained a number of unexpected selections. A handful of players who well may have gained selection were already plying their trade in Australia; namely a couple of 1970 tourists in Phil Lowe (Hull KR) and Doug Laughton (Wigan), Brian Lockwood (Castleford), Bill Ashurst (Wigan) and Mick Stephenson (Dewsbury). Two unlucky first-choice players were forced out through injury: Mike Nicholas of Warrington and Salford's Keith Fielding, to be replaced by Jimmy Thompson (Featherstone Rovers) and John Butler (Rochdale Hornets). Early in the tour, John Atkinson (Leeds) and John Bates (Dewsbury) returned home injured, and were replaced by Maurice Richards (Salford) and Bill Ramsey (Bradford Northern). The final unlucky player was David Eckersley (St. Helens), who returned home with a back injury but was not replaced. The injury to John Bates was to end the career of this splendid and underestimated second-row forward all too soon.

One touring forward who had experience of Aussie rugby league was the Widnes prop, Jim Mills. During his time as a player at North Sydney Bears, Jim had 'introduced himself' to many an Australian. In time, this tactical brand of 'self-defence', along with that of his buddy, Mervyn Hicks, had left the Bears with only one serious option, which was to release 'Big Jim' and Mervyn from their contracts, wish them bon voyage and ask them to return the keys to the club car. This they duly did, but in a highly unusual manner. For in returning the car, they drove it right into the North Sydney Leagues Club itself and left the vehicle, keys and all, right there in the foyer. Nice one, Jim! The big man's actions, though, backfired. On the 1974 tour, whenever Jim Mills was recognised as a member of the party, his fellow tourists were usually barred entry. Bad one, Jim!

As in any sizeable group, there were good lads and one or two pains in the bum. The players were measured for clothes, issued with tour numbers, told of the itinerary and provided with all relevant information required, including the names of their room-mates. Kevin was roomed with Ken Gill of Salford and, in short, it was not a good match.

The original tour party was as follows: Mr. Reg Parker (Blackpool Borough - manager), Jim Challinor (St. Helens - coach), Chris Hesketh (Salford - captain), Kevin Ashcroft (Warrington), John Atkinson (Leeds), Alan Bates (Dewsbury), John Bates (Dewsbury), John Bevan (Warrington), Keith Bridges (Featherstone Rovers), Jon Butler (Rochdale Hornets), Paul Charlton (Salford), Eric

Chisnall (St. Helens), Terry Clawson (Oldham), Colin Dixon (Salford), Les Dyl (Leeds), David Eckersley (St. Helens), Ken Gill (Salford), John Gray (Wigan), Jim Mills (Widnes), Roger Millward (Hull KR), Steve Nash (Featherstone Rovers), George Nicholls (St. Helens), Steve Norton (Castleford), Bill Ramsey (Bradford Northern), David Redfearn (Bradford Northern), Maurice Richards (Salford), Paul Rose (Hull KR), Jimmy Thompson (Featherstone Rovers), David Watkins (Salford) and David Willicombe (Wigan).

The journey to Australia was via the extra long hop to Hong Kong, then a six hour re-fuelling stop. The tourists entered Australia via Darwin, in the Northern Territory. 'We arrived in Darwin and the humidity was overpowering,' remembers Kevin. 'As tourists, we had to maintain decorum and wear our tour blazers, shirts and ties but, on arrival, this apparel was inappropriate, we were sweating cobs. Our first accommodation was at the Koala motel in Darwin. The first thing the lads saw was the swimming pool signs. Doffing our clothes after the allocation of rooms, we all dashed outside for a swim only to find two teenaged aboriginal kids with blankets wrapped around their shoulders. The pool was covered, with about one inch of water in it. We asked the two kids what was going on. "It's winter, man, and it's freezing," they told us. We had to cool down with a cold shower instead.

'Afterwards, we had a short session with a ball, but we soon found problems with the studs in our boots. They were too long and caused you to cockle over, with a danger of ankle damage. We had arrived on 25th May and played the following day before a crowd of 6,500. The weather was hot, sweltering, as we started the tour against a Darwin side that would tell the story of how they tackled the tourists with the fervour of a full-blooded Test match. It became folklore down the years. But this was the British touring team and we finished up scoring eleven tries and four goals, in a 41-2 win.'

From Darwin, the tourists travelled across Australia's 'Top End' to the beautiful coastal area of Cairns, in Northern Queensland. 'Now it was superb up there,' says Kevin. 'The people were rugby league barmy. An attendance of 8,000 turned up to witness North Queensland v GB Tourists in a breathtaking setting. We had another good win, 30-5.' Leaving Cairns, the tourists journeyed south, down the eastern seaboard of Australia, towards the distant Sydney, with the trip becoming physically harder at every stop. 'Each team seemed as if it was trying to soften us up for the big boys in the Tests,' says Kevin. 'Some areas were fairly industrialised but most were really beautiful and downright tough. After Cairns, we visited Rockhampton, Maryborough and Ipswich, and wins were recorded in each game. The first really big city we arrived at was Brisbane. We spent two very pleasant weeks there and played six games, using the place as our headquarters.'

Frequently, on tour, players are asked to fill in strange team positions, usually due to bumps and bruises caused through playing games every two days, with each set of opponents attempting to decapitate you. Kevin played in several positions during the initial games, on the wing, at loose forward, in the second row, at prop, and of course as hooker.

'Most of the players played out of position,' he confirms, 'and you helped out as much as you could. That goes with touring itself, too. You are twenty-six mates against the world and you do what you can to be a good tourist. The injuries picked up in 1974 were unparalleled. David Watkins damaged his knee ligaments in the first Test and only played six games in the whole tour. Poor John Bates never fully recovered from his injury, after playing in two games and subbing in four. John Atkinson went home early, only playing in eight games. Dave Eckersley was sent home with a back injury after eleven games and two subs, and I broke my ankle against New South Wales. I stayed on tour, though, and came back against New Zealand as substitute, having played in thirteen games and subbing once. Keith Bridges played in only eight games and it was lucky for us that, with Dai Watkins out injured, utility-player, John Gray of Wigan, could not only hook but kick goals as well.'

As with any tour, there were jokers who thought up the most diabolical tricks to play on their mates. 'I rated the pair of Steve Norton and Les Dyl as the main culprits who would stop at nothing to get a laugh,' says Kevin. 'They would go out at night looking for harmless creepy-crawlies and place them in football stockings, or let them run across the table when the most squeamish members of the squad were eating their breakfast. Jim Mills was a great tourist. I had roomed with Kenny Gill before breaking my ankle and, when recovering, had a room to myself, laid up in bed in traction for three weeks. Afterwards, I moved in with big Jim. He was a great mate and an unbelievable character.'

After the episode with North Sydney and the club car, Mills was only allowed in certain establishments, owing to his reputation of being able to handle himself. 'He was not a trouble maker,' insists Kevin, 'but his presence was such that he seemed to draw all the nutters in Australia to want to have a go at him. They must have been crackers to try, as just to see his size should have been enough to put anyone off. But for all their good humour and fun, blokes like Steve Norton were wonderful trainers. Out in the early morning with coach Jim Challinor, who was a fitness fanatic, several of the lads would go for a run on the beach or find some open grass and train on that.'

The reason the tourists had moved into Brisbane was

that they played four games in the area in nine days, starting with Queensland on 9th June, a game that the tourists won by 13 points to 12. Kevin remembers: 'This was by far the toughest match to date. Over 20,000 Queenslanders were screaming for our blood as the northern state went all out for a win. We scored two tries to their one, but the referee kept them in the game with a series of penalties. In those days, the Queensland side was selected from players playing in Queensland. No one from New South Wales could play, even if he was a Queenslander born and bred. Another reason they were playing it for keeps is that, the week after, we were due to play Australia on the same ground, Lang Park. As I was selected to play against Queensland, it was certain that I would not figure in the first Test, in fact Keith Bridges got the nod for that one.'

Great Britain's team for the opening Test of the 1974 tour was: Paul Charlton; David Redfearn, Dai Watkins, Chris Hesketh, John Bevan; Roger Millward, Steve Nash; Terry Clawson, Keith Bridges, Jim Mills, Jim Thompson, Colin Dixon and George Nicholls. The subs were David Eckersley and John Gray. The Australian team, meanwhile, included David Waite, who would go on to coach Great Britain from 2001 to 2003. Their team read: Graeme Langlands; David Waite, Bob Fulton, Mick Cronin, Warren Orr; Geoff Richardson, Tommy Raudonikis; Bob O'Reilly, Elwyn Walters, Arthur Beetson, Ray Higgs, Paul Sait and Ron Coote. Subbing were Ray Branighan and John Lang. The referee was Mr. D. Lancaster of Toowoomba and the gate was 30,280. Only one try was scored in the 12-6 defeat for the tourists that followed. Warren Orr went over for the Aussies, with Langlands adding four goals and the Warrington-born Bobby Fulton a drop-goal.

As the tour progressed, the Lions' next game was against a combined district team representing Mr. Lancaster's home town of Toowoomba '...a beautiful part of the big continent,' according to Kevin, 'lush, green and picturesque, on the edge of the Darling Downs. The inhabitants knocked bells off us, even though we won by 42 points to 16. From there, it was back up to Brisbane and a defeat at the hands of a select side picked from the Brisbane country teams. They were a strong outfit, with several former and future internationals playing, and they beat us 20-15. Then it was south to Grafton, to play North Coast, and a tough win for us this time, 19-9. Then south again, but inland, through the New England range of mountains into the Liverpool Plains, to play North Division, N.S.W at Tamworth. We won 38-14.'

And still the games kept on coming. 'West Division, N.S.W. was the next team we faced,' recalls Kevin, 'still inland at Orange, which is further west than Bathurst and really in the bush. A win by 25-10 showed that the nearer we went to Sydney, the harder were the opposition. After that, it was down to Sydney proper and into the Rushcutters Bay motel.'

At this stage in the itinerary, the tourists faced a fixture that was billed as the nearest thing to a Test match, a clash with New South Wales at the Sydney Cricket Ground. Coming into that game, Keith Bridges had suffered a bad injury against the North Coast and would not play again on tour. 'It looked as though I was in for the crucial second Test,' says Kevin, 'but first we had to get through the big one against New South Wales. Now, this was a strong side. It was crammed full of current and recent full internationals. Arthur Beetson, John Lang and Bob O'Reilly was their front row, with Ron Coote at loose forward. We were holding them pretty close when, just before half-time, I was hit in a double tackle by Beetson and Coote and, as I keeled over, I felt this crack and a burning pain in my ankle. I knew it was something serious and was whisked off to hospital where they told me it was broken. This had been one hell of an unlucky tour for a lot of the lads, and now I was sidelined. We lost the game, too, 16-11.

'When I was released from hospital, they set me up with my ankle in traction in a hotel room of my own. I was there for three weeks, obviously confined to bed, and the lads acted as nurse maids, bringing me food in my room. By the end, I was sick of the sight of eggs. Boiled eggs, fried eggs, poached eggs, egg salad, egg-on-toast, you name an egg dish, I had it. Roger Millward could only say "egg" when asked by the waitresses what it was that I wanted. He brought my meals up to me and it was always egg. Dai Watkins was the same as me, pegged up in bed, him with his strained ligaments and me with the ankle.'

After three weeks of traction, Kevin was soon hobbling around with the lads again. 'And it was then that we met up with a real character of the Sydney underworld,' he says. 'This bloke turned out to be a mate of Jim Mills and we knew him as Last Card Louie. He owned a nightclub in the Kings Cross area of Sydney called the Pink Pussy and he could get in anywhere. One of Louie's haunts was the very posh Sydney Yacht Club and we had good times in there.'

* * *

Meanwhile, back with the rugby, and it turned out to be a stroke of good fortune that the selectors had chosen to take John Gray on tour. Wigan's former rugby union player not only did a great job as a Test hooker, he also took over from the injured Watkins as a first-class goal-kicker. 'John was a wonderful tourist and a super bloke,' says Kevin. 'He kicked seventeen goals and one drop-goal in four Test matches, including three and a drop-goal in the second Test, which we won, 16-11, in front of almost 50,000 people at the SCG.'

On that day, both nations had been forced into making changes. Great Britain's team read: Charlton; Dyl, Eckersley, Hesketh, Millward; Gill, Nash; Mills, Gray, Thompson, Dixon, Chisnall and Nicholls, with Steve Norton substitute. Australia fielded: Graham Eadie; Waite, Fulton, Cronin, Orr; Richardson, Raudonikis; O'Reilly, Lang, Beetson, Sait, Gary Stevens and Coote. Their subs were Ray Branighan and Bob McCarthy. Kenny Gill, Eric Chisnall and Colin Dixon scored Britain's tries, to go with Gray's goals. Bobby Fulton, John Lang and Ron Coote crossed for the Aussies, while Mick Cronin landed one goal. After that success, the Lions' final three non-Test encounters were won at Queanbeyan, against Monaro, Wagga Wagga against Riverina, and up on the northern New South Wales coast against a very powerful club side that later became known as the Newcastle Knights.

Everything was set, then, for the final and deciding Test at Sydney. A gate of 56,000 was in attendance and, in those days, it was not quite so cut and dried as it might be today as to who would win it. 'Only six points separated us in the first Test, five in the second, so it could have gone either way,' says Kevin. 'Australia fielded another changed side compared to both the previous Tests: Langlands; Lionel Williamson, Fulton, Cronin, Branighan; Tim Pickup, Raudonikis; Beetson, Ron Turner, John O'Neill, Stevens, McCarthy and Coote. We made a few changes too, mostly because of injuries. Our team was: Charlton; Richards, Dyl, Hesketh, Bevan; Gill, Nash; Clawson, Gray, Thompson, Dixon, Chisnall and Nicholls. Our substitutes were Roger Millward and Paul Rose. It was a real nail-biter, with the difference in scores even closer than in the first two Tests. It was the Aussies, though, who held out to register a win by four points, 22-18. A try and five goals to Langlands, and tries for Williamson, McCarthy and Coote were the Aussie points, while Richards and Dyl scored tries and Gray kicked six goals for us. The Aussies did score four tries to our two, so the win was just about merited.

'The final game of the Australian section of the tour was played at Gosford, on the Central Coast, against a Southern New South Wales side. Coming to the end of this leg of the tour, we still had a tough short tour of New Zealand in front of us, with an horrendous injury list. Some of the lads were playing injured, just to make a team up. The normal things happened in the final game and, although beaten by Southern New South Wales 16-10, both sides scored two tries apiece, but they kicked five goals to our two.'

Although this 1974 Australian trip with the Lions had ended in disappointment, for Kevin the experience of a full rugby league tour was a thrill that has lasted a lifetime. 'Great, lasting friendships are made on these tours,' he says. 'Memories rush back in ones mind, years later, of the hilarious happenings and the camaraderie built up over those three months amongst team-mates. It becomes very emotional to think of them sometimes. The tour is a childhood dream come true. The vast majority of the Australian public were wonderful to us. Everyone wanted to talk to you. We all ate for free wherever we went. No one would allow you to buy a drink. It was always, "I'll get these mate." They were brilliant hosts.'

Although Kevin was by now walking with little trouble, as soon as he sat down his ankle swelled up to twice its normal size. 'I was icing and resting it as much as possible,' he says, 'but we were still on tour and there were jobs to do.' The tourists flew out of Sydney on Monday 22nd July and arrived in Auckland soon after. Their first game in New Zealand was in Huntley, about seventy miles due south of Auckland, against a North Island representative side of the central area. Auckland had their own rep side and were, by tradition, the final game of the entire tour.

Winter in New Zealand can be counted on to be wet and 1974 was no different. 'Heavy grounds and grey skies,' is how Kevin remembers it. 'In front of a 3,500 crowd, we beat North Island 37-17, but it was a rugged affair. Then came our second game in New Zealand, the first Test against the Kiwis at Carlaw Park, Auckland. As usual, the Kiwis fronted up with a huge pack of forwards and good footballers in the backs.' The New Zealand side was: Warren Collicoat; Maurice 'Mocky' Brereton, Bill Johnsen, Eddie Kerrigan, John O'Sullivan; Dennis Williams, Ken Stirling; Lyndsay Proctor, Bill Burgoyne, Doug Gailey, Tony Coll, John Greengrass and Murray Eade. Substitute Wayne Robertson replaced Proctor during the game.

'We were really struggling to field a team,' says Kevin. 'The soft going at Huntley had found one or two injuries out and, although our side looked strong enough to have won, the ferocity of the Kiwi game, together with our injuries, meant that it was one game too far for us. I was asked if the ankle would stand up, if I subbed to help the team out. I agreed as I had done a bit of jogging, but it was still swollen. In fact, the swelling was so bad that I couldn't get my usual three-quarter sided boot on the joint, so I had it strapped up real tight and borrowed a back's boot, with the low sides. So, there I was, representing Great Britain in odd boots!'

The team 'full of crocks' was: Charlton; Redfearn, Dyl, Hesketh, Bevan; Gill, Nash; Clawson, Gray, Thompson, Dixon, Norton and Nicholls, with Ashcroft and Richards the subs. The Kiwis won the game, 13-8, but Britain did score two tries to one. Bevan and Nash crossed, with Clawson kicking one goal. New Zealand replied with a Ken Stirling try and Collicoat kicked five goals. The referee was Mr. J. Percival of Auckland.

Unfortunately for Kevin, but perhaps not surprisingly, the unscheduled run-out this time finished his tour for good, as the ankle once again ballooned up. He could, though, still experience the state of the sport, overall, in New Zealand. 'In 1974, rugby league was a decidedly poor relation to rugby union,' he recalls. 'Big crowds attended all the international games at Eden Park, and the newspapers, TV and radio were full of news and views about union. In contrast, the gate at the first rugby league Test at Carlaw Park was only 10,466. Three days later, The New Zealand Maoris played us at Rotorua, where our patched-up team had a tough fight to win 19-16. Next stop was the windy city, Wellington, and a fairly easy 39-11 win. Then it was across the Cook Strait to the cold South Island, where we played the second Test, at Christchurch.'

On that day, the Great Britain team lined up as: Charlton; Redfearn, Dixon, Dyl, Richards; Hesketh, Nash; Mills, Gray, Thompson, Chisnall, Norton and Nicholls, with Alan Bates and Bill Ramsey subbing. The New Zealand team read: Collicoat; Brereton, O'Sullivan, Johnsen, Kerrigan; Williams, Stirling; Gailey, John Hibbs, Greengrass, Coll, Robertson and Eade, with Don Mann and Bob Jarvis as subs. Collicoat landed four goals for the Kiwis, but a battleworn Great Britain were to gain revenge for that earlier reverse, as Redfearn, Dyl and Hesketh scored tries, and Gray kicked four goals, in a 17-8 win played out before a gate of 6,316.

Whilst in the South Island, a game was arranged to help out with the development of rugby league in that area. 'Finances were very short down there,' says Kevin, 'and we arrived at a little club ground in Greymouth to play a team called the South Islands. It was purely a goodwill gesture to boost finances, as we were so short of playing staff, especially with this leg of the tour's two hardest games still to come. We still had a final Test against New Zealand to consider and what many people called the fourth Test, against Auckland. The gate against South Islands was 1,728.'

Indeed, so stretched were the tourists' playing resources that coach Jim Challinor turned out for the side at centre. The second Test and the game at Greymouth were only two days apart. 'Jim had been a member of the terrific 1958 touring side and it had been 16 years since then,' says Kevin. 'He was a great bloke. Shortly after scoring a try, Jim was hit by a high tackle and dropped on with the knees, which left him in a poor condition. Our players were incensed by this terrible tackle and set about the dirty player involved. All hell was let loose on the pitch - and the touchline too - as we all bundled into this huge biff. Jim was never quite the same again after this incident, and the game ended in bad taste. We won it 33-2 but that is of no consequence. The damage was the injury to Jim Challinor.'

An unsavoury incident to be sure, but for now Challinor and his weary charges were forced to turn their attention back to Auckland, where they flew to play the final Test at Carlaw Park. The Kiwis selected their strongest possible squad to try and win the three-game series. It was: Collicoat; Brereton, O'Sullivan, Johnsen, Kerrigan; Williams, Stirling; Gailey, Hibbs, Don Mann, Robertson, Greengrass and Eade, the subs being Bob Jarvis and Peter Gurnick.

'We were running on empty,' admits Kevin. 'With all the injuries the same few lads were being called on to play eight games in twenty days, including three Tests, four if you count the Auckland game. Yet somehow they responded to the challenge and won the deciding Test by 20 points to nil in front of 11, 574.' Bevan (2), Hesketh and Dyl scored tries, while Gray kicked four goals. David Willicombe came into the centre for Colin Dixon, who dropped back into the second row for Steve Norton. Terry Clawson was at open-side prop for Jim Mills. The Great Britain team was: Charlton; Redfearn, Willicombe, Dyl, Bevan; Hesketh, Nash;

Clawson, Gray, Thompson, Dixon, Chisnall, Nicholls. Subs: Alan Bates and Bill Ramsey.

'With the series won, the adventure was almost over,' reflects Kevin. 'We had one final game and then it was back home to Blighty. Literally out on our feet, the Auckland side came at us firing on all cylinders. Although only one try was scored - by Auckland - the crowd of 7, 269 enjoyed the sight of their favourites beating old Great Britain, 11-2, on another damp afternoon. The final whistle sounded and that was it. We packed our bags and, although sad to be leaving the family we had become, we were ready to meet up again with our real families.'

The 1974 tour had also been a financial success - thanks to the second Test victory over Australia in Sydney, the decider had pulled in £56,000, leaving a record total profit margin of some £93,283. Upon departure, the party flew back to Britain the same way that it had come, via Hong Kong, although, in the case of Kevin Ashcroft and a couple of friends, not without mishap.

'With the six-hour refuelling time, John Bevan, Roger Millward and I had a few drinks in a bar inside the airport,' reveals Kevin. 'We were so deep in conversation that we missed the flight home. We phoned all the relevant people and were advised that we were booked in on a later flight. One of the international supporters, Dick Cocker, a coal man from Wigan, was on his way home from the tour and linked up with us. We finally arrived home and Dick and his daughter gave me a lift from Manchester Airport to home. I shook hands with Dick and kissed his daughter's cheek for the lift, just as Janet came out of the house to greet me. Unfortunately, Janet saw the peck I gave Dick's daughter in the car and thought the worst of me. I tried to explain but it was of no use. Shortly afterwards, when things had been explained, Janet was obviously pleased to see me and I her.

"I've seen in the newspaper," Janet said, "that the tour profits are a record. We will pay the house off with your share." There was no use lying. The truth was the only way out. "Sorry, love. I owe the Rugby Football League £37." What she said in reply is another story.'

CHAPTER SEVEN

Kevin arrived home from the Lions' tour on 17th August 1974, just six days before Warrington's first game of the new season, at home to St. Helens. In order to give his injured ankle more recovery time, however, and get himself back in the right frame of mind after a hectic last few months, Kevin took a few more days off.

When he did return to the fray, on 26th August, it was in a tough 8-8 draw against Widnes at Wilderspool, a game in which his drop-goal salvaged a point for Warrington. For a while, the ankle continued to play up a bit, swollen and sore after each game. But Kevin got by, applying ice to it after every match and training session. All in all, his form was good and his fitness - the ankle aside - was in great shape. Results, though, did not go his team's way. Two away games, against Rochdale in the Lancashire Cup and Leeds at Headingley, were lost 20-12 and 23-18 respectively. The latter game, in particular, was a classic.

'Headingley was a great ground to play on,' remembers

Kevin. 'It was long and wide and, in this game, an added attraction was the expected duel at stand-off between Alex Murphy and Syd Hynes, the two leading players in the 1971 Wembley drama. A dry ground and two good footballing sides - what more could the big crowd ask for?'

Both teams selected from strength. The Leeds side read: Dave Marshall; Alan Smith, John Langley, Les Dyl, John Atkinson; Syd Hynes, David Barham; Mick Harrison, Tony Fisher, Steve Pitchford, Phil Cookson, Geoff Clarkson and Bob Haigh, with John Holmes and Ray Batten on the bench. Warrington's team was: Derek Whitehead; Billy Pickup, Derek Noonan, Alan Whittle, John Bevan; Alex Murphy, Parry Gordon; Dave Chisnall, Kevin Ashcroft, Brian Brady, Mike Nicholas, Joe Price and Barry Philbin. Ian Mather was the only sub used.

As Kevin recalls: 'Syd Hynes sold a couple of dummies to send Phil Cookson in under the posts for Leeds, and Dave Marshall kicked the goal. The referee, Harry Hunt, then disallowed a Leeds try and we swept downfield from a play-the-ball. I managed to get Chissy away and he linked with Alan Whittle, who fed Derek Noonan, who handed back to Chissy who, in turn, passed to me. I went in under the posts and Derek Whitehead's conversion levelled the scores. Leeds soon fought back, though, and after Hynes put Cookson clean through again, the forward found Atkinson who, in turn, flung an inside lobbed pass that Marshall picked up and dived over, too far out to convert.

'The game was ebbing and flowing, and then Chissy broke and surprised Leeds with his pace. He ran sixty yards before Marshall stopped him with a great tackle. Chissy and Mike Nicholas combined well, but Mike failed to see Bevan in support and a chance was missed. Pitchford then sent Atkinson away for Leeds, and he showed his class as he beat Billy Pickup and Alex, only to fall for a brilliant Whitehead tackle, with Mr. Hunt ruling that Atkinson had used two movements to put the ball over the line and ruled no try. It was that sort of game, the crowd were going bonkers.

'On the stroke of half-time, Cookson, Pitchford and Atkinson worked a move that had Dyl chasing a kick through and he scored a try, with Marshall converting for a 13-7 Leeds lead at the break. Hynes went over early in the second half, too, after Cookson and Clarkson had done the damage, with Marshall goaling. It wasn't all bad news for us, though. I managed to win six scrums on the trot and when Murph worked his magic to send Bevan over, before Parry Gordon crossed for a cracking solo try, we had pulled it back to 18-13. Up popped Murph again. This time he shimmied across the Leeds defence, drew three tacklers, and slipped me a perfect reverse pass that opened the door to the posts. I accepted it, Whitehead converted, and it was 18-18 with eight minutes to play. By now, Leeds were blowing hard. But still they came at us and, after Marshall kicked a penalty goal, Dyl scored a beautiful solo try to give Leeds the win by 23-18.'

Two defeats in a row, then, but at least Warrington had run Leeds close. And when that narrow loss was followed by successive home wins against Featherstone Rovers, 26-7, Batley, 36-3 in the John Player Trophy, and Swinton, 10-5 in the BBC2 Floodlit competition, for Ashcroft and company the ship seemed well and truly steadied.

Meanwhile, on the representative scene, Lancashire had battled their way to a play-off with Yorkshire, after finishing joint-top of the County Championship. This year, to give the competition a four-team structure, the Championship had seen the admission of an Other Nationalities side. In earlier games, Cumbria had beaten Yorkshire who, in turn had beaten Lancashire. Other Nationalities lost all three of their games, so each of the original three counties had won two and lost one. Yorkshire and Lancashire, though, had the better points difference, and so it was they who played off for one of rugby league's most beautiful gold medals.

The match in question took place on 16th October at Widnes, where the referee was Mr. Joe Jackson of Pudsey. The attendance was a meagre 3,114 and the evening was a bitterly cold one. The Yorkshire team that night was: Les Sheard (Wakefield Trinity), Mike Lamb (Bradford Northern), Peter Roe (Keighley), Bruce Burton (Halifax), John Atkinson (Leeds), Dave Topliss (Wakefield Trinity), Alan Bates (Dewsbury), Mal Dixon (York), Dean Raistrick (Keighley), John Millington (Hull Kingston Rovers), Jeff Grayshon (Dewsbury), Bob Irving (Wigan), Steve Norton (Castleford). Subs: John Hughes (Bramley) and Mick Morgan (Wakefield Trinity). The Lancashire side read: Ray Dutton (Widnes), Stuart Wright (Wigan), Chris Hesketh (Salford), Derek Noonan (Warrington), Eric Hughes (Widnes), Kenny Gill (Salford), Parry Gordon (Warrington), Dave Chisnall (Warrington), Kevin Ashcroft (Warrington), Brian Brady (Warrington), George Nicholls (St. Helens), Eric Prescott (Salford), Barry Philbin (Warrington). The red rose subs were Mal Aspey (Widnes) and Tommy Martyn (Leigh).

That Lancashire went on to win the game, 29-11, owed much to the amount of possession won by Kevin in the set scrum. His superiority over Raistrick allowed Lancashire to register five tries. Noonan (2), Wright, Hesketh and Gill were the beneficiaries, while Dutton added seven goals. The Yorkshire reply came in the form of tries to Roe, Atkinson and Norton, and one goal by Burton. The medal Kevin received remains a particular favourite of his to this day.

* * *

Though Kevin had again enjoyed individual success on the representative stage, Warrington's form was now settling into an alarming pattern of up and down. Losses to York away, 10-5, Wigan at home, 17-11, and Dewsbury away, 11-10, along with wins over Dewsbury at home, 29-7, and Keighley away, 13-12, showed that inconsistency all too well. At least two further wins in the John Player Trophy and Floodlit Trophy, against Huyton and New Hunslet respectively, brought some relief.

Kevin had missed the Dewsbury loss and the New Hunslet victory because of a two-match ban, incurred for being sent off at home to Wigan. In the four games after beating Huyton, Warrington lost three more: Bradford Northern at home, 12-6, Salford away, 11-7, and Whitehaven away, 5-0, the latter result ending their interest that year in the John Player. The one victory during this time was against Featherstone Rovers, away, 13-7.

Hopes for the Floodlit Trophy, however, continued to burn brightly. After walloping Leigh 32-0 at home in the semi-final, Warrington were scheduled to face glamour side Salford, who had seen off Huddersfield, 16-2, St. Helens, 11-7, and then Hull Kingston Rovers, 27-10, in the other semi. Along with the victory over Leigh, the victims in Warrington's run to the final were Swinton, 10-5, and New Hunslet, 36-17. Salford won the toss for home ground and the game was played on Tuesday 17th December 1974 at the Willows.

Games between these two teams were usually tough, as seen in late November, when Salford won at the Willows, 11-7, in the league. Later, in mid-January, Warrington enjoyed a reversal of fortunes, 7-2, at Wilderspool. So, so, tight. The scene was set, then, for a close-run thing, although only 4,473 people turned up to watch it live, the rest tuning in on BBC2. The weather was cold and damp, as might be expected one week away from Christmas. Each coach had just about a full-strength squad to chose from, although the game's most notable gamebreaker, Alex Murphy, remained content to leave the job to his younger players, and did not come into contention. Alex had, in fact, only played four times since the start of the season. His influence, particularly in big cup-ties, was often missed.

On this particular occasion, the Salford team read: Paul Charlton; Keith Fielding, Chris Hesketh, Gordon Graham, Maurice Richards; Tom Brophy, Peter Banner; Mike Coulman, Ellis Devlin, Alan Grice, John Knighton, Colin Dixon and Eric Prescott, with David Taylor subbing. A confident Warrington side lined up: Derek Whitehead; Dave Sutton, Dave Cunliffe, Alan Whittle, John Bevan; Wilf Briggs, Parry Gordon; Dave Chisnall, Kevin Ashcroft, Dave Wright, Wayne Gaskell, Tom Conroy and Barry Philbin. Subs: John Lowe and Peter Jewitt.

The match turned out to be a dour forward-dominated affair, with Philbin conspicuous early on with his usual hard and straight-running. In such conditions, the dual threat of pacemen Fielding and Richards posed no problem for Warrington, especially with Kevin winning the scrums by a handsome margin. Gaskell went near to a try, as did Dave Chisnall, while Kevin was thrown back from the tryline on a couple of occasions, as he attempted to lunge over from a number of close-in play-the-balls. But after eighty minutes the stalemate refused to be broken and the teams would be forced to meet again to decide a winner, this time at Wilderspool.

For the Wire, their following five games continued to be marked by inconsistency. Two were lost, Wigan away, 20-6, and Castleford away, 20-8. Three were won, Rochdale Hornets away, 13-3, Leeds at home, 15-5, and that second league match with Salford, won 7-2 at home. Then, nine days after beating the Red Devils in the league, it was time to front up again in the replayed Floodlit Trophy final.

Both sides made changes for this rematch. A dry ground made the danger of the two Salford speedsters, Richards and Fielding, more real. At the Willows, the deep mud brought everyone down to the slowest speed, but the perfect Wilderspool pitch was made for the fast men. Alex Murphy reacted accordingly. His team read: Dave Cunliffe; Derek Whitehead, Billy Pickup, Alan Whittle, John Bevan; Derek Noonan, Parry Gordon; Dave Chisnall, Kevin Ashcroft, Bobby Wanbon, Tom Conroy, Mike Nicholas and Barry Philbin. His subs were Wilf Briggs and Brian Brady. Salford, desperate for a cup success, welcomed back key stand-off Ken Gill and moved David Watkins into the centre. The Salford front row was rejigged, too, in an effort to get some more ball to the speed merchants on their flanks. The Salford team read: Frank Stead; Keith Fielding, David Watkins, Chris Hesketh, Maurice Richards; Ken Gill, Peter Banner; Alan Grice, Peter Walker, Graham MacKay, Colin Dixon, John Knighton and Eric Prescott. The referee was again Billy Thompson from Huddersfield and the attendance was 5,778.

As before, Kevin again won the lion's share of ball from the scrum, but the biggest difference between this game and the original draw was that Salford, on the firmer surface, moved the ball more sharply out wide and, despite it being another very close game that could have gone either way, the pace of Fielding and Richards did the rest. Both of these wingmen raced over for tries, while Watkins added two goals against Warrington's reply of a superb Bevan try and one goal from Whitehead.

Fielding's try, in particular, was a beauty. Derek Whitehead's penalty kick at goal fell just short and 'Dai' Watkins caught the ball. From there, he ran into a gap, before passing to Fielding, who tore sixty yards for a magnificent solo effort. Referee Thompson immediately awarded a further penalty under the posts, as Fielding was fouled in the act of touching down, which Watkins converted to give his side a seven-point lead.

Whitehead reduced the arrears with a penalty goal of his own, but Richards then scored from deep, when a Warrington attack halted after a poor pass. Chris Hesketh swooped onto the ball to intercept and send Richards sprinting over for an unconverted try. John Bevan briefly raised Warrington hopes with a try that was the end product of a smart attack by Kevin, in which he beat two tacklers in midfield and put in a diagonal punt for Bevan to collect brilliantly and speed over by the corner flag. But as the weather again deteriorated, and the rain swept across the field, the five point advantage turned out to be enough to earn a win for Salford. The final score of 10-5 was about right, although the Red Devils had needed to fight to maintain their advantage.

Again, the Wire had missed the great matchwinner that was Alex Murphy. For Warrington, both of these games against Salford lacked that touch of brilliance that only Alex could bring. But he was the coach and had decided that the team he had purchased were good enough to win without him. Either way, the four cup season of last term was now but a fading a memory. Already gone were this season's Lancashire Cup and the Floodlit Trophy. The two left to play for were the Challenge Cup and the Championship play-off.

Kevin recalls: 'The Challenge Cup began with a home draw against Halifax. We were bang on form and recorded a 32-6 win. So into the draw we went, where we were given a plum tie against Wigan at Central Park.' In between those cup-ties, Warrington had a tricky game at home to Wakefield Trinity. 'They were a side full of pride and, whenever you played against them, they made it very difficult.' A try by Tommy Martyn and two goals by Derek Whitehead saw the Wire through, in a confidence-boosting 7-6 win.

'Wigan were waiting for us in round two,' continues Kevin, 'but our backs had a sharp look about them. As usual, Derek Whitehead was at full-back, while Paul Wharton, Wilf Briggs, Derek Noonan, John Bevan, Alan Whittle and Parry Gordon formed the rest of an excellent back division. The pack was fairly regular with Dave Chisnall, myself, Bobby Wanbon, Tom Conroy, Tommy Martyn and Barry Philbin starting, and Mike Nicholas on the bench. It was a rousing cup-tie which moved end to end from the very first whistle. And we again struck good form to beat the Wiganers by 24 points to 17.'

The third round of the Challenge Cup is traditionally accepted as the crucial one, and Warrington went into it on the back of a disappointing 38-20 defeat to Bradford at Odsal. This time, though, they were lucky enough to draw one of the less-fancied clubs, New Hunslet, albeit away.

'The weather had been bad over in the Leeds area,' remembers Kevin, 'and New Hunslet played on a ground that was just inside the legal size allowed by the Rugby Football League. It was short and narrow, with American gridiron-style tuning fork posts. The small pitch was under water almost all week, but we were told it would be cleared for the game day. It was too, but in a very unusual way. The New Hunslet club hired a helicopter to hover over the swimming pool-like pitch and blow the water away. Remarkably, the plan worked and the pitch was left soft but definitely playable. New Hunslet played in the middle of the Elland Road greyhound stadium, so that tells you all you need to know about the size of it.'

According to Kevin, Alex Murphy was worried that his players might be put off by all this, not to mention the fact that the New Hunslet players were notoriously hard tacklers on a narrow field that tended to make for down-the-middle rugby. 'It was a tough game,' says Kevin, 'but our bigger pack suited the pitch and we took Hunslet on at their own game. Mick Philbin (2), Dave Chisnall, Alan Whittle and Derek Whitehead scored our tries, and Whitehead landed four goals as we won, 23-3. The draw for the semi-final took place on Monday evening, with the games to be played the following Saturday. The four teams through were ourselves, Wakefield, Widnes and Leeds. No matter which team we drew, we knew it was going to be hard. And, as it happened, we drew Leeds. If they turned up ready to play, then it could be goodnight Vienna - we all remembered that cracking match at Headingley in September.'

Warrington, though, were about to clinch their second Wembley appearance in two seasons. And the atmosphere at Wilderspool when they did so was terrific. 'Ossie Davies put on an appreciation of the supporters night,' remembers Kevin. 'The fans were singing and chanting. There was a top table for the players and staff, and a question and answer session from the floor - it was a great night. Mick Philbin helped to make it so. When Brian Pitchford began paying his respects to the team, suddenly, out from the side of the stage, ran Mick, totally naked, to do a streak which left the astonished Mr. Pitchford speechless.'

Brian Pitchford was a very wealthy man indeed. 'He lived in a huge house in the the beautiful rural village of Appleton, south of Warrington,' says Kevin. 'And he had an expensive hobby in that he collected Napoleonic treasures. Brian had everything one could think of belonging to the great Emperor: saddles, hats, swords, medals, coats and even some of Napoleon's favourite statuettes in china clay. Before the team left for Wembley, he invited us players around to his house for tea. Alone in Brian's study, surrounded by possibly millions of pounds worth of treasures, Johnny Lowe picked up a small statue of the Emperor on horseback, brightly coloured and done in exquisite bone china. Not knowing its vast value, Johnny called out "catch" and passed the statue, rugby-like, to Alex, who dropped it! Off came the head of Napoleon and a hush fell over the squad. In a flash, Alex ran out to his car and back again, quick-time, carrying a tube of Superglue, which had then just gone on sale to the public. He carefully glued the head back on, making sure it was looking the right way, and the statue was restored. But from then on, every time Alex or Johnny saw Brian Pitchford they expected the worst, but it was never noticed.'

The Leeds route to the Challenge Cup semi-final was via Whitehaven away, Salford away and Bradford Northern home, all tough games. Their semi-final showdown with Warrington would be staged at Wigan's Central Park, while the Widnes versus Wakefield clash was at Odsal.

'We set our stall out to sicken the Leeds pack with heavy tackling,' says Kevin, in looking back on a memorable game. 'If we could hold the Leeds pack, that would starve their fast backs of the ball and stop the dangerous runs of Steve Pitchford and Phil Cookson. We also had to stop the ball-playing Ray Batten, who was so dangerous in midfield by slipping great passes to the fast-supporting Les Dyl and Bob Haigh. We talked about that game at Headingley, where we could so easily have won if we had taken our chances. Murph told us early that he wouldn't be playing and that his half-backs would be Alan Whittle and Parry Gordon. The side suddenly had taken on the look of last season's Wembley winners. Frank Reynolds was back in the centre, Mick Philbin on the wing and our confidence grew. These were hard-nosed professionals who knew how to win big matches.'

Warrington's semi-final team was: Derek Whitehead; Mick Philbin, Derek Noonan, Frank Reynolds, John Bevan; Alan Whittle, Parry Gordon; Dave Chisnall, Kevin Ashcroft,

Bobby Wanbon, Mike Nicholas, Tommy Martyn and Tom Conroy. The subs were Wilf Briggs and Brian Brady. Not surprisingly, the local newspapers had noticed that, should Warrington beat Leeds and Widnes beat Wakefield Trinity, the two final coaches would be Murphy and his mate Vince Karalius, now back coaching at Widnes.

'They made that a big story,' says Kevin. 'Alex and Vince had been friends in many a fabulously successful team for both St. Helens and Great Britain. They had been involved in wins at Wembley and in Australia, including the famous Battle of Brisbane in 1958, when Great Britain won against all the odds with only nine fully-fit men on the field.'

First, though, Warrington had to get past a formidable outfit. Kevin recalls: 'The pitch was nice and dry, which suited us and our quick backs. We worked to our strengths and our tackling that day was wonderful. Our trump card was John Bevan who was in great form, scoring a terrific hat-trick of tries. Each one was true international finishing. John was tremendous that day at Central Park and he broke the hearts of the Leeds side and supporters. Derek Whitehead kicked one goal and, in front of 14,000 spectators, we marched on to Wembley with an 11-4 victory.'

Once again, Warrington succumbed to a bout of Cup fever. 'There were so many people watching us train at Wilderspool that Murph took us down to Lousher Lane field to do our ball work, as there were no parking places left near the ground,' Kevin remembers. 'One evening, we snuck back to train at the stadium because no-one was there, they were all down at Lousher Lane. Somehow, someone heard we were up at Wilderspool and, suddenly, those big blue gates at the scoreboard end of the ground burst open and in rushed over 2,000 people, singing, shouting and cheering. Alex said: "I've never seen anything like this before, its incredible." But Warrington was a fairly demanding town. It had some very big works, breweries and business concerns. There was always plenty of work and its people were as well off as any in Lancashire. This was a rugby league town and they wanted a successful rugby league team.'

* * *

With a Challenge Cup final still ahead of them, Warrington faced another ten games in the league at least; more if they made the Championship play-offs. The first of those was against a Widnes team that had, by now, been confirmed as their Wembley opponents. 'Widnes away was always tough going,' reflects Kevin, 'and this certainly was. Alex wanted to make a big show as we knew that we would be playing them at Wembley and he loved to play mind games with the opposition.'

As it turned out, Warrington beat Widnes at Naughton Park in a very tight game, 11-7, thanks to tries by Mick Philbin and John Bevan, plus two goals from Derek Whitehead and a drop goal by Kevin. 'Of those ten games, we won nine and lost only one,' Kevin recalls, 'to Wakefield Trinity away, by 18 points to 10. The remainder we won comfortably. The hardest game score-wise was against Keighley at home, when we won 16-7.' Then came another visit to Bradford's Odsal Stadium, two weeks before Wembley, in a Championship play-off.

'I had missed a couple of games because of the ankle flaring up,' says Kevin, 'the win against Bramley at home by 23-8, and the defeat at Wakefield. Charlie Middlehurst stood in and did well in both games. I came back for the Odsal trip but, despite Dave Chisnall and Tom Conroy scoring tries, and Derek Whitehead kicking four goals, we lost 22-14. Northern were very much up for it. We now had what seemed an eternity to wait for the big one at Wembley.'

Alex Murphy prepared his side for this latest Wembley final in exactly the same way as he had approached the 1971 and 1974 showcases. It was Southport on Monday, through to Thursday morning, with players allowed to go home each afternoon. 'This was the way that Alex did things and he had been extraordinarily successful,' says Kevin. 'We used Hendon Hall, as we had done with Leigh, for our HQ, but the training was not as intense at Southport, as quite a few of the Cup final team were carrying knocks. So Murph nursed the squad through training and had meetings where he talked about Widnes, what made them tick, their strengths and weaknesses, what each key player did on the field and what Vince Karalius, their coach, would be telling them about Warrington.'

One of the directors at Lockers, Kevin's place of work, was Mr. John Dutton, who had since taken over the chairman's job at Leigh. He sought Kevin out, to see if everything was all right with him at Warrington. Kevin knew that Mr. Dutton wanted to sign him, but he was committed to Warrington.

In any case, for now, Kevin's eyes were only on the Challenge Cup final. Warrington travelled down to London on the Thursday afternoon and Alex warned his players not to talk back to Peter Geraghty, the referee from York, as he would be sure to award penalties against them. As the big day approached, Murphy hammered it home: no back-chatting the ref. Once at the hotel, things were free and easy all day Friday and, once again, it was off to the dogs on the Friday evening. From there, it was back to the hotel and a relaxing time playing cards or reading, before an early night to awake fresh as a daisy on matchday morning.

There was one problem on the horizon, however. Parry Gordon had complained about a sore throat when training at Southport. The club doctor diagnosed a slight throat infection and Parry took his antibiotics religiously right up to Alex's deadline for a decision. To play or not to play, that was the question. In the end, the half-back said that he was fit, thereby ending any speculation that Murphy himself would feature somewhere in the playing of this game.

This year, the dignitary presented to the teams was Her Royal Highness Princess Alexandra, the Hon. Mrs Angus Ogilvy, who also presented the Challenge Cup itself. For a change, there was little talk between the rival factions ahead of the game, because the two coaches had too much respect for each other than to start a slanging match. There was one interview, though, in which Vince Karalius made a very good point indeed. When asked about the likely outcome, he said: 'I shall take thirteen athletes onto the field for what is ninety-nine per cent a physical game. Widnes will not be found wanting for lack of physical condition.' So did it come to pass. As Jack Winstanley, the great rugby league writer, noted at the time: 'And outstanding athletes they turned out to be. Widnes were a homespun team of lads who beat the Cup holders, Warrington, making them as despondent in defeat as they had been deliriously happy in winning the Challenge Cup twelve months earlier.'

The teams for what was, sadly, a rather colourless final played out before a crowd of 87,000 were as follows. Widnes: Ray Dutton; Alan Prescott, Mick George, Mal Aspey, Chris Anderson; Eric Hughes, Reg Bowden; Jim Mills, Keith Elwell, Barry Sheridan, Mick Adams, John Foran, Doug Laughton. Subs: Tony Karalius and Nick Nelson. Warrington: Derek Whitehead; Mick Philbin, Derek Noonan, Frank Reynolds, John Bevan; Alan Whittle, Parry Gordon; Dave Chisnall, Kevin Ashcroft, Bobby Wanbon, Tom Conroy, Tommy Martyn, Barry Philbin. Their subs were Wilf Briggs and Mike Nicholas.

John Bevan's early try and a Whitehead conversion did

nothing to damage the Widnes spirit and, for once, Warrington's fearsome pack was bettered. In a 14-7 win, full-back Ray Dutton's five goals and a one-point drop goal, plus a Jim Mills try, gave Widnes their points, whilst Warrington could only find Bevan's try and two Whitehead goals in reply. Kevin tells of a conversation that took place afterwards, with his Lions tour room-mate Jim Mills. 'Big Jim greeted me in the tea room and said: "Well, Ashy, how bad was that? It was one awful game." That just about summed it up because both of us missed vital scoring chances that normally would have earned points. I was so frustrated with Peter Geraghty's decisions that I actually couldn't help saying to him: "Peter, do you know the laws of the game?" Quite rightly, he gave a penalty against me. Possibly, Peter let the magnitude of the occasion get to him. But I can't blame Peter for us not playing well, and a thought did cross my mind that we might all be growing old together at Warrington.'

Kevin continues: 'Arguably, we had been the best side in the country for two seasons, but we were all knocking on when we first got together, and that great four-cup season may well have been the peak. It could be all downhill from here. Could that thought have been brought on by us being so confident before the final? We thought at Wilderspool that we were untouchable. Not big-headed in any way, but we were so confident that when we were beaten, albeit by a mere seven points, it really made us think about our vulnerability. On the day, I suppose, Widnes were the better side, and that was a big reason for thinking that the Cup-winning party for this Warrington team could be over. It was certainly food for thought.'

And speaking of food: 'We had our usual after-Wembley banquet with the wives and partners at the hotel,' says Kevin, 'and we all felt terrible. It was like a bad dream. But we survived and the trip home on the coach the following day was again strange, as a lot of the players were asking "What about the supporters? Will they be out in strength or will they shout abuse?" Well, as we approached Warrington, the crowd began to thicken and it was obvious well before the Town Hall that the supporters were still with us, bless 'em. There were thousands upon thousands milling around the Town Hall, calling for the players and cheering when we waved at them. It was very moving that so many people could be so much behind us, even when we had just let them down at Wembley.'

Kevin had easily topped the Warrington tackle count in the final. Vince Karalius was as forthright as ever when he said after the game: 'We murdered 'em. We were too fit and fast.' Alex had simply said: 'Things can go wrong despite all your preparations. After all, the Titanic sank, didn't it?' All these things were going through Kevin's mind, along with another fact that he had been contemplating for a while. In playing at this high-profile level, he found that more and more he was being targeted by all the young gun hookers, who wanted him on their CV under: 'I did Ashcroft'. Increasingly, his time on the field was spent practising self-defence rather than playing rugby league. Cut head, split eyebrow, black eyes... he was coming home each weekend to Janet with injuries great and small. Now, Kevin was always one for a challenge, so long as he was enjoying it. At this stage of his career, his enjoyment in playing was draining away. Kevin needed another outlet in the game; not because he was spitting the dummy or anything like that, this was a genuine feeling of needing a change of direction. It never really dawned on him that he had played his final game for Warrington but, in fact, he had.

* * *

Mr. John Dutton, the Leigh chairman and Lockers director, was a very persuasive gentleman and a good friend of Kevin and his family. After the dust had settled on the Wembley final, he and Kevin discussed the latter's feelings about being in the big league. Mr. Dutton listened intently to Kevin's description of how, at thirty years of age, he wanted his career to take a different direction. Mr. Dutton suggested that a role at another club as, say, coach or player-coach might be more suitable for Kevin, as his playing retirement approached. And with that he offered him the job of captain and coach at Leigh.

There was no real doubt that Kevin would accept such an offer but, before he did, he knew he had to make it right with two gentlemen of whom he thought the world, Ossie Davies and Brian Pitchford. Firstly, he had to ask to be transferred. Secondly, he had to leave, football-wise, two very dear friends. Kevin explained his need for a different direction and that he thought coaching could be the answer. Initially, both men were against the move but, with the help of Mr. Dutton, a deal was eventually done with extreme sadness.

Kevin's coaching predecessor at Leigh had been the highly-respected Eddie Cheetham. The club were relegated into division two with Les Pearce as coach in 1973/74 and, under Cheetham, had not managed to bounce straight back. Kevin understood the game and felt he knew what was needed to gain promotion and return Leigh to the big league of first division football. He went to Salford and asked for his old pack-mate Paul Grimes and John Corcoran on loan. Similar requests to Whitehaven and Dewsbury brought John McVay and Phil Evans to Hilton Park. In the cases of Corcoran, McVay and Evans though, only seven games in total were realised from the three players. Corcoran played three times, Evans three times and John McVay once.

As usual, Kevin maintained his fitness throughout the close-season and the new experience of handling a coach's job gave his enthusiasm the impetus it needed. His interest in the game returned. Kevin's team began to look right and he began by building his pack as a driving force. Size always helps up front and, under Kevin, the Leigh props were all big men. Steve Breheney, who went on to wrestle in the WWE in America, was signed from Blackpool Borough. Other props included Alf Wilkinson, Geoff Fletcher, Maurice Platt, Dennis Carden and Allan Rowley. Kevin's back three was made up of big units too, whether it be Paul Grimes, Clive Jones, the tough Welshman signed from Warrington, Dave Mako from Widnes or Keith Clarke in those roles. A couple of front-rowers, Platt and Rowley, often doubled up as second-rowers. At loose forward, was Dennis Boyd, renowned for his blitzing defence and hard running. With Kevin slotted in at hooker, the Leigh pack was sound.

In the backs, Mick Hogan was a very good full-back, a local boy signed from the Leigh 'B' team. The wingmen, too, were excellent local(ish) lads; John Davies from St. Helens 'B', Kevin's old mate Joe Walsh, Alva Drummond, brother of Des, and Terry Bilsbury from Leigh Colts. The centres were Mick Stacey and Steve Grimshaw from Leigh Colts, and Wilf Briggs, whom Kevin brought from Warrington. Stand-off John Taylor came from Oldham and others who filled in at number six were Mick Hogan and John McAtee, who signed from Langworthy Juniors in Manchester. McAtee also filled in at scrum-half for the regular choice, Cliff Sayer, who also signed from Oldham. Kevin's goal-kicker for his first season as player-coach was Mick Stacey, who did an excellent job. Stacey had 137 successful shots at goal, while also notching nineteen tries.

With Kevin Ashcroft at the helm, Leigh enjoyed a far better season and did indeed gain a surprise promotion back to division one. Concentrating on the league, with any Cup runs a bonus, they did however make a disastrous start with two defeats, albeit by very close margins, Whitehaven away, 2-0, and Rochdale Hornets at home, 5-2. The Cup campaigns began with the Lancashire Cup and a good win over Blackpool Borough away, 11-3. But the second round pitched them against first division Salford at Hilton Park, where a crushing defeat followed, 23 points to 6. A good home win against Hull FC then set Leigh up for a home cup-tie with Featherstone Rovers, and a cracking 17-12 victory in the first round of the John Player Trophy. League wins against Huyton away, 26-5, York away, 15-14, and Batley at home, 30-7, were the preamble to a 12-7 defeat at Craven Park, Barrow, in the first round of the Floodlit Trophy. Only three days after that defeat, Leigh played at Barrow again in the league and lost 9-6, before falling 21-11 away at Hull FC and going down 23-8 to Hull Kingston Rovers away in round two of the John Player, despite enjoying a good 31-4 win over Whitehaven in between.

As the league season progressed, a run of five wins followed: Bramley at home 13-4, Halifax on the road 39-24, York at home 29-12, Blackpool away, 9-6, and Blackpool at home 44-2. In their final fifteen games, Leigh were beaten only three times: Rochdale away, 10-9, Workington at home, 14-7, and Keighley away in the third round of the Challenge Cup, 13-7. The return league game against Barrow showed the competitive nature of the division. After losing in the two previous meetings, this time the game at Hilton Park was a punishing 9-9 draw.

In the 1975/76 season, it was a case of four up and four down when it came to promotion and relegation between the two divisions. Leigh found themselves promoted in fourth place and so back into the first division they proudly went. As a coach, Kevin had been a revelation. He handled all coaching matters with aplomb, including the buying and selling of players and the organisation of training schedules. Above all, Kevin led by example, playing in all thirty-four games in Leigh's season, scoring three tries and dropping three goals in the process.

Not surprisingly, his experiences as a coach were also teaching Kevin how to handle players. Mick Hogan, for example, was a very special player. The full-back played in thirty-three games that season and was a key figure in the side. As a coach, Kevin had one really strict condition for his players: no boozing the night before a game. Mick Hogan liked a pint or two but, as far as Kevin was concerned, all the players accepted his condition.

Early one Sunday morning Kevin was awakened by a phone call. It was Mick Hogan's dad. 'Can you come round and speak to our Mick,' he asked. Kevin went around straight away. There, in the house, sat Mick Hogan, battered and bruised. He had been pulled into a fight at a nightclub. Mick said he was sorry and that he couldn't play that afternoon. 'You will play,' said Kevin. 'Your mates are relying on you playing. Get to the ground a bit earlier and let the physio have a look at you.' This the lad did, before repaying Kevin's trust by scoring a one hundred-yard try. After winning the game, the players were all getting ready to go out for a pint until Kevin stopped Mick and said to him: 'Where are you going? You had your drink last night when the rest of the lads were at home. Now, you go home and I will phone you some time during the evening and you had better be in.' Kevin did phone and Mick's dad answered. 'He is here, Kevin,' he said. 'He is sat watching a film on TV, eating a packet of crisps. I don't know what you said to him, but it did the trick.'

Kevin's return to Hilton Park was initially viewed with suspicion by some Leigh supporters, who had earlier considered his move to Warrington an act tantamount to treason, even though it was actually Alex Murphy, Dave Chisnall and Geoff Clarkson who had left first, almost immediately after the Challenge Cup win of 1971. In fact, Kevin played thirty-two games and subbed four times for Leigh after that. Returning Leigh to the first division as coach, though, reinstated Kevin Ashcroft as a local hero.

With promotion confirmed, work now had to begin on strengthening the team for the first division. Kevin swooped for his old pack-mate, Dave Chisnall, who had since moved from Warrington to Swinton. He signed three juniors from the Leigh Colts side who went on to play for Great Britain: John Woods, on his day one of the best footballers ever to play the game; Des Drummond, a regular at international level for many years and a great finishing wingman; and the tough-as-teak Alan Rathbone, a fine forward who later played for Bradford Northern and Leeds. All three made their debut under Kevin's leadership. The return to his beloved hometown club was going well.

* * *

For all his varied track record in the game, when talking to Kevin nowadays, he can be relied upon to wax lyrical about one particular club. One might imagine that his first side, Dewsbury, must still be Kevin's favourite. If so, one would be wrong. Maybe Warrington, where he won so many honours, top the list? No. Perhaps surprisingly, nor does that honour fall to Leigh. In fact, Kevin will tell you that his favourite club was Rochdale Hornets.

Looking back, Kevin says that his days at the Hornets with his childhood hero Stan Owen were the best. 'Stan taught me more about scrummaging than anyone else,' he confirms.' When I had big Stan with me I was as safe as houses. When he set those legs of his and he got a grip of the opposite prop, he was immovable, a rock. I had plenty of good props in my career, Peter Birchall, Bill Payne, Charlie Winslade, Dave Chisnall, Dennis Hartley, Cliff Watson, Brian Brady, but of all those great scrummagers Stan Owen was the best.'

With his youthful dreams of packing at the side of big Stan fulfilled, Kevin also greatly admired the chairman at Rochdale, Arthur Walker, a real character. 'Arthur was an entrepreneur, into nightclubs, pubs, anything that could maintain his super Rolls Royce motor car,' says Kevin. 'There was a very tough council estate near the old Athletic Grounds and I would say to Arthur: "You have a bloody nerve driving the roller through that estate, it's a wonder they don't ambush you and dip you." But Arthur Walker could look after himself.' Kevin liked Arthur because whilst he was a successful businessman and dealt sometimes with dodgy characters, if he said the players would get £1,000 then they would get it. He was a man of his word.

Season 1976-77 began well for Kevin and the Leigh side. A 41-13 win over Whitehaven in the first round of the Lancashire Cup at Hilton Park had the Leigh faithful in seventh heaven. They were even happier the following week, when Leigh went to Central Park in the second round and beat Wigan, 16-14. Barrow were then beaten at home, 18-8, before two defeats by Widnes at home, 24-16, in the Lancashire Cup semi-final, and Castleford away, 28-12, in the league introduced a note of reality. Then Warrington came to Hilton Park, in round one of the Floodlit Trophy.

Kevin's try helped to beat the Wire, 11-10, and that narrow success was followed by a marginally more comfortable 19-13 win at home to Oldham. By then, though, Kevin had gradually come to realise that the thinking of his chairman, Mr. Dutton, was not entirely at one with his own.

One or two suggestions were being made with regard to cutting the players' winning money, perhaps by as much as £45 for a win to £30. Kevin advised his chairman that to do so would cause eruptions in the dressing room. Mr. Dutton had come to Leigh with the intention of sorting the club out financially. This he did, in a very short time, but, like many men before him, he tried to make more money for the club on the backs of the players.

The situation grew uneasy between the chairman and Kevin as the board, along with the coach, knew the problems that a cut in player payments would bring. As the season progressed, St. Helens won at Hilton Park, 20-5, and Leeds beat Leigh at Headingley, 19-10. Salford were the next visitors to Leigh in round two of the Floodlit Trophy and, in a tremendous game, Leigh were victorious, 22-18. Five days later, though, Featherstone Rovers came to Hilton Park and won, 8-4. Things were busier than ever on the field, as the Floodlit games were being played on Tuesday evenings, the league games on Sundays and the start of the John Player Trophy was due to start soon too.

Despite all these matches, Leigh were holding their own in the first division. A 27-15 defeat at Widnes was followed by a thrilling draw at home to Bradford Northern, 12-12. Swinton were entertained at Hilton Park in the first round of the John Player Trophy and Leigh saw them off with a fine 29-7 victory. After a heavy defeat at Post Office Road, Featherstone, by 29-9, Leigh went on a terrific six-match winning run: Oldham away in round two of the John Player, 28-13; Leeds at home in the league, 25-11; Hull FC at home in round three of the John Player Trophy, 17-12; Wigan at home in round two of the Floodlit Trophy, 12-5; Rochdale at home in the league, 17-6; and Huddersfield at home in the BBC Floodlit Trophy semi-final, 19-10.

Instead of building on such a growth in confidence, this

fantastic run of form again prompted Mr. Dutton to resume his efforts to cut winning money by £15 per game. On 11th December 1976, Leigh travelled to the west coast to play division two side Blackpool Borough in the John Player semi-final at Borough Park. The Seasiders had fought their way bravely to the semi and beaten some good teams to get there. Kevin remembers with a grimace: 'We made the mistake of thinking that all we had to do was turn up and they would surrender. It was a mistake.' Playing well above their league position, Blackpool pulled off another giant-killing performance with a 15-5 win. The game was full of incident. 'We went over their line four times and recorded one try,' says Kevin. 'The biggest miss was when John Taylor ran clear and, with only yards to run to score, his hamstring pulled and he had to stop short of the line. It was one of those games. Blackpool harried us into making mistakes. We couldn't put three passes together before we dropped the ball. As it was, we were lucky to find our way to the dressing rooms.'

Three days later, on Tuesday 14th December, Kevin had to get his troops up for the Floodlit Trophy final. Their opponents were an excellent Castleford side, captained by Malcolm Reilly. The feeling around Hilton Park was still one of disbelief that the semi-final against Blackpool had gone badly. At least the luck of the draw was with Leigh this time, the final would be played at their home ground.

The Castleford team that evening read: Geoff Wraith; Steve Fenton, John Joyner, Phil Johnson, Jamie Walsh; Bruce Burton, Gary Stephens; Paul Khan, Bobby Spurr, Alan Dickinson, Mal Reilly, Sammy Lloyd and Steve Norton. Leigh lined up: Mick Hogan; Alan Prescott, Mick Stacey, John Woods, Joe Walsh; John Taylor, Cliff Sayer; Dave Chisnall, Kevin Ashcroft, Geoff Fletcher, Dave Macko, Paul Grimes and Dennis Boyd.

After the debacle at Blackpool, Kevin was determined not to let the club's supporters down again. He set about firing his side up which, with home advantage, was not too difficult to do. Stephens, at half-back, was a box of tricks for classy Cas, but Leigh responded well to Kevin's prompting and his drop-goal gave them a half-time lead. In those days, in-form Castleford were top of the league but Leigh, too, had enjoyed a good return to the higher division and could take on anyone.

As usual, only the second half of the game was televised live on BBC2 and Castleford, completely shocked by Leigh's tigerish defence in the first half, saved their best for the cameras. Stephens continued his good work, while Reilly and Khan, the big Aussie prop, began to find little gaps in the home defence. Despite the tackling heroics of Taylor, Hogan, Ashcroft and Grimes, the 1-0 lead was lost as Jamie Walsh and Bruce Burton raced in for tries, and Sammy Lloyd added the conversions and a penalty goal. Game to the end, Joe Walsh produced one of his special tries to restore home pride with a blockbusting run, but the Trophy went back over the hill to Yorkshire thanks to a 12-4 Castleford victory.

Kevin was pleased with the effort after the terrible showing at Blackpool, but his meetings with the chairman were turning into verbal battles over his intention to cut the winning pay. Having straightened out the Leigh finances, Mr. Dutton seemingly now wanted to justify his reputation as a good manager further at the expense of the men in the front line. Kevin, forthright as ever, told him this and relations between the pair became strained.

In the next away game at the Willows, Salford were put to the sword in cracking style, 13-12, with another Ashcroft drop-goal the deciding factor. Leigh were now well and truly back on track. Then, Kevin's worst fears came true and winning pay was cut by £15. Kevin should have been given a medal for keeping his team from upping sticks and walking out on the spot. The following game, away to Hull Kingston Rovers, not only ended in a 23-9 defeat, it saw the debut of an all-time great in the red and white of Leigh, Des Drummond. That was followed by a 9-4 loss at Wilderspool and a home game against Castleford, which ended 12-2 to the visitors. Rightfully, the players were disgruntled and out of sorts at the apparent rough-riding over their agreed terms. There had been no warning of a pay cut, until it came into place after the great win at Salford. Kevin had known it may be imminent, but hoped that Mr. Dutton may see sense and withdraw his intention.

Attendances were as good as they ever had been with an average of around 4,000 per game, some as high as 6,500, and 6,000 for the cup-ties with Wigan and Hull FC. It was the Salford game at home, though, that brought the match money crisis to a head. As Kevin tells it: 'I just could not make the chairman realise what the outcome of pay cuts would be. These players had an agreement with the chairman to pay £45 a win for this season. It was standard pay in the first division and, no doubt, if the club had suddenly gone skint then the players would have helped out by taking a cut to support it. But this was a dirty trick. The chairman had done a turnaround on his word and that was something that even I could not heal. The players were numbed by this seeming lack of thought. No matter what anyone says about loyalty by players to clubs, it goes out of the window when the players are cheated by the chairman. Not many players play just for the money. Some do and did in the days we are talking about, but the vast majority of players are ordinary lads wanting to play for Leigh, Rochdale, Oldham, Bramley, Featherstone or any team, to accept the challenge of playing at the highest level their own ability allows. But when a guy, who shows no loyalty or respect for them, suddenly decides to strip one third of their winning pay simply to enhance his own standing, then he is in for trouble. Mr. Dutton was a managing director for a massive business concern and, if you ask me, had no idea of the working class culture of the Leigh people. They just could not accept the way he rode roughshod over their feelings.'

Increasingly, the Leigh faithful on the terraces grew to suspect that something was totally and irrevocably wrong with their side. 'Naturally,' says Kevin, 'many of them thought this was something to do with me! Throughout the first half of a game against Salford we were being slaughtered and the chanting of "what a load of rubbish" didn't help. Walking off at half-time, we had to endure further cat calls and I was livid that this inexperienced rugby league chairman could turn the great folk of our little town, that prided itself on its rugby league team, against us. Calling the kit man over to me, I asked him to nip up into the board room and ask the chairman if he would kindly come into the dressing room, immediately, to talk to the players. I had taken enough, what with trying to hide his incompetence. The kit man came back to tell me that the chairman would not allow me into the board room or listen to me. We went out for the second half and I knew that if he didn't see sense then my position was untenable.'

The result of the game, not surprisingly, was a good hiding for Leigh by 45 points to 8. Kevin had to go and find the chairman and fronted him there and then. 'This season will end in disaster if you don't honour your word to the players,' Kevin told him. Mr. Dutton retorted by asking Kevin if he knew to whom he was speaking. Kevin told him what he could do with himself - which was a physical impossibility, actually - said goodbye to the players, his assistant Tommy Grainey and walked out of the club, never to return.

The season, as predicted, fell apart. Up until the cut in pay, Leigh had won fourteen Cup and league games, drawn one and lost only eight. They had beaten the old enemy, Wigan, both home and away. After the win at Salford, Leigh won only three of their remaining nineteen games. The club was in turmoil. Wigan visited Hilton Park in the league and won by 40 points to nil! A grand servant of Leigh, Billy Kindon, took over as caretaker coach, but the die was cast and the club was relegated. At the final league game of what became a dreadful season, only 1,500 supporters attended.

Some eight years later, John Dutton's long-serving secretary phoned Kevin to tell him that John was dying. Kevin went to see him and it was a good reunion. In fact, Kevin visited his former chairman several times over the following months and, to add to John Dutton's misery, his wife died suddenly, leaving him completely alone. He was well enough off to hire live-in help but, when he did finally pass away, Kevin was glad that he and John had managed to become friends again.

* * *

So, for the first time ever, Kevin found himself out of football on the 23rd January 1977. Asked what he did with his time during that period, he says: 'worked and slept'. It wasn't long, though, before he received a phone call from an old friend, the secretary of Rochdale Hornets, who asked Kevin if he would come to meet Ray Taylor and himself at the club. Kevin was asked if he would consider helping Hornets for around ten matches, until they could sort things out. His strong feelings for the club made him jump at the chance of playing there again; Rochdale had given him such a lift early in his career.

His mind made up, Kevin trained hard throughout the

summer and joined in pre-season training. Going back to Hornets reminded Kevin of the days when the club's famous Fijians had first arrived there. Stan Owen was at training one night and the coach, Johnny Noon, had asked him if he would nip around to the Fijian boys' lodgings. Stan arrived at the house and knocked on the door, but there was no answer. In went big Stan, up the stairs and into a bedroom, in which there were two double beds. In the beds were four Fijians. Each one was dressed in wartime surplus Army great coats, with lots of blankets piled on top of them, shivering with cold. 'Come on boys,' Stan said. 'Up you get, you're late." And, with that, Stan flung back the blankets, pulled them all out of bed, and took them off to training. Kevin agrees that it was so cold at Rochdale he once had to train in his sheepskin coat.

One giant Fijian, Liatia Ravouvou, took size fifteen boots, Kevin remembers. Only problem was that, back in Fiji, the players didn't wear boots, they played on those hard sun-baked grounds in bare feet. Over here, it was freezing mud and so Kevin had to take the newcomers over to Walsh's boot makers in Bolton, to be measured up for a handmade pair. When Norman Walsh came to measure Ravouvou, he turned to Kevin and, in his rich Bolton dialect, said: 'Them others were all right at £15 a pair, but yon fella, you'll need more than £15 for 'im. Have you sin them feet? They're like battleships.' So, big Ravouvou had his boots made but hated wearing them. Kevin still smiles when he says: 'He took them off to train one evening and little Jimmy Gaskell, the half-back, was coming back from a torn hamstring. Ravouvou had just thrown these kangaroo skin boots worth £40 down and little Jimmy was steadily running a circuit of laps. He tripped over one of Ravouvou's boots and did his hamstring again.'

In this latest spell at Rochdale, Kel Coslett had also just

come to the club from St. Helens as player-coach, and he had a decent squad at his disposal. It included John Maloney, Norman Brelsford, Paul Longstaff, Tony Wainwright, Alan Hodkinson, Warren Ayres, Bob Irving, Charlie Birdsall, Alan Grice, Paul O'Neill, Tony Halmshaw and Tony Gourley. With Coslett himself and Kevin thrown in for good measure, that was not a bad side at all.

In time, the ten games that Kevin promised to play turned into twenty-three, as the club saw great potential in young hooker Paul O'Neill but did not want to rush him in too soon. Paul learned much under the guidance of Kevin, who enjoyed his return to Rochdale. Hornets had some good results during his second stay, including an impressive 4-4 draw with St. Helens in the Lancashire Cup, although the replay favoured Saints, 16-5. There was also a 49-8 win over Halifax at Rochdale, in which Kevin scored a hat-trick of tries, two doubles over Huddersfield and Keighley, and a great double over arch-enemies Oldham. Soon, though, Kevin was on his way again.

This latest move began with a telephone call from Alex Murphy, who was by then coaching Salford. It was followed by a further call from the highly-respected chairman at the Willows, Mr. John Wilkinson. The Red Devils had a star studded back division in those days, full of internationals and crowd-pleasing entertainers. Their pack, though, just lacked a bit of true devil in them, or what the Australians call 'mongerel'. Some of the Salford forwards had it but, if the club was to be a world-beater, then they all must have it. No doubt that is why Murph and John Wilkie, as he is affectionately known, went for Kevin in the first place, along with his old Warrington pal, Barry Philbin.

Salford were and are a great club with great traditions. Their signings prove that. They can also boast the sport's first purpose-built Variety club inside the ground, where a tremendous evening's entertainment could be had with big name turns and a civilised meal. On the playing side, Kevin was pleased to be linking up with his tour-mates, Chris Hesketh, Dai Watkins, Colin Dixon, Maurice Richards, Steve Nash, John Butler and Kenny Gill. He also linked up again with his childhood friend and former Leigh team-mate Tommy Grainey, as well as another one-time Leigh team-mate from the glory era, Bobby Welding. Both Tommy and Bobby were on Alex Murphy's coaching staff although, later that season, Grainey returned to Leigh as coach, in place of John Mantle.

Despite being settled at Salford and enjoying his time there, Kevin had little luck in the various Cup competitions staged throughout that first season. After good wins in the Lancashire Cup in rounds one and two against Oldham, at home, 30-15, and Whitehaven away, 19-6, Workington Town came to the Willows in the semi-final and won 9-8. A bitter disappointment. The John Player Trophy brought home success against Rochdale Hornets in round one, 25-7, but another close defeat in round two at Craven Park against Hull KR, finished 16-14 to the opposition. Still, when Salford were then beaten 17-15 by St. Helens in the Floodlit Trophy, it showed just how near they were to winning a major trophy.

In February, the Challenge Cup came around and, in the first round, Salford were drawn to play Bramley at the Willows. At that time, Bramley were coached by the tough former-player, Les Pearce. This particular cup-tie produced a most unusual series of games, three in all, as the first round, expected by most to be a walk-over, was a death or glory battle which ended 6-6. The replay at McLaren Field was a carbon copy, a real battle ending in a 2-2 draw. The second replay was then held on the magnificent old Station Road ground at Swinton, where an unbelievable scoreline of

7-5 to Bramley ended one of the most exciting and controversial Cup encounters in the history of the game. Legend has it that, in one of the games, played between 11th February and 1st March, an irate Salford fan and renowned tough customer made the mistake of 'calling out' Les Pearce as he walked from the pitch. Les proved too much of a handful for the upset supporter and the argument was over in double quick-time. After settling matters, Les walked away to the dressing rooms leaving the sorry man asleep, to cheers from the travelling Bramley contingent.

With no further interest in any of the Cups, Salford's good but ageing side just about cleared the top-flight's four-team relegation zone. In fact, they finished twelfth in a division of sixteen. The four who took the drop were Barrow, Featherstone, Rochdale Hornets and Huddersfield. The teams replacing them were Hull FC, New Hunslet, York and Blackpool Borough. Kevin's appearance record was an exemplary thirty-five games played, and one as substitute, from a season total of forty.

When Tommy Grainey moved to Leigh, Kevin moved up to the role of player-assistant coach, as Salford entered season 1979/80, the Centenary year of the club. By now, Kevin was easing away from the playing side of the game and bolstering his coaching experience. He did play in key matches, including the run to the John Player Trophy semi-final, played at Warrington's Wilderspool stadium, against Widnes. Unfortunately, Salford were heavily outplayed on the day and the Chemics won their way to the final with a 19-3 win. Progress in the BBC Floodlit Trophy was halted by a 15-10 defeat against St. Helens at Knowsley Road in round two, after a great first-round win over Wigan at home. Knocked out of the County Cup in round one by the hard Workington Town outfit up at Derwent Park, things looked rosey in the Challenge Cup, with wins over Huyton away,

25-0, and then Rochdale Hornets away, 20-5. The third round, though, brought a meeting with nemesis, Widnes, the Cup kings, and with it a dreadfully unlucky 9-8 home defeat. Out of all the Cups again, Salford's league form was nevertheless good enough to earn them fourth position in the final league table and a home draw in the top-eight Championship play-offs. Fifth-placed Leeds were the opponents and, in the warm conditions, a fast and open gala of a game ensued from two sides known for playing attacking football. In the end, though, it was Leeds who won an entertaining tussle, 27-13.

A further highlight of this season without silverware was the Willows' Centenary game, played against the stadium's first visitors of one hundred years before, the dreaded Widnes. Again, this was a good open and entertaining game that, this time, produced a 16-16 draw.

* * *

Season 1980-81 saw Kevin start in only three games: Oldham away in the Lancashire Cup; Halifax at home in the league; and Leeds away in the league. He also subbed in four games: Castleford away in the league; Workington Town at home in the league; and Wigan and Castleford at home in the John Player Trophy. In the Oldham County Cup game, Kevin played at blind-side prop.

Then, on 9th November, Salford were beaten 42-18 by Wakefield Trinity at Belle Vue and their coach, Alex Murphy, resigned a day later. Kevin was asked to take over in the role and that is exactly what he did. The retirements of Mike Coulman, Dai Watkins, Kenny Gill, Chris Hesketh and Colin Dixon had left a huge hole in the Salford armoury. Kevin also lost one of his toughest pack men when loose forward Eric Prescott was transferred to Widnes. That pack was strengthened a little when Mike Coulman returned to help out along with the experienced Bill Sheffield, but a downward spiral was established that proved almost impossible to escape. Most teams who lose a respected coach during a season hit the skids and Salford were no exception. They were relegated into division two in a most unusual season in which all four bottom clubs had a fairly large number of league points. Halifax went down with twenty-two points, Salford and Workington twenty-one apiece, and bottom club Oldham on sixteen points. Normally, twenty-one points would keep a club from relegation so Salford, Halifax and Workington were all very unfortunate. Another of Kevin's problems was the loss of players whose calibre formed the backbone of the side. Such talent could not be replaced quickly enough. The very good youngsters coming through were denied that vital element of time to adjust to the speed, strength and power of first division football.

With the arrival of the following season, Kevin all but gave up playing, standing in for Paul O'Neill on only three occasions. His mind now was most definitely centred on coaching. Salford began their 1981-82 campaign bravely, with Lancashire Cup wins against Oldham away, 17-7, Fulham at home, 19-3, and a league win at Ninian Park over the Blue Dragons of Cardiff, 26-21. The semi-final of the Lancashire Cup was too big an ask, though, and Widnes sailed through at Naughton Park with a score of 33-2. This particular season saw Salford win twenty and draw one of their thirty-two league games, to finish four points behind Halifax, who were promoted in fourth place. Of the promoted teams above them, Salford could win only one of those eight matches. Silly points were dropped against lesser sides, including a 3-0 loss to Blackpool Borough away, a 10-10 draw away to Hunslet, and defeat at home to Cardiff, 17-14. The crucial double against Salford, though, was that by Halifax. Those four points proved to be the difference between going up and staying down.

In March 1982, Kevin was asked to return as coach to Warrington and he left Salford under very friendly terms with the board who thanked him graciously for his efforts. The man who enticed Kevin back to Wilderspool was Brian Pitchford, who wanted his former hooker to replace the former Saints centre, Billy Benyon, as coach. At this stage in his life, Brian was not in the best of health and he needed to know that the post was in secure hands. As usual, when Kevin rejoined the club it was without a written contract; a handshake with Brian Pitchford was as good as that. In the press conference that accompanied Kevin's appointment, he stated that he would set Warrington alight. Two weeks later the main grandstand burnt down to the ground. Kevin said that he hadn't meant it literally!

Kevin Ashcroft's entrance into the Warrington camp was welcomed by the players. Here was a winning player turned into a winning coach. Huyton were demolished 43-5 in the County Cup first round at Wilderspool. A draw and two losses preceded that victory, before a cracking win in the league at home to Wigan, 19-13, was followed by defeat to Oldham, 22-12. Four days later, Oldham returned to Wilderspool in round two of the Lancashire Cup, where a thriller ensued, before Kevin's men marched on to a semi-final against Fulham, which they also won 17-8, thanks to tries from Ken Kelly, Mike Kelly and Bob Eccles, with Steve Hesford kicking four goals.

The prize for that victory was a place in the Lancashire Cup final against St. Helens. Already, Kevin was repaying the trust that Brian Pitchford had in him. The date of the final was 23rd October and the venue was Central Park, Wigan. St. Helens very much fancied their chances, although it seems the fans didn't very much fancy the game. On a cold and showery day, the attendance of 6,462 was the lowest County Cup final crowd since 1913.

Even so, precious silverware was at stake and St. Helens lined up as follows: Brian Parkes; Barrie Ledger, Chris Arkwright, Roy Haggerty, Dennis Litherland; Steve Peters, Neil Holding; Melvyn James, Graham Liptrot, Gary Bottell, Gary Moorby, Peter Gorley and Harry Pinner. The Saints subs were John Smith and Roy Mathias. Warrington's team read: Steve Hesford; Paul Fellows, Ronnie Duane, John Bevan, Mike Kelly; Paul Cullen, Ken Kelly, Neil Courtney, Carl Webb, Tony Cooke, Bob Eccles, John Fieldhouse and Mike Gregory. Substitute: Dave Chisnall. The pace of Fellows and the two Kellys, Ken and Mike, together with the power-running of Eccles and the kicking of Hesford proved too much for Saints on the day, and Warrington returned home comprehensive 16-0 winners. When they got there, the scenes in Warrington were reminiscent of their golden year of 1974. Thousands saw the Lancashire Cup come back to Wilderspool.

In one of the town's main streets is a statue of Oliver Cromwell. Directly opposite is a gents toilet. Steve Hesford and Ken Kelly were great practical jokers and, the week after the Lancashire Cup final, they pulled off a beauty. After mixing some of the white lime paste used to mark the pitch, they approached the statue of Oliver and, with the aid of a piece of wood and a pair of wellies, made boot tracks right the way down the plinth, onto the path in front and across the road into the toilet. The prank even made the pages of the local Warrington newspaper. 'Oliver taken short,' read the headline.

Meanwhile, in the John Player Trophy, home victories over Halifax, 19-8, Blackpool, 36-15, and Hull Kingston Rovers, 11-10, put Warrington into the semi-final against Wigan. Sadly, unless you are a Wigan fan, that was as far as they went. Wigan produced a tough, fighting performance and went through to the final, 15-14. The luck of the draw was with Warrington in the Challenge Cup, too, as Bramley and Huyton were both beaten at home, before Hull FC came to Wilderspool in the third round and edged a brutal game, 10-4. The good early-season results which coincided with Kevin's return to Wilderspool had not proved sustainable and the side eventually finished eleventh, just below halfway in the league table. The winning of the Lancashire Cup gave some satisfaction, as did reaching the semi-final of the John Player, but overall league form had been sketchy.

Happily, 1983-84 saw a vast improvement in the club's league standing. At the end of that season, Warrington were sitting in a very creditable third place, tucked in behind Hull Kingston Rovers and Hull FC. After a great start, in which they drew 22-22 draw at the Boulevard, Hull, and beat Leeds 14-12 win at Headingley, they won at Blackpool in the County Cup, and then beat Leeds away. Three days later, the Wire went to St. Helens in the Lancashire Cup and won by 30 points to 26. Hull Kingston were beaten at home, 26-10, and then Warrington played Barrow at Wilderspool in the County Cup semi final, only to lose it by 19 points to 18.

'Our league form was good going into the John Player games,' says Kevin, 'and a great win [32-18] at Belle Vue, Wakefield, plus another win over Trinity the week after in the league [17-9], had us in good spirits to take on Saints at home in the second round. But they beat us 15-10. Again, we were playing really well but then Castleford beat us [23-16] at Wheldon Road, in the first round of the Challenge Cup. The old top-eight Championship play-offs came around and our position in the league gave us a home draw against St.Helens, who had finished sixth.' But further success was not to be and Saints won the tie, 19-13.

214

* * *

That final defeat to Saints came on 29th April 1984 and, less than one month later, Kevin had rejoined Salford in order to take up the position of football manager, with Tommy Grainey as coach and Bob Welding assistant coach, as a replacement for Mike Coulman.

The first job for the new coaching regime was to get Salford back into the first division, having been relegated in 1983-84. And they did it too. The Red Devils bounced straight back up into the top division at the end of season 1984-85. 'We enjoyed our football that season,' says Kevin. 'Swinton finished top of the league and we came second, after losing only five of the twenty-eight league games played. Back up with the big clubs, we had to start thinking of bringing some decent overseas players in. John Wilkinson and I discussed several players who would do well for us. The quota we went for was Steve Stacey, Mark Brokenshaw, Neil Ritter and Todd Riley, all Australians. I also went back to Warrington and brought in the tough Kiwi, Roby Muller. On the home signings we captured Clive Griffiths, the former Welsh rugby union international and goal-kicking full-back at St. Helens. Clive joined us on a £4,000 transfer fee. We also signed Wigan's outstanding loose forward, John Pendlebury for £16,000, a club record at the time. These signings enabled us to gain our first priority which was promotion.'

In preparing for 1985-86, Kevin had signed two further Australian players in Neil Baker and Brian Battese, as well as the experienced Keiron O'Loughlin, the former Wigan, Widnes and Workington Town middle back. Unfortunately, it was a season composed largely of ups and downs. As Kevin remembers: 'We lost away to York, who had finished below us the previous season. Then, the following game, we beat Wigan at home by 12 points to 8. We won three games on the trot prior to the Challenge Cup and then blew it at Doncaster away in the first round, losing 18-12. Our league form was good enough to achieve our second goal, which was to maintain first division football. We did that by finishing in tenth place.'

The spirit in the club, though, was excellent. 'Tommy Grainey was just the man to get the best out of players,' says Kevin, 'as was Bob Welding. Tommy had a special sense of humour and also was one of those people who could laugh at himself. In the '86-87 close-season, we were invited to take part in a four-team competition in Paris. The other teams were XIII Catalan of Perpignan, Paris Chatillon and a BARLA select side. We won the competition and the players and staff let their hair down on the final evening in the French capital. As coach, Tommy had the job of ensuring that all the players made it to the plane on time, armed with their passports. Getting the taste of the beautiful French wine, Tommy was still Franz Liszt when he arrived at the airport. Before that, he had drilled into the players not to put their passports in their cases as they were put on board the aircraft before the players cleared passport control. "Don't bloody forget about the passports," he had warned them. At passport control, Tommy, still gassed, fiddled in every pocket trying to find his passport until, at last, it dawned on him that he had, in fact, put it in his case, which by now was on the plane as predicted. Refused entry, Tommy started to carry on and a gendarme was summoned. Tommy began to try to explain where his passport was, holding his arms full out to his sides and making engine noises. "Passport-o on-o plane-eo," he said, sounding more Spanish than French. His explanations to the typically French policeman, who had the pencil moustache, pillbox hat, and that suave French look, went on for what seemed hours, until the gendarme finally said: "What you are trying to say, old love, is that your bloody passport is on the plane." The gendarme was a Manchester lad. The players were rolling about in hysterics.'

Kevin agreed that the four overseas players for this coming season would be Australians. He went over to Sydney with chairman John Wilkinson and vice-chairman Stan Bibby, to run the rule over the fancied players. While there, he signed Greg Austin from North Sydney, Mark Wakefield from Cronulla, and the nineteen-year-old Gary Schubert from Taree United, a New South Wales country team. Cream of the crop, though, was the talented young back-row forward Geoff Selby, from the St. George club in Sydney. Big, strong, quick and a beautiful footballer, Geoff played his heart out for Salford but, at the end of his short contract, went home to see his family and whilst there, was fatally injured in a car crash. His death was a tragic loss, not only to his family but to the game in general. Kevin, to this day, firmly believes that Geoff would have made the Australian Test team. Greg Austin, too, gave his all to the cause. His ability to score exciting tries thrilled the Salford faithful and the league form improved slightly this term, with one move up the league ladder to ninth on twenty-eight points. Widnes were in eighth as a result of a superior points difference, the halfway position in the league. The end of the season brought the relegation of four teams in Oldham, Featherstone, Barrow and Wakefield Trinity. Only two teams, Hunslet and Swinton, were promoted in their place, making the first division a fourteen-team competition rather than sixteen.

The signs ahead of the 1987-88 season were promising as, very secretly, Salford had nipped back down to Australia to sign the current Australian Test full-back, Garry Jack. Kevin recalls: 'We played a pre-season friendly with Springfield Borough at the Willows and lost heavily, 24-10. We then lost the next two games, before beating Fulham in the Lancashire Cup first round, 58-4. After that we played Hull Kingston Rovers at home and, early in the second half, we were trailing 26-6. We came up with a tremendous fightback, though, and ended up winning 34-32. In our next game, Wigan knocked us out of the County Cup with a 42-2 tonking. Garry Jack's stay with us was not a happy one. After basking in the spotlight of a high-profile club and international career for almost the whole of his time in Australia, coming into a struggling Salford side was not to his liking.' Jack's sixteen appearances produced only seven wins and the outlay for him was in no way returned. After Jack's return to Australia, another Aussie, Steve Gibson, stood in at full-back and was a revelation.

'We signed Peter Williams, Orrell's union international stand-off,' recalls Kevin, 'but it was a struggle. We dropped down the league ladder and it all rested on the final game of the season against Halifax at the Willows, as to who was relegated. In a titanic psychological game, we pulled out all the stops to register a fine 36-16 victory and stay up.'

If season 1987-88 had been disappointing, the 1988/89 campaign kicked off in the most positive manner or years. Home league games against Hull Kingston Rovers, 24-14, Warrington, 25-18, Widnes, 15-12, and Oldham 38-20, were all won. An away victory at Belle Vue against Wakefield Trinity, 36-18, further maintained a healthy early position in the league table and, when the Lancashire Cup came around, Whitehaven were overwhelmed 42-8. In future rounds, Oldham were seen off 18-2 and, in the semi-final, Warrington were dispatched, 15-2, meaning that Salford would make their first County Cup final appearance in thirteen years.

Their opponents in that game would be the ominously strong Wigan, and the venue, Knowsley Road, St. Helens.

The Salford team read: Peter Williams; Tex Evans, Keith Bentley, Kenny Jones, Adrian Hadley; Paul Shaw, David Cairns; Steve Herbert, Mark Moran, Peter Brown, Ian Gormley, Mick Worrall and Mark Horo. Subs: Ian Blease and Mick McTigue. Playing for Wigan were: Steve Hampson; Tony Iro, Kevin Iro, Dean Bell, Joe Lydon; Shaun Edwards, Andy Gregory; Ian Lucas, Martin Dermott, Adrian Shelford, Andy Platt, Andy Goodway and Ellery Hanley. Subs: Ged Byrne and Dennis Betts. Although the Australian at stand-off half for Salford won the man of the match award for a fine game in both attack and defence, it was soon-to-be all-conquering Wigan who took the spoils with a 22-17 win.

Such an outcome was far from unexpected as Wigan had bought richly and well, meaning they would finish the season second in the table behind a tough Widnes outfit. Salford, on the other hand, finished tenth, one up from last season. The scorers for Wigan in the County Cup final were Kevin Iro (two tries and three goals), Bell and Shelford. Salford's scorers were Evans, Bentley and Herbert, with Brown kicking two goals and Worall a drop-goal.

With the final behind them, five successive league defeats had Salford tumbling down the table although, yet again, they managed to cling on to a place in the top echelon. Kevin says: 'We played well in the Lancashire Cup but could not find any rhythm in our league matches. I signed Ian Bragger from Keighley and Steve Kerry from Preston Grasshoppers rugby union and both did well in the fight to stay up.'

Kevin's final effort as Salford's football manager came in 1989-90. Five defeats on the trot left the club rooted firmly to the foot of the table and Kevin explains what happened next. 'I tried to look at things positively,' he says, 'and decided that a change of direction was required. I spoke to John Wilkinson, who was dismayed to hear my decision but came to terms with it. I had a very special relationship with John. He was and is a wonderful chairman with a deep love of Salford and the game of rugby league in general. As far as I am concerned, his contribution is beyond compare. Anyway, John thanked me for all the hard work put in by the entire coaching staff. The former New Zealand international forward, Kevin Tamati, took over as coach at the Willows and I wished him well.'

* * *

Whilst Kevin was striving away at Salford, Leigh were going through a bad time financially. Relegated in 1989-90 under Billy Benyon, the club brought in Alex Murphy for another spell as coach and Murphy just failed to gain promotion in his first season, as his charges finished fifth in the league. The club went into administration during the summer of 1991 before a local businessman, Tim Maloney, bought them out at the eleventh hour to save the club from extinction. Maloney installed Tony Cottrell, a Leigh player who was building up a nice business in the town, in the unusual double role of player-chairman.

Tony Cottrell had the business acumen to put the club back on an even keel, but he needed a good coach in place and Kevin was back in amateur football, coaching Leigh Victoria. In fact, Tony had played for Kevin at the Vic on permit.

Away from rugby, Kevin and Janet had taken over as mine hosts at a nice pub, The Albion, better known as the 'Topshop' in Atherton, between Leigh and Bolton. The pub was refurbished ready to move into and Nat Lofthouse, the former England international centre forward, opened the couple's new premises. On the whole, though, the locals were soccer fans who followed Bolton Wanderers and, try as he might, Kevin couldn't get enough players interested to start a rugby league team under his pub's name. So, when an old pal Terry Ryan, who was then running the Vic team, came to see Kevin and asked him to come and 'put a bit back in', Kevin obliged.

Meanwhile, at Hilton Park, Tony Cottrell called Kevin to a meeting where it was resolved that Kevin would return to Leigh. There was a little job to do before the team could be called to pre-season training, however. First, Kevin and Tony would have to actually find some players! There was another problem, too. There was no money in the bank to pay wages. The club was skint.

Kevin and Tony's final meeting, one week before the opening match, was held on the car park at Hilton Park. Tony said: 'Right, how many bloody players have we got for this match?' To which Kevin replied: 'About nine.' They needed, therefore, six players to make up a side. 'I'll go watch Leigh East, you go down to the Miners Welfare,' said Kevin. 'We will get three players each and sign them as amateurs until we get sorted out.' And that is exactly what they did.

Those few players left who had signed under Billy Benyon or Alex Murphy and stuck with Leigh formed the cornerstone of this new side. The remainder were the aforementioned kids signed from amateur rugby league by Kevin and Tony. As chairman, Tony was straight as a die with the players. He told them that it was impossible to tell them what the playing terms would be and that the money from this week's attendance would pay all expenses, the tax bill and an amount to the players as wages, once the following week's expenses had been deducted. Those great-hearted kids accepted these terms, knowing that the future of Leigh RLFC itself was at stake.

The first game that this patched-up team played was

against Ryedale-York at Hilton Park. Kevin remembers well the feeling of the unexpected as the side listened to his final words and disappeared out onto the field to be rapturously greeted by a healthy crowd of around 3,500 supporters. The players were well-motivated and played some excellent attacking football in walloping York by 26-10. Tony Cottrell was delighted, as was Kevin. The Leigh faithful were delighted too as they had sweated on whether or not they would have a team to cheer on.

The Leigh side that fateful day was: Paul Topping; Mick Round, Simon Booth, Ian Jeffrey, Neil McCulloch; David Ruane, Jason Donohue; Mark Sheals, Andy Ruane, Ian Potter, Andy Collier, Jim Moore and Andrew Collier. Another local businessman who sponsored the side, Mr. Bill Parkinson, was so pleased with this first unexpected win that he promised a week's holiday for the team in Tenerife at the end of the season, should the side finish in the top six.

During the season, Kevin and Janet moved out of the Albion and Kevin started work for Tony Cottrell. The trips to see the amateur teams of Leigh East and Leigh Miners Welfare were worthwhile as John Costello was signed from the Miners Welfare and Gary Pendlebury, Tommy Hayes and Mark Dainty all arrived as professional players from Leigh East. Another amateur, Sean Fanning, was signed from the Hare and Hounds club in St. Helens. Real bargain buys such as David Tanner from Saints, Lee Hansen from Orange United in Australia, Andy Ruane from Oldham and Andrew Collier from Wigan helped build a sound footballing backbone.

In the Lancashire Cup, Leigh beat Chorley 59-12, but Wigan in round two at Central Park beat Kevin's boys 42-12. In the old John Player Trophy, now renamed the Regal Trophy, one of the toughest draws sent Leigh to play the ultra-tough Hull FC, away. The result was a 22-7 win for

Hull. Another very tough draw in the Challenge Cup saw Leigh play Dewsbury at Owl Lane. The Yorkshiremen knew how to play on that big slope and won the tie 14-6.

For this season, 1991-92, the league was split into three divisions; the first containing fourteen teams, the second eight and the third fourteen. Second division sides played each other four times in the season, twice at home, twice away. The idea was nicknamed 'The Hetherington Plan', due to it being pushed through in an RFL Council meeting by Gary Hetherington, then owner of Sheffield Eagles. The idea was to stop the yo-yo effect of a team not quite good enough for the first division going back into division two and being too good for that group. It was thought that playing a select group of good middle-rated teams who were all as good as each other, with no easy games, would gradually make for a stronger first division.

In essence, the idea was good, but in reality it could not work. Leigh had a great season in the league without doing anything in the Cups. Tony Cottrell had done a fabulous job at Hilton Park in getting hold of the club, maintaining professional rugby league football in Leigh and keeping the ground out of the hands of land-grabbers. But the staunch Leigh man was then reluctantly forced to concentrate on his business and ease his way out of the game, which he did very successfully indeed.

During that 1991-92 season, Leigh had a huge 70-0 home win against Ryedale-York, in which John Woods scored four tries and kicked eleven goals. Workington were beaten 68-6, also at home, four weeks later. In the end, Leigh were promoted in second place behind Sheffield Eagles, whom they beat once at home and once away over the four games in which the teams played each other. The match that clinched promotion was a win at Oldham in the final game of the campaign. If Oldham won, they would go up and the same could be said for Leigh. After a true nail-biter, Kevin's men won at the Watersheddings, 15-14! What an end to a truly great season. Furthermore, the lads had won themselves a week in Tenerife, courtesy of Bill Parkinson and they had a ball. No one was safe that week, including Mr. Parkinson himself, who was was lifted silently from his bed and eased into the swimming pool as he slept on one particularly sultry night.

The high spirits evaporated when the party arrived back in Leigh only to discover that Kevin had been sacked as coach by Tim Maloney, who was now the club's chairman. When asked why he had lost the job after such a good season, Maloney told Kevin that he thought a change was needed to take the club onward and upward! So, Kevin left Leigh again, but with his head held high. His replacement at Hilton Park was Jim Crellin, who lasted only a few weeks before the Australian Steve Simms came in.

CHAPTER EIGHT

So, the old warhorse was put out to grass, but only on the coaching front. For Kevin's career now took an upward turn, when he was asked to become part of the rugby league commentary team on BBC Radio Manchester, or GMR as it was in those days known.

Kevin's partnership with ace-commentator Malcolm Lord soon became the envy of the various Sunday afternoon local radio rugby league programmes broadcast across the North of England. The two characters called the game as they saw it, with no frills attached. The laughs generated on-air were unrehearsed and spontaneous. The laughs off-air were even more hilarious.

One Sunday, the second Sunday in November, Malcolm and Kevin were on duty at Central Park, as the teams walked out ahead of a Wigan versus Widnes game. Up to the halfway line the players walked, before facing each other in two rows. When a request came over the public address system - 'Please be upstanding for one minute's silence' - the crowd rose as one and removed their caps and hats. Malcolm covered the mike with his hand and whispered over to Kevin: 'Who's died?' Kevin looked aghast. 'Malcolm,' he said, 'it's Remembrance Sunday.'

Kevin and Malcolm became a radio double act and this very entertaining duo continued in a similar vein for many years. They introduced a lively hour to the Sunday rugby league show each week, by running a question and answer spot immediately after commentating on a game. At almost every ground it was a matter of climbing many steps up to the press box. Malcolm Lord had difficulty walking and this made it progressively difficult for him, until he retired from a job he had done so professionally for many years.

This meant that Kevin would henceforth be paired with Jack Dearden, a commentator better known for his soccer work than rugby league. In time, Kevin found himself being edged out in favour of Trevor Hunt. Soon, the new duo had taken over the question and answer section, leaving Kevin to bow out of broadcasting.

The Ashcroft-Lord partnership, while it lasted, had grown to become a local radio institution. Malcolm's expert calling, then a thoughtful word and quip from Kevin, were looked forward to by thousands of devoted listeners. The crunch for Kevin came when Wigan winger Martin Offiah pulled out of a game with injury and was replaced by Henderson Gill. Repeatedly, the commentator Kevin was working alongside credited the non-playing Offiah with his replacement's efforts, including a Henderson Gill hat-trick of tries!

Enough is enough, thought Kevin, who had worked for so many years with the ultra-professional Malcolm Lord, only to be paired with co-commentators who didn't know the difference between Offiah and Gill. Kevin had loved working with Malcolm Lord, and loved his time as a radio personality, as it allowed him to stay in touch with his old mates in the sport.

During Kevin's playing career, various damaged bits and pieces were either removed or cleaned up. As he grew older, the wear and tear on his knees became most painful, so he saw his doctor and had two new knee joints fitted. Still, his work for BBC Manchester kept the brain in good nick, as it both maintained his interest in, and association with, rugby league. So, when Blackpool Borough were re-admitted to the professional body, after having earlier been removed from the league on account of a series of poor seasons, along with Nottingham and Chorley, Kevin was ready to go when asked to take over from Mark Lee as coach at the seaside resort's super Bloomfield Road ground in March 2005.

'The facilities were beautiful,' says Kevin, who ended thirteen years of retirement in taking on the role. 'We trained at Newton-le-Willows rugby union club. An old friend of mine, Dave Rowland, was the rugby league club chairman and he laid it on the line when he told me that we had to avoid finishing bottom of National League Two. Dave was a smashing chairman and, although I had been away from the sharp end for quite a few years and had just turned sixty-years-old, I felt good in the position.'

Kevin's first game in charge at Blackpool was against the top French side, Toulouse, in the Challenge Cup. 'A reporter from the local Blackpool newspaper came to see me,' recalls Kevin, 'to feature this cup-tie in his column. "Do you know anything about this French side Kevin?" he asked. I think he was testing my up-to-date knowledge of the game. "Oh, yes," I replied. "They have a big fat prop who is as soft as shite, a second-rower who hides on the blind side, a stand-off who is afraid of his own shadow but is very quick, a hooker who will kick your head in if you don't watch him and two centres who are bit-players in French cinema." The journalist looked at Kevin in amazement. "Kevin, that's brilliant. How have you picked up so much information?" Kevin gave this novice writer an old-fashioned look and said, "I haven't. All French teams are like that." Don't bandy words with Kevin without knowing what you are talking about first.

In the end, Blackpool lost to this very good Toulouse side and the revival of the club was stretched to the limit when it all came down to the last game of the season, away to London Skolars. Now, Kevin is the product of an extremely tough era of top-flight rugby league football. One knew how far to go talking to referees and the like, it was an art form. Openly, at least, there was very little offence taken, for example, if one person joked about another person's colour. Nobody thought they were being racist. The players at Blackpool were like players all over the world. If a coach knows the game, has had experience in coaching and is a fair man, then players will respect his experience and listen, no matter what his age. Kevin tells of a famous Australian full-back who questioned his right to tell him how to play. 'I am a full-back, Kevin,' he said, 'you were a hooker. You can't tell me how to play'. The shrewd Ashcroft looked him in the eye and said: 'No I can't tell you how to play, but I am telling you how I want you to play.'

Several tales abound surrounding Kevin's return to the game during this latter period. One is that he was watching his first game as coach, when he supposedly said to an assistant: 'How far back is this referee taking us at the play-the-ball?' The assistant answered: 'The normal ten metres, Kevin.' The coach looked horrified and said: 'What? It's five yards like it always was, not ten metres.' Another time, at training, a young player said to Kevin: 'That's a long haul next Sunday, Kevin, up to Gateshead.' Again Kevin looked horrified. '*&^%$ Gateshead? How long have they been in the league?' But the most comical remark was surely when the same player said: 'This fixture at London Skolars will be a tough one.' Kevin was bemused. 'What?' he said. 'Don't tell me we play *&^%$ schoolboys now.'

Tales such as those are only told about real rugby league icons. Whether or not they are true, they show the humour of the man and anyone facing the Australian front-row as a hooker in Kevin's day had to have a sense of humour or be deemed crazy. Kevin loved the coaching days at Blackpool but it wasn't all buns and cake. Some of the players at the club were the type who were looking to pull a few quid a week on their past reputation. They had held a gun to the head of the previous coach, Mark Lee, when he was trying to get a decent team together and there were a handful on £300 per week, win, lose or draw. They came to Blackpool and went through the motions, before picking up their £300 on Thursday evenings. Kevin got rid of them like a dose of salts and brought in players whom he knew would shed blood for the club. And, when it came to that final game at London Skolars, Kevin's faith in human nature was restored as his boys won in style, 20-6, to avoid the dreaded wooden spoon.

The old army song 'Old soldiers never die, they only fade away' certainly holds true where Kevin is concerned. Talk to him today about his days as the number one hooker in this country and the fire returns, along with the tales of true heroes. He still lives in Leigh and a favourite pastime is to do the shopping in Leigh market. There Kevin meets his old playing mates, like his childhood hero at Rochdale, big Stan Owen. Former Great Britain tourist and international prop Norman Herbert can also be found there, along with many other ex-players. Kevin loves nothing better than swapping stories about the game and roars with laughter when reminded of this or that player.

His respect for the men he hammered into the ground, or who gave him a smack, is still there and Kevin will often say, on concluding a discussion, that such and such a player was 'a good 'un, him' or 'a hard bastard.' Kevin loves to use the term, 'he took no prisoners' when talking about some hard-case of the past. He is from that era of part-time players who maintained their fitness in their own time. Their day job took care of much of the strength work, but there was still time for blokes like Kevin to train in their own garage gyms.

Wherever Kevin went in the game, he found characters. His own playing career was surrounded by characters, so too his coaching and working environment. He has thousands of Tommy Grainey tales, for example, from playing with Tommy at Leigh, coaching with him, and being mates since they were kids. Kevin even worked with Tommy fixing fences. One particularly warm day, the pair were fixing concrete posts and, just before dinner, Kevin had a thought. 'Here, Tommy. Do we have a partnership in this firm?' he asked his oppo. 'Course we bloody have,' replied Tommy, who was weighing up why Kevin had asked. 'Well,' said Kevin, 'how is it that I'm lifting, carrying and setting these *&^%$ posts, and you are just sat there at the side of the hole with your spirit level, saying left a bit, right a bit, okay, fill it in?' Tommy said: 'You see, Kevin, you are the managing director, whilst I am the technical director.'

When discussing Alex Murphy, Kevin talks with high regard and respect. 'I can't think of another man in our game who knew as much as Murph,' he says. 'Alex was born just before World War Two and a lot of people think he started it. He knew players and what they were capable of. I went with Alex to South Wales to watch a young wingman who had been recommended to us. His name was Dennis Curling. Also playing in this game was a young, strong wing forward, who knocked everything down in front of him. "I could make something of him," said Alex, and he signed that player too, as well as Curling. That loose forward's name was Mike Nicholas.'

Alex Murphy didn't only have an eye for new players, as Kevin points out. 'When Bobby Wanbon was being put out to grass at Saints, Murph said "Bob has a lot left, they have been playing him injured and all he needs is a rest and change of club." So he signed Bobby for nowt and he was brilliant for us at Warrington. All Alex's signings were tough men. The lads used to say he signed all these tough bastards so they would look after him on the field. Good thinking, but Murph could look after himself in any company. When he moved clubs as a coach, he took a group of players around with him, Dave Chisnall being one case in point. But Murph was not one to stand on ceremony when bollockings were being dished out. Top player or otherwise, everyone was in danger. Yet when he came to sign you for whichever club, he would say: "Come with me and I will look after you." And he did. He fought the directors to get things right for the players, over money, conditions, everything. Alex was a great bloke to play with and work for.'

During his supposed retirement years, Kevin did briefly work for the newly-named Wigan Warriors in a one-season spell as media manager. This job entailed releasing news from the club and ensuring that all the information leaving Central Park was good propaganda. He announced new signings, kept the newspapers up to date with injury news and dealt with reporters and television pundits who were always on the look-out for a story. But although that might sound like a dream job, it was made unbearable by constant in-fighting behind the scenes. One faction of the club wanted stay at Central Park, the other was determined to sell up and move to the JJB. As media manager, Kevin was caught fairly and squarely in the middle. Of the Wigan directors at that time, Mike Nolan, Martin Ryan and John Martin were the men who wanted Kevin to stay in the job. But, as at any club with a split board, there were some who wanted things changing. Kevin's inside knowledge would have blown the club apart if it had been leaked to the media. And so his time there ended.

CHAPTER NINE

When discussing the state of modern-day rugby league, and full-time professional Super League in particular, Kevin is adamant about its good and its bad points.

He says: 'The good points are that it is played in a more favourable spectator environment during the summer, making it a more attractive package as a family game. The full-time aspect also makes for fitter players and gives far more scope for the various media outlets, although we are still the poor relations of soccer and cricket. But the changes in the fabric of the game, due mainly to the incoming and over-riding influence of Sky TV, and its demands in making rugby league purely a television product, have damaged the structure of the game as we, the former players, knew it.

'Nowadays, rugby league is a watered-down sport that is not producing the sort of earthy characters of which it was once so proud. Our rich, spicy game is now gone. In its place we have a game played in exactly the same way by every single team, with no variation. As an instance, in the past, coaches and players did not know when approaching a scrum which side would win the ball. We were coached to have moves from the scrum in various parts of the field. That was also the case with tap penalties and from the play-the-ball. Now, we see nothing, just one run off the play-the-ball for five tackles, and then a kick downfield. I am forever reading and hearing about the development of the game in this country, yet still sixty-five per cent of our Super League players are from overseas. One or two clubs are giving chances to young local players, but these chances are given because the club is either skint or can't afford top players, or because the club is not high-profile enough to attract the better class of Aussie or Kiwi. The bigger clubs still bring over players from abroad whose careers are on the wane, or who can't get a contract in their own country.'

On overseas coaches, Kevin has a simple philosophy. 'Overseas coaches should all go home and take the game's money with them,' he says. 'The two overseas coaches who I have the most respect for are Graham Lowe, the New Zealander who transformed Wigan, and Justin Morgan, currently at Hull Kingston Rovers. The current overseas coach at most clubs is coaching the same thing, in the Australian way. This method of playing suits the Aussies, but it does not suit us. Our culture is different. The Aussies fancied the ten metre rule at the play-the-ball, so we changed. Any dummy-half with an ounce of pace now has a field day. This on-side ruling has opened the door to a spate of Australian hookers, such as Danny Buderus and Shaun Berrigan, who can boss games. We have Keiron Cunningham, who delights in running from dummy-half, and not many others.

The Aussie game is based around a half-back bossing things too, hence the demise of the stand-off half. If we could somehow instruct our British coaches to use the set-piece at both scrum and play-the-ball, we would at least offer more than the head down, bums up approach to coaching we have now. We will never beat the Aussies at their own game and this is the type of game that our own British coaches and the current Australian coaches are preaching right now in this country.'

In looking to the future, Kevin, like most people involved with rugby league, is not sure how the proposed Super League franchise system, scheduled to begin in 2009, will move the game forward. 'If the deal put before the clubs in the National Leagues is not perfectly acceptable, then a breakaway to form a new Rugby Football League could well be the answer,' he says. 'The original breakaway was done in a far different world than today. But somehow the climate for the change may be even better now than it was in 1895. Nowadays, we have things like television, the internet, easier travelling and the experience of over one hundred years behind us. As we are right now, our governing body, the RFL, is not in control of the game. Super League and Sky TV run the sport, even in the National Leagues. Whatever the deal on offer from the RFL, it will be cut and made by Sky and Super League.'

The so-called dinosaur, it seems, roars on!

KEVIN'S DREAM TEAMS

Having played with and against the best players in Great Britain, Australia, France and New Zealand throughout his illustrious career, Kevin was only too pleased to provide us with two teams which he considers to be the best of the best.

Team one	Team Two
Steve Hampson (Wigan)	John Woods (Leigh)
Des Drummond (Leigh)	Tom van Vollenhoven (St. H)
Alan Davies (Oldham)	Reg Gasnier (St. George)
Eric Ashton (Wigan)	Neil Fox (Wakefield Trinity)
Billy Boston (Wigan)	Brian Bevan (Warrington)
Roger Millward (Hull KR)	Wally Lewis (Brisbane)
Alex Murphy (St. Helens)	Alex Murphy (St. Helens)
Kevin Ward (St. Helens)	John Wittenberg (St. George)
Phil McKenzie (Widnes)	Tommy Harris (Hull FC)
Stan Owen (Leigh)	Artie Beetson (Easts)
Phil Lowe (Hull KR)	Ron Coote (South Sydney)
Mike Gregory (Warrington)	Wayne Pearce (Balmain)
Ellery Hanley (Wigan)	Johnny Raper (St. George)
Subs:	*Subs:*
Alan Hardisty (Castleford)	Trent Barrett (St. George)
Shaun Edwards (Wigan)	Arnie Morgan (Featherstone)
Bob Haigh (Leeds)	Mal Meninga (Canberra)
Jim Mills (Widnes)	Brian Edgar (Workington)

EPILOGUE

Kevin Ashcroft had two wonderful careers in the game of rugby league football. First, there was a long, distinguished stint as a player, and then another long period in which he was coach to some of the biggest clubs in the game.

Kevin's position on the playing field was just about the most unglamorous one in the team; that of hooker. Hookers are rarely as well remembered as the slick-haired, pin-up glory boys at stand-off and centre. On the contrary, hookers were supposed to wear a beat-up face and be known as 'that bloke in the middle of all those big horrible men'. But Ashy defied that stereotyped niche to become one of the first truly modern hookers. He ran with the ball and was privy to everything going on around him. Sure, he was at every play-the-ball and distributed with pin-point accuracy, but he also tackled hard and secure. He could drop goals, always a handy skill for a dummy-half, and he supported well enough for him to collect vital tries in crucial games.

Kevin's ability and knowledge of how to play this game

of rugby league to its highest professional standards were highlighted by him being the confidant of the world's greatest ever player and thinker, Alex Murphy, when the pair worked together so well at Leigh and Warrington. Kevin's record as a hooker is exemplary in so much as he played in two World Cup tournaments; Australia in 1968, and Britain in 1970. A full Great Britain tour followed in 1974 and, in his four appearances for Lancashire, he was only once on the losing side. Kevin Ashcroft played in three Wembley Challenge Cup finals, winning twice, and was also in the Championship-winning Warrington side of 1974. His personal collection of silverware includes Lancashire Cup, John Player Trophy, BBC Floodlit Trophy and Captain Morgan Trophy winners medals, along with various man of the match awards.

Kevin's coaching achievements, too, take some beating. After assisting Alex Murphy at Leigh, he was later head coach at Leigh twice, coach at Warrington and football manager at Salford for five and a half years, before bringing the curtain down at Blackpool Panthers in 2005, at the tender age of sixty!

Kevin Ashcroft is always a pleasure to meet and brings a ray of sunshine with him. To say he was a credit to rugby league is an understatement. Kevin was much more than that. Upon every playing field he graced, he was a true character and a real giant of the game.

Maurice Bamford
June 2008

A summary of Kevin Ashcroft's playing career

Club Career

	P	S	T	G	D/G	P
1963-65 - Dewsbury	14	0	2	0	0	6
1965-67 - Rochdale H	82	0	2	0	0	6
1967-72 - Leigh	198	5	19	12	0	81
1972-75 - Warrington	123	1	20	18	5	101
1975-77 - Leigh	58	0	6	0	6	24
1977/78 - Rochdale H	24	0	3	0	0	9
1978/81 - Salford	55	5	4	0	4	16
Club Totals	554	11	56	30	15	243

Representative Career

	P	S	T	G	D/G	P
Lancashire	4	0	1	0	0	3
G B Tests	4	0	1	0	0	3
G B World Cup 1968	3	0	1	0	0	3
G B World Cup 1970	2	0	0	0	0	0
G B Lions Tour 1974	13	1	2	0	0	6
Total Career	580	12	61	30	5	258

AFTERWORD

BY KEVIN ASHCROFT

I was delighted when Maurice Bamford told me about his plans to write a biography of my career, and have found the last few months something of an emotional rollercoaster, reminiscing about my life in rugby league.

I must pay tribute, in particular, to some very close friends of mine, without whose sponsorship and support this project may not have been possible. John and Elaine Wilkinson, Peter and Tom Clay, and Dave Rowland are all superb people. I would like to thank them for their support and, most of all, their friendship over many years.

Looking back over the last few months, the experience of putting this book together has been a hugely enjoyable one. I could talk to Maurice all day and frequently have done. We are both on the same wavelength and share a passion for the game of rugby league that is infectious.

Maurice has a wicked sense of humour, an appreciation of the game's traditions and history and its place in many people's lives. His love of the game is beyond reproach.

The main thing that has been reinforced for me is that, throughout my career, being involved in rugby league was like being involved in one huge family. The memories I have got and the friendships I have made are things that money just cannot buy. Sadly, some of these traits have been lost in aspects of the modern game. Rugby league was a family sport for working class communities and I hope that the game's enduring traditions are not abandoned in the years to come.

Since ending his distinguished playing and coaching career, Maurice has taken up the pen with a vengeance and become known as the Barbara Cartland of rugby league. It is a huge honour to be the subject of his fifty-third book since last Christmas.

One thing I have learned during the production of this book is that, when I first signed professional forms for Dewsbury to embark upon my playing career, Maurice himself had only left the club three months previously. I believe he was a prop forward, so we came within an inch of packing down in a scrum together. What a near miss that was!

Finally, I would like to thank some other great friends who have helped this book come to fruition. In particular, I am particularly grateful to Mike Latham. His infectious enthusiasm and encyclopaedic knowledge of the game was an immense assistance with this project. Thanks also to John Woods and Alex Murphy for contributing their kind words, and to Tony Hannan and all at Scratching Shed, for their expertise in putting it all together.

Above all, I would like to thank everybody with whom I have come in contact during what has been a hugely enjoyable career. I hope that you, the reader, gets as much pleasure from reading the book as I have in helping with its preparation. You never know, there may be several more chapters to be written.

Kevin Ashcroft, Leigh, July 2008

TESTIMONIALS

AN APPRECIATION

BY JOHN WOODS

Kevin Ashcroft was my first professional coach and is someone I have been proud to call a friend for many years.

What you see with Kevin is what you get. He is friendly, down-to-earth and passionate about the game of rugby league - one of those people who always lights up your day whenever you meet. He has an infectious sense of humour and the ability to instil confidence and belief into players.

Kevin was player-coach at Leigh when I was first making my way in the professional ranks and he always led from the front, setting a tremendous example for others to follow.

Kevin never feared any challenge and where he went others followed. But he also had that knack of remaining one of the lads at the same time.

Looking back on my career in the game, some of the times I spent with Kevin are amongst the happiest. He was a tremendous player - you only have to look at the number of games he played and the honours he won to realise that. And he also had a long and successful coaching career.

It is quite remarkable that he played as many games as he did at a time when the game was far more brutal than it is today. Being a hooker in the days of competitive scrummaging was probably the toughest and most uncompromising position of all. But it was a challenge that Kevin rose to year after year.

I still see Kevin regularly around Leigh and his is always jovial, straight to the point and loud. He remains as he always was - outspoken, truthful, passionate and, above all, honest.

I am delighted that his great career in this great game has been marked by this book and feel sure that, like the rest of Kevin's career, it will prove to be a tremendous success.

It is a great honour to be asked to contribute a few words for a man I consider to be one of my closest friends. When they made Kevin Ashcroft, they threw away the mould.

John Woods,
Leigh,
July 2008

THE LAST WORD

BY ALEX MURPHY OBE
(WHO ELSE?)

I first signed Kevin Ashcroft when I was coaching at Leigh. We had played Rochdale Hornets and Kevin and I were involved in a scuffle during the game. I ended up with a broken nose. Someone asked me later why I had signed him. I simply said that I don't want to play against that mad bugger again, I want him on my side!

Kevin was arguably the best signing I ever made. His assets were comprised of him being a winner; a trustworthy friend; a great learner of things to do with the game; a wonderful professional; he would never take a backward step; a terrific trainer; and just the type of lad I wanted to build two great teams around, at Leigh and Warrington.

He was and still is a very confident and strong-willed person. He was one of the major cornerstones from which those two great sides were constructed. All the other key men I took to both Leigh and Warrington had that same winning streak running through them.

I honestly consider Kevin to be the best hooker I ever

played with or against and I met some great hookers in my time. His physical and mental toughness, plus his ability to play football in a very shrewd and knowledgeable way, made Kevin an awesome opponent and the driving force behind him was that he was a terrific competitor.

Kevin may well have been underestimated by some as a footballing hooker but not by me. He was, as I said, the best of the best. Finally, he is a one hundred per cent nice bloke too and I wish his biography all the very best of success.

Alex Murphy OBE